LIVING WITHOUT SALT

Kärin Bundesen Baltzell

Terry Martin Parsley

Foreword by Graham Kerr

D1265201

The Brethren Press, Elgin, Illinois

LIVING WITHOUT SALT

Cover design and illustrations by Ken Stanley and Kathy Kline

Library of Congress Cataloging in Publication Data

Baltzell, Kärin B., 1941-
    Living without salt.

    1. Salt-free diet—Recipes.   I. Parsley,
Terry M., 1943-   II. Title.
RM237.8.B34   641.5'632   81-21684
ISBN 0-87178-539-0   AACR2

Published by The Brethren Press, Elgin, Illinois 60120

Printed in the United States of America

To our families:

With love and thanks for their patience, support, and encouragement.

Acknowledgments

We would like to acknowledge the assistance received by families, friends and community members. Without their encouragement and interest, this effort probably would have been impossible.

Special thanks are expressed to: Lynn Ellwein, Susan Maley, Judy Richards, John and Esther Eichelberger, Debbie Faller, Dr. Thomas Richtsmeier, M.D., and to The Brethren Press for its continued service to people. We are also grateful for the spiritual guidance that sent us on this path to help others.

Contents

Foreword

I began my working life in the hotel business in Europe; here I learned that one's sole reason for living was to creatively cause the customer to desire to return.

Later I entered the world of audio-visual gastronomy; here I learned that one's sole reason for living was to creatively cause the viewer to desire to switch on again.

Later still I became involved with food technologists; here I learned that one's sole reason for living was to creatively cause the customer to desire to purchase again.

Later even than that I became involved with the natural foods movement; here I learned that one's sole reason for living was to creatively cause everyone that I had previously "served" to drop all their desires and plunge their heads into a kind of horse's feed bag . . . and attempt to smile in the process!

Finally I became involved with Christians. Here I learned that one's sole reason for living was to love God with considerable fervor and gratitude and in much the same manner to embrace my fellow man . . . and to creatively live out my life in a celebration of my close family relationship with Jesus Christ so that others would desire to live also for Him.

I've said all this in order to applaud this book. It sidesteps, with reasons clearly stated, the rich, fatty, sweet and especially salted manipulations of High Cuisine. It explains the pitfalls of High Technology and its chemical assaults . . . yet it seems to me to avoid the out-of-balance zeal of the ascetic naturalist. What it does do is show the love, care and responsibility that two Christian wives have for their husbands.

They are giving an attractive and practical witness to a world plunging ever deeper into increasingly harmful addictions . . . will we stop, will we care, can we be responsible? . . . By the Grace of God and with tools of guidance such as this well-thought-out cookbook . . . we shall!

Graham Kerr

Preface

Low sodium eating is more than just cooking the low-sodium way—it is an attitude! This attitude is a major force for changing dietary habits.

The resolve that "I just will not add any salt" works well for a few days and a few meals. But when you and your family are tired of broiled chicken, baked potato plain, and lettuce with straight oil and vinegar dressing, then what do you do for variety in the meals? You would love to have a pizza? How about that Mexican food "freak out"? Oh, how tempting to go off "the diet"! Here is where attitude is so important.

It is up to the cook to help make things seem "normal" so that the temptation to stray off the proper diet rarely occurs. It is *your attitude* that will make meals cheery rather than dreary.

It is *your* attitude that will motivate you to go through your cupboards and take out everything that contains sodium—including baking powder and baking soda. It is your attitude that will make shopping for many new unsalted spices, seasonings and products from the health food store a moment of triumph.

Many cooks will need the low-sodium cooking for themselves, some for their spouses. Which foods will be put before the important people of their lives?

What if cooking is less than enjoyable to you? What if you have relied upon commercially prepared foods? Your frame of mind when looking at this new diet and way of life is vital! Cooking can be viewed as a pleasant challenge. Think of learning to cook the low-sodium way as something that makes you unique and very important to your family.

A tendency toward hypertension can be inherited. Hypertension possibly can be avoided altogether if the proper preventative diet is started early enough. When cooking for a hypertensive person, remember that it is a matter of life and death that that person remain on the low-sodium diet especially if a physician has recommended it. Hypertension can go unnoticed for years because of its silent nature. High blood pressure, however, is like a time bomb ticking away, and the longer it goes unnoticed, the shorter time you have to defuse the bomb.

You will find the recipes and tips provided in this book tasty as well as full of healthful foods and ingredients. Our purpose has been to give you, the cook, a book of "basic" low-sodium recipes that continue to make you feel that you can and are presenting foods you have always been eating. This diet also is beneficial to the whole family, as Americans consume far too much sodium.

Specific milligram counts per serving are not included in this cookbook. This is because milligram counts are so low for the recipes and suggestions that a low-sodium diet is naturally maintained. Another reason the milligrams per serving is not included is to make the cook and diners feel that they are eating normally rather than feeling that they are ill and must constantly worry over their food.

Many of the recipes listed herein suggest complementary foods in order to make a complete meal. Combine recipes as if using any other cookbook. That is the beauty of this cookbook—everyday foods are to be used in an everyday way! Why feel that you have to be "special" or plan your meals in any way other than you did before?

Ingredients should be fresh to assure the desired results. Make sure that shelf items are stored properly, rotated when new goods are purchased, and that they are discarded when no longer fresh. Flours, baking powder substitute, baking soda substitute, yeast, herbs, spices, eggs and many other ingredients do deteriorate as they age and can ruin the results of a recipe. When time and money are invested in a recipe, the outcome should be a success.

These recipes were tested and retested in our own kitchens. Copies of the recipes were then given to friends and relatives to test for flavor, clarity of instruction, and inclusion of all ingredients in an order that was easy to understand. It should be noted that we gave these recipes to people who are experienced and accomplished cooks as well as to those who were beginning their cooking experiences.

Of course, when embarking on dietary and lifestyle changes, check with your physician. Good health is a combined effort.

It has been suggested to us that cooking the low-sodium way becomes easier the more it is done. That might be a note of encouragement to a cook who feels a bit overwhelmed at first. This feeling should dissipate with practice. Keep on keeping on!

Kärin Bundesen Baltzell
Terry Martin Parsley

Introduction

High Blood Pressure: An Epidemic

According to the U.S. Department of Health, Education and Welfare, hypertension is the chief 20th century epidemic. Today, there are more than 23 million adult Americans afflicted with hypertension.

"High blood pressure" is often called the "silent killer" because of the absence of visible symptoms. It is estimated that *over half* of those with hypertension are unaware of their plight. Perhaps even more disconcerting is the realization that only one in seven with "high blood pressure" presently has his/her condition under control through some form of medical intervention.

Hypertension causes more than 60,000 deaths annually in the United States and has been implicated as a "contributing factor" in the deaths of *twenty times* that number each year. Without question, hypertension is a life-threatening condition which if left untreated can be every bit as serious to the victim as terminal cancer or a fatal plane crash.

As with any serious epidemic, the human ability to cope with hypertension is dependent on a variety of factors. Foremost in combating hypertension is the need for increased knowledge by both the layperson and the medical practitioner. A program of public education regarding what is known about "high blood pressure" is beginning to show results, but much more needs to be done to heighten public awareness of the problem. America's very lifestyle is being impugned as her citizens fail to get enough exercise, work in a stress-laden business world, and eat themselves into a premature grave with dietary excesses. The average American daily consumes from 15 to 30 times the amount of sodium required for good health. Much medical evidence suggests that one to three grams per day would be more than enough.

It is probable that as the causes of hypertension are better understood considerable attention will be focused on environmental and dietary factors which appear unique to the 20th century. Of these dietary factors, a high-sodium intake is now suspected as a major factor in causing human hypertension. Researchers have established that high intakes of sodium can develop various types of human and experimental hypertension and that on the other hand salt restriction often decreases the blood pressure of hypertensive subjects. Because of this, treatment for many hypertensive patients includes diuretic drugs which have the ability of a saluretic agent to decrease blood pressure.

It is known that for many patients with mild hypertension, a low-sodium diet may be the only treatment necessary. Many physicians also recommend a low-sodium diet along with one or more other treatments such as psychological or stress-reducing therapy (meditation, biofeedback, relaxation, etc.), exercise (often in combination with a recommendation for weight loss), and/or drug therapy (diuretics or antihypertensives). Unfortunately, no single approach seems appropriate to all cases of hypertension and some modes of treatment carry with them the possibility of having no controlling effect or inducement of undesirable side effects (as potentially the case in drug therapy).

Even though certain treatments may be accompanied by side effects, it is obvious that non-treatment of hypertension is simply not an acceptable alternative. Mortality rates for those with untreated hypertension are indeed sobering. One simply needs to check the actuarial tables with any life insurance agent to be persuaded by the overwhelming weight of statistical evidence. Without question, treatment *is* of crucial importance to the hypertensive patient.

High-sodium Diet: A Modern Day Hazard

Our culture has placed a premium on convenience foods. Unfortunately, such foods are inordinately high in sodium content. Sodium chloride (common table salt) is but only *one* of the culprits in todays's pattern of dietary sodium excess. Among some other sodium preservatives and ingredients commonly used are:

baking soda	baking powder
brine	MSG (monosodium glutamate)
di-sodium phosphate	sea salt
sodium alginate	sodium benzoate
sodium hydrozide	sodium propionate
sodium sulfite	sodium casseinate
sodium nitrite	

Sodium preservatives have become an "essential" ingredient in virtually all commercially prepared foods. Add the taste habits of a generation which has been brought up on convenience foods and you can frequently witness the spectre of table salt being added to an already sodium-laden diet. One illustration of the problem is found with ordinary canned peas. Because of commercial processing, they contain 250 times the amount of sodium as fresh produce. To this the average cook would probably add a generous pat of butter while cooking (one tablespoon of butter has 139 mg. of sodium) and salt to taste (one teaspoon of table salt has 2,500 mg. of sodium). Without much imagination, it is easy to visualize the problem.

Apart from a recommendation to avoid convenience foods, throw away the salt shaker and totally forgo junk foods, there yet is a serious and overriding dietary consideration—taste! The motivation for this book came out of that overriding consideration. The authors were abruptly confronted with a dilemma: for medical reasons, their husbands were directed to low-sodium diets by physicians. The dilemma became acute, however, when a quick examination yielded a dearth of low-sodium recipes and when finicky husbands (and dinner guests) compared standard recipes with low-sodium versions of these same dishes. All concluded that the new "taste" was akin to something between wallpaper paste and cardboard fricassee.

Anyone recently departing a doctor's office with the same suggestion for a low-sodium diet will also note that a physician becomes virtually mute when confronted with the question, "How can I cook without salt?" Perhaps if you are really lucky, your doctor will provide you with a six-page pamphlet containing as many as eight recipes (four involving boiled chicken served over salt-free melba toast) which are supposed to take care of your dietary need for the rest of your life. Add to the scenario a busy lifestyle that requires entertaining and dinner parties and the stage is almost set for *Living Without Salt!*

One important consideration remains: What about the rest of the family? Are they also exiled to a life of cardboard fricassee? Or is the chef to prepare separate menus for each member of the family?

First, it should be emphasized that each member of the American family is probably ingesting far beyond the sodium level required for optimum health. It also would seem to follow that by controlling the sodium intake of children, many could be spared hypertension in later life. Today's emphasis on convenience and junk foods with a high sodium content may well be contributing to a whole new generation of hypertensives in the future.

Research in the 1960s illustrated that sodium levels in commercial infant foods were lethal for rats and that such high levels served no useful purpose in the infant diet. As a result, the Committee on Nutrition of the American Academy of Pediatrics recommended the reduction of salt in commercial infant foods. Most producers have complied; however, many parents insist on adding salt to infant food to match their adult taste and thereby assure continuation of the problem. Clearly, all the members of the American family are in the same boat. There is a strong case for substantial reduction in sodium intake for each member of the family regardless of age. There is also a need for appetizing and realistic recipes which meet the realities and demands of today's lifestyle. The stage is now set.

Our Safe, Practical Answer: *Living Without Salt*

The authors have succeeded in making available highly appetizing recipes that have a low-sodium content. Also stressed in their work has been a recognition that a busy lifestyle requires not only a daily "bill of fare" that is practical and appealing but that there are those special occasions when entertaining requires a menu that is something special. The recipes have been developed and refined by the authors and tested by their "finicky" husbands. Both husbands are enthusiastic in their high appraisal of *Living Without Salt*.

Recipes from hors d'oeurves to desserts have stood the test of family approval. Dinner guests have praised many of the recipes never having suspected that a "low-sodium" meal had just passed their palates. Most importantly, *Living Without Salt* contains healthful recipes that are highly appetizing and happily allow a smooth transition to saner dietary habits.

The book is intended for patients following medical advice or for anyone who simply wishes to use an "ounce of prevention" rather than face the prospects of later searching for a "pound of cure."

James W. Baltzell, M.D.

James F. Parsley, Jr., Ph.D.

Salt Is Not The Only Seasoning

Throughout the centuries salt has been a precious commodity. A daily ration of salt was given to the Roman soldiers. The portion alloted was known as the "salarium" from which our modern word "salary" is derived. This salarium was eventually converted to an allowance to buy salt.

Indians traded their most valued handiwork for salt to feed their tribes for a year, but only those in charge of the cook pots were allowed access to the salt. The soldiers of ancient times wore quilted jackets padded with salt to insulate themselves against the cold. In medieval England those seated "below the salt" were not privileged to have salt at all! (Who were the lucky ones?)

Lot's wife was told not to look behind her. She did and turned into a pillar of salt! (Gen. 19:26.) In parts of Central Africa, salt is still a luxury available only to the rich. The habitual use of salt is connected intimately with the advance from nomadic to agricultural life. Peoples of ancient nations usually included salt in their offerings to their gods.

Covenants were made (and in some countries still are) over a meal in which salt was a necessary element. The preservation qualities of salt make it a symbol of an enduring compact. Thus, the word salt is equated with something held in high esteem. The Arabs say, "There is salt between us." The Hebrews have an expression "to eat the salt of the palace." And one of the sayings of Jesus was, "You are the salt of the earth." There is an old Spanish saying—"A kiss without a mustache is like an egg without salt."

Salt has historically been a valued commodity—used wisely and *sparingly*. In the present time of massive food processing the food industry has cheapened the value of salt by using it indiscriminately. Therefore it is up to you, as the consumer, to put value back in salt. Use it sparingly. Change your buying and eating habits. Let's keep salt in the history books and not in food!!!

For Starters . . .

Keep these items on hand as staples. If these items are not readily found, ask the store manager—often they will order for you if an item is not regularly stocked.

Baking powder substitute: can be found at health food stores.

Bouillon cubes: unsalted varieties can be found in health food stores or the special diet section at the grocery store.

Bran flakes: found in health food stores or look for "untreated" bran in the grocery store, usually near the flour/sugar section.

Bread: look for unsalted bread in the frozen food section or bread rack in grocery stores or ask at a bakery. Some health food stores also carry low-sodium bread.

Brown sugar: dark or light brown, preferably cane sugar as this sugar tends to blend with other ingredients easier than beet sugar.

Chili sauce and catsup: unsalted varieties can be found in grocery stores or health food stores.

Garlic and onion powder: be careful to get powders rather than salts!

Honey: there are many flavors and all are acceptable.

Margarine: unsalted margarine is sold in grocery stores. Some stores keep it in the frozen food section and some stores keep it in the refrigerated section with the other margarines.

Mustard: unsalted varieties can be found in grocery stores or health food stores.

Nuts: all varieties can be purchased raw at health food stores, grocery stores, or specialty nut stores. Walnuts, cashews, almonds and peanuts provide a great variety for cooking and eating alone. Store in freezer until ready to use as nuts have oils that can turn rancid with prolonged shelf storage.

Paprika: a great addition to many dishes and also decorative when lightly sprinkled on top of many dishes.

Potassium bicarbonate (baking soda substitute): available at most pharmacies. Ask for "food grade" potassium bicarbonate and tell the pharmacist that it will be used for cooking.

Raisins: any color, light or dark. Great for cooking and snacks. Nutritious.

Salt substitute and seasoned salt substitute: found in health food stores and grocery stores.

Sesame seeds: found in health food stores in bulk quantities which tend to be more economical than buying the small packages in grocery stores. Brown sesame seeds do not have the hull removed so are more nutritious and contain more potassium.

Skim milk: This is recommended because the cholesterol content as well as calorie content is lower than whole, one percent, or two percent milk. The amount of sodium remains the same no matter what the fat content of milk. Skim milk and nonfat milk are comparable.

Spices and herbs: Check labels for salt listed in ingredients. Also, be careful of any ingredient listed with the word "sodium." See *Potpourri of Flavor,* pg. 25.

Soups: order unsalted soups by case lots for extra savings. Cream of mushroom and tomato can be used in many recipes.

Tomato paste: unsalted varieties can be found in grocery stores—read labels carefully.

Unbleached flour: use instead of "white" flour.

Vegetables, canned and frozen: unsalted vegetables are available in cans and may be purchased in case lots for economy. Many frozen vegetables are unsalted. Read labels for any salt or sodium additives.

Wheat germ (raw): store in freezer as oils have a tendency to turn rancid rapidly.

Whole wheat flour: whole wheat flour adds flavor as well as vitamins to the daily diet. Fresh, stone ground flour contains bran which provides fiber.

A Comparison in Sodium Content
The amount of sodium in spaghetti sauce prepared three ways

Prepared Mix	Mg of Sodium	Homemade with Salt	Mg of Sodium	Homemade Low-sodium	Mg of Sodium
1 3/8-ounce package with mushrooms prepared as package directs	3940	½ cup onion, sliced	0	½ cup onion, sliced	0
		1½ pounds lean ground beef	354	1½ pounds lean ground beef	354
		2 cloves garlic, minced	0	2 cloves garlic, minced	0
		4-ounce can mushrooms	533	¼ pound sliced fresh mushrooms	0
		2-pounds canned tomatoes	400	2 1-pound cans unsalted tomatoes	15
		2 8-ounce cans tomato sauce (seasoned)	1500	2 6-ounce cans tomato paste (no salt added)	0
		1 6-ounce can tomato paste (salt added)	65	1 cup red wine	0
		¼ cup parsley, chopped	8	¼ cup parsley, chopped	8
		1½ teaspoons oregano or sage	0	2½ teaspoons oregano or sage	0
		1 teaspoon salt	2500	½ teaspoon seasoned salt substitute	4
		½ teaspoon M.S.G.	815	½ teaspoon thyme	0
		¼ teaspoon thyme	0	1 bay leaf	0
		1 bay leaf	0	1 cup water	0
		1 cup water	0	1 green pepper	8
		Total Milligrams Sodium	6175	1 teaspoon brown sugar	4
				Total Milligrams Sodium	393

Mg of sodium per serving of sauce	Mg of sodium per serving of sauce	Mg of sodium per serving of sauce
985	1029	65.5

Helpful Hints for Avoiding a Few of the Pitfalls

Acid Indigestion or Heartburn? The sodium in just five tablets of the leading roll antacid exceeds over half of the daily allowance of sodium doctors recommend for strict low-salt diets. But certain tablets have virtually no sodium—less than one percent. Check labels for sodium ingredients.

Anti-depressants (MAO Inhibitors) and Antihypertensives: Check with your physician about the consumption of foods that are tyramine-rich if you are on some form of drug that is either an antidepressant or is antihypertensive medication. The combination of food and drug may possibly be dangerous—if not lethal!

Adapting Recipes is really not too difficult, but be careful of hidden sodium. Watch out for cottage cheese, cheeses, corn syrup, molasses (some types are worse than others), bacon, ham, tomato sauce, bouillon cubes, baking powder and soda, monosodium glutamate, most canned foods unless specifically low-sodium, luncheon meats, frozen dinners, prepared foods, soups. Eliminate the salt in recipes and learn to be adventuresome with other spices and substitutes that are lower in sodium. See the bibliography for a listing of guides to low-sodium eating.

Caffein: Be careful of caffein! One cup of coffee has 150 mg of caffein and can raise blood pressure 10-15 points—plus it remains in the body 8-12 hours. A cup of instant coffee has 60 mg of caffein, 50 mg per cup of tea, 30 mg per cup of cocoa, and 30 mg per can of soda pop. A candy bar has 10-20 mg of caffein and a commercially prepared caffein tablet may have 100 mg of caffein. Caffein has many adverse side effects, one of which is irritability.

Women who are breast feeding should avoid coffee with caffein as it is often transmitted to the infant and can cause side effects.

Carob Powder: This powder is ground from the carob pod, which comes from a tree of the locust family. Toasted, carob powder strongly resembles chocolate, but it has none of chocolate's undesirable features. Whereas chocolate is high in fat, carob is not. For many people, chocolate is an allergen, especially for migraine headache sufferers. Carob has no such adverse effect. Chocolate contains theobromine, a stimulant similar to caffein, carob is free of stimulants. Carob is rich in minerals and natural sugars. Toasted carob powder more closely resembles chocolate in flavor. Carob powders vary in flavor, so keep experimenting until you find the one you like.

Celery: One outer stalk of celery has 50 mg of sodium, so judge for yourself as to how much your diet will allow. Celery adds taste to many dishes and can be used sparingly.

Chili Powder is a blend, so read the label to ascertain whether it contains any salt. Different brands have varying blends.

Cocoa Mixes have lots of sodium, plus caffein, plus tyramine. A recipe to make your own cocoa mix is included in the appetizer section.

Compliance: Many specialty cookbooks and/or low-sodium cookbooks use no salt substitute and use fewer spices in recipes than those in this book. Consequently, people do not comply with their diet—that means they do not stay on the diet. This may be for a variety of reasons such as: (1) the recipes come out tasting so bland, (2) ingredients are difficult to obtain, and (3) figuring out charts, graphs, quantities, and milligrams becomes tedious.

Freezer: Use for freezing dairy products. All dairy products can be frozen, so don't hesitate to buy in quantity. Also, freezing your own vegetables ensures that they are salt-free. Use the freezer to store nuts, leftovers, prepared mixes, extra quantities for later use, breads, and flours.

Horseradish: Horseradish without added salt may be found in the refrigerated section of the grocery store.

Licorice: A substance contained in natural licorice root causes salt and water retention that can lead to elevated blood pressure and an increased possibility of heart attacks. (See *Potpourri of Flavor* section.)

Frozen Juices: Read labels for brands which are free of any additives.

Molasses: The light molasses tends to be lower in sodium than the unsulphured, blackstrap, and medium molasses.

Salt Substitute: Salt substitute is a natural ingredient. It is not artificial and has a "plus" because it contains potassium. Recent studies indicate that potassium, when combined with a low-sodium diet, further reduces blood pressure levels. It is also important in the diet because some medications prescribed for high blood pressure cause potassium depletion. Some recipes included in this book call for the use of salt substitute (potassium chloride). This is for three reasons: (1) it makes the food taste more like "normal food"; (2) it adds needed potassium to the diet; and (3) salt substitute added to bread mixtures that require yeast replaces the function of regular salt in retardation of the growing action of yeast. Thus, breads do not rise too quickly and leave a coarse texture.

Sugar: Granulated sugar in any recipe may be replaced with honey (using half as much honey as you would sugar) or fructose (following the label directions).

Soda Pop: Diet drinks tend to be 30 mg of sodium per can higher than non-diet drinks. Be careful with cola drinks, as they contain caffein and tyramine as well as sodium.

Spices: Go through your spice cabinet and read the labels—you'll be surprised at the number of spices that have salt already in them. THROW THEM OUT! Then, be adventuresome and try lots of new spices.

Stamps: They have salt, as does the envelope closure. Use a sponge, lick the non-sticky portion of the envelope, or lick your finger—OR, use self-stick envelopes.

Tomato Paste is usually unsalted—read the label. Use tomato paste instead of tomato sauce. Some tomato puree has no salt and may be used as tomato sauce (just add a little water, garlic powder, minced onion, seasoned salt substitute, and a squirt of lemon).

Toothpaste has salt in it. The moral of this is to try not to eat your toothpaste!

Toppings: Use pure maple syrup, apple butter or honey as a topping for pancakes or waffles. Many syrup brands have sodium and corn sweeteners.

Water: Check the sodium level of your local water supply. Avoid drinking softened water as salt is used to soften water. In the kitchen, the cold water can be hooked up to by-pass the softening system—check with your plumber.

Wheat Germ: Use the untoasted wheat germ. This has more food value and tastes more flavorful. This must be stored in the freezer, as it turns rancid and may even get weevils.

Whipped Toppings: The authors had a philosophical question when including either non-dairy whipped toppings or whipped cream in the recipes. There are two ways to view this issue: non-dairy whipped toppings have the advantages of low cholesterol and low sodium levels, but they have the disadvantage of the inclusion of artificial ingredients. Conversely, whipped cream has high fat content which contributes to a high cholesterol content. *However, whipping cream is lower in sodium than a cup of skim milk.* It is hoped that the reader will make the right judgment for his/her diet and philosophy in the use of either non-dairy whipped toppings or whipped cream. If only one of the ingredients is listed, the cook should make the decision to use what is requested, make a substitution, or eliminate the topping altogether.

Baby Food

A number of years ago, a study revealed the dangerous level of sodium in prepared baby foods. A warning went out to the manufacturers of the possible fatalities due to the amount of salt. Manufacturers complied with regulations and eliminated the salt additive. But a danger still exists!

Parents still add salt to the baby's food, not realizing the dangers. Salt acts as a poison and the child's body has a low salt tolerance level. Plus, adding salt to the child's food develops the undesired taste for salt which causes the victim to become a saltoholic—one who adds salt at the table and often even before the food has been tasted.

What can you do to remedy this situation and give the child the healthy, nutritional beginning he/she deserves?

First, if you purchase prepared baby foods, DON'T ADD SALT—OR SUGAR! Keep up this practice as the child grows. Remember, heredity plays a strong part in hypertension.

Secondly, prepare your baby's food from your unsalted leftovers. This way you're providing good nutrition at an economical cost.

Adding salt is only a habit. *You* can make sure this habit is not developed!

Start immediately your family's education about the dangers of adding salt at *any* time to food.

Toward a Potpourri of Flavor

The flavor backbone of any diet, particularly a low-sodium diet, is the seasonings. Our dilemma in this chapter is the proper way, in one quick word, to tell you about the various ingredients with which you will want to become familiar. Hence, "Potpourri," the meaning of which is "medley." A creative cook will use a medley of ingredients. These ingredients may include:

| herbs | seeds | flavorings |
| spices | extracts | seasonings |

Many suggestions follow for flavoring your foods. Mix-your-own blends have been presented so that the cook can make them easily and economically. They taste so much better when freshly made! The flavor of whole spices will last almost indefinitely. Ground spices will maintain good aroma and flavor for up to six months if properly stored. Protect spices from heat, moisture and light. Keep them tightly sealed in opaque containers.

Along with your attitude, spices and herbs provide the key to your "new" adventures in eating. The following guide will help you know what flavorings are available for your use.

ALLSPICE — Allspice is the dried, unripe fruit of a West Indian tropical evergreen, now commonly grown in Jamaica. The berry is picked green and dried in the sun, thus intensifying the aroma. Allspice has a flavor reminiscent of clove, cinnamon and nutmeg combined.
Uses: Pickling, meat stews, fish, fruits, fruit pies, relishes, puddings, breads, and fruit drinks.

ALMOND EXTRACT — Almond extract is the oil extracted from the kernel of the bitter almond. The almond tree is related to the peach tree.
Uses: Gives flavor to cakes or pastry, sauces, dessert puddings, gelatins, and other dishes; marzipan.

ALUM — Alum is a chemical which has an astringent effect. It is available in drugstores.
Uses: Gives crispness to cucumbers for pickling, as well as crisping up melon rinds, onions, green beans, and other foods. It is often used as an ingredient in some baking powders.

ANISE — This Mediterranean plant is of the parsley family and has a distinctive licorice flavor. Anise seed is the dried fruit. The Hebrews, Greeks and Romans valued anise for its reputed medicinal qualities. The full flavor of the seeds is released by crushing the seeds between two sheets of waxed paper and then used in baking. The star anise is from the fruit of a tree of southeastern China and Vietnam.
Uses: Liqueurs; breads, stews and seafood cocktails; enhances carrot, cauliflower and beet dishes; baking and candy-making such as in licorice confections; flavors sausages.

ARROWROOT — The edible starch obtained from the rootstocks of various tropical plants. The roots produce a white fluid which is then made into a powder. Arrowroot is an excellent thickening agent, especially in sauces and custards containing eggs, which must not boil or are heat sensitive. High temperatures and excessive stirring will cause marked thinning. When substituting arrowroot for flour in a recipe, use half as much arrowroot as the called-for amount of flour.
Uses: Soups, sauces, pie fillings, puddings; useful in invalid cookery because of its easy digestibility.

BASIL (Sweet Basil) — This sweet-flavored leaf is a member of the mint family. "Basil" is Greek for "royal" or "king." Native to the Middle East and the Mediterranean. Hindus regard it as a sacred herb, protecting one from the misfortunes of life and as a guide to heaven in death. It offers protection against malaria and assured fertility to those desiring children. The Hindus feel uprooting the herb can only bring evil. Available either fresh or dried.
Uses: It is helpful in almost any dish that can be herbed and especially flavorful with seafoods, salads, poultry, potatoes, vegetable soup, and dishes that contain tomatoes.

BAY LEAF (Laurel Leaf) — Native to the Near East and the Mediterranean, the bay or laurel shrub or small tree is also grown in the southern United States. The California laurel is grown mostly for its volatile oil. The laurel tree occupies a semi-mystical place in Greek life and mythology. "Winning one's laurels" is an expression originating when a laurel leaf was placed on the brow of the winner of the Olympic games. Being crowned with laurel was a custom for gods, emperors, and heros of ancient Rome. The word "baccalaureate" means "laurel berry." Bay leaves are available whole, crushed, and ground.
Uses: Potatoes, onions, vegetables, and tomato-flavored dishes; a familiar ingredient

of bouquet garni; popular in French and Mediterranean cooking.

BELL PEPPERS—Bell peppers are related to chili peppers, cayenne, and paprika. This is an excellent all-around addition to foods. The red peppers are sweeter tasting than the green peppers.
Uses: Pickling, sauces, stews, soups, meat dishes, salads, appetizers; a wide variety of uses.

BOUILLON—Bouillon is extracted from boiling poultry, fish, or beef parts or vegetables in water. DO NOT USE COMMERCIAL BOUILLON IN ANY FORM as it is made with a high concentration of sodium—use low-sodium bouillon cubes, low-sodium soup base concentrate, or make your own. When a clear broth, or consomme, is desired, the bouillon must be clarified.
Uses: By itself or as a base for other soups, flavorings in main dishes, or to provide moisture to rices and potatoes.

BOUQUET GARNI—A "varied bouquet" of herbs and spices tied together in a muslin or cheesecloth bag for easy disposal after cooking. Usually contains parsley, thyme, and a bay leaf.

Uses: Flavors soups, such as bouillabaisse.

CARAWAY SEED—Caraway seeds are actually a fruit from a plant of the carrot family. They have a pleasant, aromatic odor when crushed and an agreeable spicy taste. The oil from the seed provides the distinctive flavor of the liqueur kümmel.
Uses: To season soups, meats, vegetables, breads such as rye, cakes, and pastries.

CARDAMOM—Cardamom is a precious spice, second only in cost to saffron. An acre of land will yield only about 250 pounds of cardamoms and hand labor is required for harvesting. Cardamom is native to the moist forests of Southern India. It may disintegrate and disappear during the cooking process in soups, curries, or stews. The aroma and flavor is slightly reminiscent of camphor.
Uses: Soups, curries, or stews; bread and pastries; relishes; Indian and Scandinavian cooking, bouquet garni.

CASSIA—Cassia is the inner bark of an Asian evergreen tree. Available in bark, bud, or ground form, cassia is more strongly flavored than cinnamon even though the cassia tree is botanically the same tree as the cinnamon tree. It is just grown in a different area.

Uses: Same general uses as cinnamon; pickling, preserving, and flavoring puddings and cooked fruits.

CAYENNE PEPPER — Also called red pepper or chili pepper, it is ground into a powder from the dried fruits of several species of the capsicum plant. Cayenne has a hot, biting taste and should be used lightly to flavor foods.
Uses: An ingredient of sausage seasonings and curry powders; adds flavor to meats, fish, poultry, cheese and egg dishes; sauces, salad dressings, and ethnic dishes.

CELERY SEED — Celery seed is from the wild celery plant. Obtained mostly from India, celery seed is stronger in flavor and tougher in texture than celery cultivated for the table. Available whole or ground.
Uses: Pickling; salad dressings; fish and vegetable dishes, or any dish calling for celery.

CHERVIL — This delicate herb is a favorite in American herb gardens. Chervil resembles parsley. One of the most famous of *fines herbes,* or the "fine herbs," this herb is an essential ingredient in Bearnaise Sauce. The Greeks and Romans ate chervil as a vegetable by eating the leaves and boiling the roots. It was considered by a Roman writer to be a hiccup remedy when chervil seed was put in vinegar.
Uses: Flavors soups, salads, stews, omelets, and potato dishes.

CHILI CON CARNE SEASONING — A blend of seasonings used to flavor chili con carne. This blend contains ground chili peppers, garlic, cumin, coriander, and oregano.
Uses: Eggs, poultry, cheese, and pasta sauces. Hamburgers or meatloaf, sprinkled over corn, summer squash, or lima beans to accompany a Mexican dinner; marinades for pork and roast.

CHILI POWDER — Milder than cayenne pepper, chili powder is a blend. It combines Mexican chilies, marjoram, cumin seed, oregano, garlic, cloves, allspice, bay leaves AND SOMETIMES SALT — be cautious and read the label for ingredients.
Uses: Mexican dishes, sauces, stews, and meat dishes; eggs, meat marinades and with shellfish and sweet vegetables.

CHOCOLATE — Chocolate and cocoa are made from the beans of the cacao tree, a perennial evergreen tree of the cola family. Native to the hot humid forests of the Amazon basin, it flourishes only in tropical climates. Chocolate is a mixture of roasted cocoa, cocoa butter, and very fine sugar. Chocolate was the royal drink of the Aztecs and cocoa beans were used as money. Chocolate has a considerably stimulating effect on the heart and general musculature of the body.

Uses: Baking and in drinks; also, when combined with milk and other ingredients, is used for general eating. Unsweetened or bitter chocolate, semisweet or candy-making chocolate, pieces, sweet cooking chocolate are a few of the types of chocolate available.

CIDER VINEGAR—A milky yellowish-brown vinegar made from hard or fermented cider.
Uses: Pickling, canning, salad dressings.

CINNAMON—From the laurel family, cinnamon is from the dried bark of a shrub-like evergreen tree. Native to the Orient and India, the ancient Romans used cinnamon not only to spice their foods but to make love potions. Cinnamon can be purchased in sticks or ground form, or as an oil.
Uses: In ground form cinnamon can be used to spice desserts, cookies, vegetables, toast. In stick form can be used as an attractive stirring stick or to flavor hot drinks; good in hearty soups and vegetable dishes.

CITRON—Citron is probably native to India and was the first of the citrus fruits to be used by Europeans as long ago as the fourth century B.C. Similar to lemon, citron has a greenish-yellow, tough and warty, fragrant peel, and a scanty, acid pulp.
Uses: The peel is used in baking, especially in fruitcakes. The peel is first soaked in brine (SALT and water)—use in small quantities!

CLOVE—Clove is the nail-shaped, unopened bud of the clove tree. This tree is grown mainly on the islands of Zanzibar and Madagascar. Used since before Christ, this spice was coveted and valued. Native to the Spice Islands of the Far East, clove trees were limited in production by the Dutch in the 17th Century. This created a productive monopoly until the French were able to get a few trees transplanted to various French colonies.
Uses: A wide variety of uses in its whole or ground forms in desserts, chili sauce, pickles, vegetables, meats, soups, and hot drinks.

COCONUT—The fruit of a palm, native to Malaya, coconut is now grown in all parts of the tropical and subtropical world. This fruit is twelve to eighteen inches in length and six to eight inches in diameter. Requiring about a year for this fruit to mature, the outer covering is smooth, the husk fibrous, and a woody brown shell encases the coconut that is available in grocery stores. Inside the brown shell is a layer of firm white meat with a milky fluid at the center. The meat can be purchased already grated or shredded.

Uses: Eaten fresh, used for cooking, a delicious accompaniment to curry, and as an ingredient in baking and candy.

COCONUT MILK — When a recipe calls for coconut milk, this does not mean the liquid contained in the coconut shell — it is the juice squeezed from the meat of the coconut. If a fresh coconut is not available, packaged coconut may be purchased, soaked in the proportions of four cups of packaged coconut to one cup of boiling water for five minutes. Squeeze out and strain the liquid and set aside. Add another cup of boiling water to the coconut meat and repeat process, keeping liquid separate from first squeezing. May be processed a third time for large quantities of curries. When the recipe calls for two cups of coconut milk, use one cup of the first extract, and one cup of the second extract.

CORIANDER — The dried fruit of a foot-tall herb which belongs to the parsley family. Native to the Mediterranean and the Orient, coriander was used in ancient times by the Egyptians and has been found in tombs of 960 to 800 B.C. This seed has a pleasant flavor, not unlike that of a combination of anise seed, cumin seed, and orange. It has the unusual quality of becoming more fragrant the longer it is kept.

Uses: Ground coriander is used to spice cookies, candies, soups, pastries, and gingerbreads; blended spices, condiments, and curries contain coriander.

CREAM OF TARTAR — A fine white powder made from pressed grapes. A natural fruit acid, cream of tartar is used as a leavening agent and is used in commercial baking powders. Before the production of a reliable baking powder, cream of tartar and baking soda were combined to make a leavening agent.

Uses: Used for making frostings and candies (keeps food white and gives it a creamier consistency and a less-sweet taste). Used for beating egg whites, it makes the whites firmer for greater tolerance of the oven heat.

CUMIN — A delicate member of the parsley family, the cumin plant produces the cumin seed which is tiny and oval, with a strong, warm and slightly bitter taste. Native to the Mediterranean countries, North Africa, and Western Asia, the cumin plant has been used since ancient times to stimulate the appetite and flavor fish, meats and breads. Available either whole or ground.

Uses: Used widely in oriental meat cooking, curries, and Mexican cooking, as well as cheeses and liqueurs such as kümmel; this seed has a wide and varied appeal.

CURRY POWDER—Probably the world's earliest spice blend, curry powder ingredients vary depending upon the dish that it will flavor. Columbus discovered America and many members of the pepper family (capsicum). The Portuguese brought capsicums to India and it was at this time that curries became hot. The basic ingredients in curry powder include turmeric, fenugreek, cumin seed, coriander, and red or cayenne pepper. It may also include peppers, aromatic spices, and mustard.

Uses: Indian dishes, soups, white sauces and creamed dishes, mayonnaise, and salad dressings.

DILL—Native to Asia Minor and Europe, dill is a favorite herb now as it was for the Greeks. Decorative garlands of flowering dill purified the air of banquet halls in Roman times. Dill seed is the dried fruit of the herb and dill weed is its dried leaves. Available as fresh or dried weed or whole or ground seeds.

Uses: Pickling and canning; soups, cheese, fish, meats, poultry, vegetables, and breads.

FENNEL—Native to the Mediterranean, this plant belongs to the carrot family. The flavor is reminiscent of anise. Fennel seed is available whole or ground. Fennel has a strong taste and a little fennel seed goes a long way—use sparingly. Use one fennel seed per serving, until it is discovered how much of this flavor is desired.

Uses: Flavors soups, breads, candy, liqueurs.

FENUGREEK—Native to Asia and southern Europe, fenugreek is a member of the pea family. Cultivated chiefly for its seeds, the seeds are removed from the parent plant and dried with artificial heat. The seeds have a pleasantly, bitter taste, somewhat like burnt sugar. Fresh fenugreek plants are eaten as a vegetable in India.

Uses: To flavor curry powders, chutney, spice blends, soups, legumes such as black-eyed peas, breads, and cookies.

FINES HERBES—a French term meaning "fine herbs," this blend is a combination of two or more finely chopped herbs.

Uses: French cookery, egg dishes, fish, chicken, salads and salad dressings.

GARLIC — A member of the lily family, the hardy, bulbous plant is widely cultivated in both temperate and hot climates. Garlic has been long used for medicinal purposes, as a love potion, and in expelling evil.
Uses: Pickling and canning, soups, sauces, stews, dressings, vinegar, sausages, meats, salads.

GINGER — The thick, tuberous root of a perennial plant, ginger comes from Jamaica, India, Sierra Leone and Nigeria. Ginger was considered in ancient times to be a medicine as well as a spice, reputedly curing troubles of love and prolonging life, as well as being used as a cure against the plague. Presently used as a digestive stimulant.
Uses: Oriental dishes, cakes and pies, Indian pudding, stewed fruits, pot roasts, broiled and roasted poultry, chutneys, pickling, and preserves and conserves.

GLYCERIN — A clear, colorless, thick, sticky, sweet-tasting liquid belonging to the alcohol family of organic compounds. Glycerol remains as a solution in water when acids are set free and is purified by coagulating and settling extraneous matter, evaporating the water, and distilling. Thus, glycerin is used when acids need to be neutralized and a thicker consistency is desired.
Uses: Liqueurs, candies, pickling, to preserve broad leafed plants in a dried state.

HORSERADISH — The large, fleshy, white, and cylindrical root has a pungent odor. Native to southeastern Europe, horseradish is one of the five bitter herbs of the Jewish Passover festival. It has been used long before Christian times. It grows wild in some states such as Nebraska and Iowa. Sold fresh, dried, or bottled. Do be careful buying horseradish. Some horseradish spreads contain *SALT!*
Uses: Flavors seafood sauces or served as a condiment for meats, game or fish.

INVERT SUGAR — Recipes do not call for invert sugar. Rather, this is the resulting mixture from a cooking process, particularly those involving the cooking of jelly, jam, candy and frosting. Invert sugar is formed when sugar is changed from sucrose to glucose and fructose. This change occurs with the use of heat and acid. Invert sugar keeps the sugar crystals small; therefore, the end product will be of a smoother texture. Many recipes require heating the sugar and acid (lemon juice, vinegar, cream of tartar). Remember this step is important. Not only will the sugar granules be less apparent, but the acid will stop jellies and jams from recrystallizing. They will, therefore, be more clear, smooth and palatable.

LEMON—Native to Asia, this citrus fruit has been long used for preserves, medicinal purposes such as preventing scurvy on long voyages, flavoring, and removing stains. Lemon oil is used for flavoring and is extracted from the rind taking about 1,000 lemons to make one pound of oil. Lemon juice is available in bottles or frozen, and the lemon rind can be found dried in the spice section of the grocery store.
Uses: Preserves, flavors, beverages, remove stains.

LICORICE—A perennial herb of the pea family, licorice grows wild in southern Europe and in western and central Asia. It has been known as a flavoring since remote times. This plant is now cultivated commercially for its root which is dried and produces an extract used for flavoring. Most licorice in this country is artificial and not harmful, but imported licorice candy and flavoring from Europe is often natural. This natural licorice contains a substance which may cause salt and water retention that can lead to elevated blood pressure and heart attacks.
Uses: The extract from the root is used to

flavor medicines, tobacco, cigars, cigarettes, soft and alcoholic drinks, candy, and chewing gum.

LIME—Quite similar to the lemon, this green citrus fruit has a slightly more pungent juice. The lime tree originated in eastern and southern Asia. It was growing wild in Asia and was then brought to the East Indies and domesticated in the 16th century by Portuguese and Spanish explorers. Packaged like lemon juice and rind.
Uses: Preserves, flavors, beverages.

LOVAGE—This herb has a celery-like taste. The lovage root has a strong taste and smell, but resembles its relatives, celery and parsley. Native to southern Europe and Asia and India, lovage was used extensively in Greek and Roman cooking. Astrologists have claimed that it is a sun herb, whose sign is Taurus the bull. "If Saturn offend the throat," lovage is recommended as a cure.
Uses: Flavors stews, salad dressing, meats, and vegetable juice cocktails.

MACE—An aromatic spice that is made from the seed covering of the nutmeg. More pungent than nutmeg, mace has the sweet strong flavor and odor of the nutmeg. The Moluccas or

Spice Islands, in the East Indies, is the originating source of the nutmeg tree and it is also grown in the West Indies. Mace imparts a rich, yellow color to pound cakes.
Uses: Comes in blades (whole) for pickling and preserving; ground for pound cakes and chocolate dishes, stewed cherries, apricots, or peaches.

MALT—Malt is made from sprouting or germinating grains, and then drying and grinding them. This process partially converts starch to sugar and changes proteins to amino acids, changing the raw, hard grain into a mellow, crisp, and sweet-tasting malt. This adds proteins and carbohydrates to the diet. When using malt in the breadmaking process, decrease the amount of sugar slightly.
Uses: Brewing beer, breads, milkshakes.

MARJORAM—This member of the mint family is related to oregano. It is native to Europe, Asia and Australia. It is a delicate herb with a sweet taste and gentle fragrance, with a mild sage-like flavor. Traditionally used at joyous occasions, marjoram accompanied newly weds on the road to a long and happy life together hidden in hope chests and tucked into wedding wreaths and crowns. The Greeks and Romans used it extensively at funerals to symbolize the happiness of the loved one. It was found to be effective in the cure of burns and headaches in the Middle Ages.
Uses: Enhances the flavors of almost any dish —salads, vegetables, seafoods, meats, eggs and game, pasta, tomato dishes and soups.

MINT—There are a number of mint varieties and many uses. In cooking, the term mint usually refers to peppermint or spearmint. Named by the Romans and Greeks, it was believed that Pluto, the god of the underworld, had fallen in love with a beautiful nymph, Menthe. Pluto's wife, Persephone, angrily changed the maiden into a plant that would grow where it could be stepped upon. Mint was quite valued at one time and is mentioned in the Bible as forming part of a tithe. It has been used for religious incantations and throughout history for medicinal purposes.
Uses: Mint has a large number of uses for its leaves, both dried and fresh, as well as the oil derived from these leaves. Removes strong tastes from meats such as lamb and game; enhances vegetables, soups, fruits, fish, salad dressings and juices.

MUSTARD—While mustard can be any of several herbs cultivated for the pungent seeds and leaves, most of the mustard seasonings come from the mustard seed of the black or white mustard plants. Mustard originates in the Mediterranean region or western temperate Asia. The French acquired the technique of making mustard from the Romans in the first century B.C. Reputed to be effective in the curing of hysterical females and persons suffering from pains, mustard has also been used as a cure for colds and sore muscles. When eaten, it stimulates salivary secretions and peristaltic action of the stomach.

Uses: The seeds are used for pickles and in pickling, in boiling fish and vegetables, and as a garnish for salads. The powdered mustard is widely used for seasoning meats, vegetables, salad dressings and is used in baking. Prepared mustards generally have salt used in the processing so care must be taken to purchase low-sodium prepared mustard. Mustard greens have a peppery flavor and can be boiled for use as a pot-herb or used raw in salads.

NUTMEG—The nutmeg tree produces an apricot-like fruit. The hard kernel of this fruit contains the nutmeg seed. The nutmeg is dried and is sold either whole or ground. Native to the Spice Islands, nutmegs were traded by the Arabs in the Near East. They became favored and valued in the Middle Ages. Oil was extracted from the nutmeg and used to flavor butter.

Columbus sought nutmeg when he sailed in search of the West Indies. Valued by the early settlers of America, nutmeg was sold or bartered often by traveling peddlers. Connecticut is named the Nutmeg State.

Uses: Baking, sauces, puddings, custards, bananas, berries, cauliflower, spinach, eggnogs; try a pinch in pastry for fruit and meat pies.

OREGANO—Also known as wild marjoram, oregano is native to the Mediterranean region. It grows widely today in northeast Canada and the United States. Belonging to the mint family like sweet marjoram and thyme, oregano has a similar but more bitter and pungent flavor and therefore should be used with discretion. It is sold dried, crumbled, and ground. Occasionally, fresh oregano can be found in specialty food stores.

Uses: Mexican and Italian dishes; marinades, salad dressings, vegetables, potato salad, vegetable juice cocktails; and soups.

PAPRIKA—Paprika is made by grinding the ripe, dried pods of the sweet red bell pepper, a member of the capsicum family. Not strictly classified as spices or herbs, members of the capsicum family include paprika, cayenne, chili peppers and bell peppers and are not related to the black pepper. The quality, color, flavor and pungency vary depending upon the variety of the bell peppers used and the processing method, thus resulting in a number of paprikas. The name is Hungarian and paprika is an essential element in Hungarian cooking. Available ground.

Uses: Hungarian Goulash and other Hungarian dishes; a seasoning and a garnish on practically all nonsweet dishes.

PARSLEY — Parsley is native to Southern Europe and is widely used for flavoring and as a garnish. The parsley family includes many herbs and spices such as anise, dill, angelica, chervil, caraway, coriander, cumin, fennel, lovage, sweet cicely, as well as the vegetables celery and carrots. There are more than thirty varieties of parsley. This herb is available fresh or dried. Parsley is a Greek word meaning "celery growing among rocks." The ancient Egyptians sprinkled parsley on the bodies of loved ones in Greek and Roman times. Associated often with death, an old English proverbial expression was "to be in need of parsley" which means to be at death's door. Used to ward off intoxication, a wreath of parsley was a common companion at Greek and Roman banquets to protect from the consumption of too much wine. Parsley is a good source of Vita-

mins A and C when eaten in quantity.

Uses: Garnish; in bouquet garni; flavors soups, meat dishes, fish stuffings, cream or cheese sauces, eggs, breads, flavored butter, marinades, and most vegetables and salads.

PEPPER (Black and White) — The pepper is the fruit of the pepper plant, and is native to the forests of southwestern India. It is now widely cultivated in warm climates throughout the world. Black and white pepper come from the same plant with the black pepper being the unripe, reddish berry of the pepper plant. The berries are dried, with the riper berries being fermented or soaked in water to remove the outer coating of the seed. The white pepper is not as pungent-tasting as black pepper. Not always as plentiful as it is today, black pepper was traded for centuries and was as precious as gold. It was the most prized of all spices during the Middle Ages and was often used as money. Pepper is available whole, cracked, coarsely or finely ground.

Uses: Use white pepper where black specks are not desired, as in white sauces, clear soups, mashed potatoes, etc. Use whole peppercorns in pickling, soups, and stews. Cracked for salads, vegetables, meats; ground for general use in almost all nonsweet dishes. Remember that a little pepper goes a long way!

PEPPERMINT—Peppermint is a wild herb found in damp, lowland areas of Europe, Asia and America. The crop is harvested for its leaves and its oil. Peppermint oil is the most important use for this plant and over one million pounds are produced yearly in the United States alone. Peppermint has been grown since medieval times for medicinal purposes as a soothing balm. It consists principally of menthol, also called mint camphor. The oil can be purchased in drugstores.

Uses: The oil is used in medicines, dental preparations, and chewing gums. Oil and extract of the peppermint plant are used for flavoring mint candies, frostings, jelly, cakes, ice cream and other desserts, and beverages.

PICKLING SPICE—A blend of whole spices. Among the most common ingredients are allspice, bay leaf, cardamon, celery, chilies, cinnamon, cloves, coriander, dill, fenugreek, gingerroot, mace, mustard seed, and black pepper.

Uses: For pickling and preserving meats, vegetables, and relishes, and to season gravies, sauces, stews, fish, and shellfish.

POPPY SEEDS—The green pods of the poppy plant produce opium. After the pods have dried and lost the narcotic properties, the seeds form and have a gentle, nutlike taste that complements a variety of foods, especially noodles, breads, and other baked goods. Poppy seeds are used extensively in Austrian, Czechoslovakian and Hungarian cooking and baking. The popularity of the poppy seed declined markedly during the Opium Wars in China in the 1800s. The Chinese government, in an attempt to outlaw the drug, crossed purposes with the greedy English merchants who capitalized on widespread Chinese addiction. The seeds need to be heated for 15 minutes to stimulate their full nutty flavor and enhance their crunchy texture. If the seeds will not be cooked in the recipe, toast them in the oven or sauté in unsalted butter first. This heating will release essential oils.

Uses: Sprinkled on rolls, bread, cake, cookies, and pastries. Crushed and sweetened, they are used as a filling for cakes, coffeecakes, and pastries. Added to cooked noodles and some salads, they contribute both taste and texture. Available whole or ground. The ground poppy seed may be purchased in bulk in Hungarian or Czechoslovakian food specialty stores.

POULTRY SEASONING—A ground blend of sage, thyme, marjoram, and savory, and sometimes rosemary.

Uses: Used with poultry, pork, veal, and fish;

in croquettes and meat loaf; in stuffings and biscuits.

PUMPKIN PIE SPICE — A ground blend of cinnamon, cloves and ginger.
Uses: In pumpkin pie, spice cookies, gingerbread, breakfast buns; in pumpkin, squash and sweet potato dishes.

ROSEMARY — The leaves of this perennial evergreen shrub are used as an herb seasoning. This shrub grows wild in southern Europe and is cultivated throughout the rest of Europe and the United States. If purchased dried, the leaves should be crushed to release full flavor.
Uses: Fruit cups, soups, meats or poultry, fish stuffings and creamed seafood dishes, cheese sauces and eggs, herb breads and stuffings, many sauces and marinades, fruit salads, and vegetables such as lentils, mushrooms, peas, potatoes, spinach and squash.

SAFFRON — Saffron is a hybrid herbspice which is the stigma of a small crocus, cultivated principally in Spain. Each flower stigma is picked by hand thus making the price in the United States over $1,300 per pound. Saffron is an ancient flavoring with an elusive and indefinable flavor. It is used to impart color as well as flavor. Saffron, with its deep-yellow color and aromatic properties, has been used since antiquity for dyeing, for flavoring foods, and for medicinal purposes. The Egyptians anointed their royalty with saffron-tinted oil. The gods and goddesses of the ancient Greeks were dressed in saffron-colored robes. It was used as a fragrant essence by the Greeks and Romans for sprinkling in the streets and theaters to sweeten the air and it was also used as a personal cosmetic. Available either ground or whole, it should be remembered that a little saffron goes a long way.
Uses: A necessary ingredient in bouillabaisse and in certain Iberian rice and chicken dishes like arroz amarillo con pollo and paella; breads and cakes; rice dishes, especially those of Spain, Italy, the Near East and India; it also enhances cream soups, sauces, potatoes, and veal and chicken dishes.

SAGE — This herb is native to the Mediterranean region. It is an aromatic perennial. Its leaves are used fresh or dried; crushed or ground. Sage is known in the United States especially as a flavoring in stuffings for poultry and pork or in sausages. Sage is a bush and the leaves are a gray-green or whitish-green in color. Sage is said to have slightly stimulating properties and has been used historically as a folk medicine. Sage tea has been used as a spring tonic for centuries. In the Middle Ages sage was believed to promote wisdom and strengthen the memory. Sage is now grown in many parts of the world. The sage that grows wild in the western United States is not suitable as a food flavoring.

Uses: Flavorings for poultry, pork, sausage, soups.

SAVORY (Summer and Winter)—A native of southern Europe, savory was known to the Greeks and Romans who used it for all sorts of medicinal remedies. It was reputed in France to cure lethargy if worn on the head as a cap or garland. The summer savory is milder than the winter variety. It is sold dried, either in whole leaves or ground.

Uses: Savory is an excellent companion to bean dishes; it adds flavor to paté, vegetable juice, consummé, chowder, and bean and lentil soups; chicken loaf, hamburger, lamb, veal, stews, and poultry stuffings; barbecue, fish, seafood, or poultry sauce; artichokes, beets, cabbage, peas, rice, sauerkraut, salad; stewed pears and quinces.

SESAME—Sesame is also called benne. It is the oldest herb known for its seeds. The plant is an erect annual of many types and varieties. The sesame seed is a tiny grayish-white or black seed which has a sweet nutty flavor and, when pressed, yields a bland oil. The cake residue from the oil pressing process is used for food and fodder and is a rich source of protein. The term "open sesame," which was used in the Arabian Nights to open the door to the treasure, was used because of the ease with which the seeds pop out of their hulls. The African slaves introduced the sesame seed to America; the seed is popular in Southern cooking, especially in cakes and cookies. It is crushed into a paste to spread on bread in the Middle East, and it is made into a rich candy called halvah. Available whole, either with or without hulls, and as oil. To toast seeds, bake in preheated 350° F. oven for 10 to 15 minutes until golden brown.

Uses: Turkish halvah; garnish for appetizers, salads, and almost any dish calling for nuts; in baked dishes, sprinkled over breads before baking, used instead of bread crumbs as a topping for meat and poultry casseroles, served instead of nuts in cakes and cookies; tasty combined with cheese or used in sweet sauces; good with butter over noodles and vegetables.

SPEARMINT—Spearmint is a herb native to the temperate sections of Europe and Asia and has become widely naturalized in the United

States. Often available commercially under the name of "mint," spearmint also is grown fresh in home gardens, dehydrated, or as an extract or oil.

Uses: Adds flavor to cranberry juice, fruit cups, and soups such as pea soup; meat ragouts or fish; minced in cottage cheese or cream cheese and salad dressings; with vegetables such as cabbage, carrots, celery, potatoes, and snap beans; jellied salads; mint sauce and mint jelly, the usual accompaniment to lamb roast; desserts such as ice cream, custards, fruit compotes; and fruit beverages.

SUGAR — Sugar is a sweet substance which, when purified, is colorless or white. It occurs in many plant juices but the commercial sugar products are produced from either the sugar cane or the sugar beet. Used in India as early as 1000 B.C., the sugar cane was chewed because of its sweet taste. In 500 B.C. a process was developed to extract the sweet juice from the center of the cane. A crude process yielding a substance of sugar crystals and molasses, this was the forerunner of the present day process. The juice from the sugar cane is extracted, treated with lime to remove impurities, filtered, and evaporated to crystallization. Molasses is the liquor removed in a cen-

trifuge, and brown sugar is refined from this process by redissolving, clarifying, decolorizing, and recrystallizing. Christopher Columbus brought the valuable cane to the New World in 1493. It was originally planted in Santo Domingo and later in Puerto Rico, Cuba, and various countries in Central and South America. Early American colonists had a hard time obtaining sugar and had to pay high prices when they were able to get it. As a result, they used molasses and honey to sweeten foods.

TARRAGON — The tarragon plant is believed to be native to Siberia. Tarragon is a herb with an anise-like flavor. An extremely useful herb, it should be used with discretion as it tends to dominate dishes. Avoid using it in herb bouquets that contain delicate herbs like chervil, parsley, or savory. It may be an ingredient in fines herbes.

Uses: A perfect accompaniment to green salads; chicken livers, vegetable juices, chowders, and consommés; pheasant, sweet breads, tongue, veal; chicken or turkey dishes; fish, scrambled eggs; butters, marinades, mustards, mayonnaise, and vinegar; asparagus, beans, beets, broccoli, and cabbage.

THYME — Thyme is a relatively powerful and

sweetly-fragrant herb which is widely available in leaf or ground form.
Uses: Traditional in New England clam chowder and many creole dishes; vegetable juices, soups, meat and poultry dishes, fish, cheese, stuffings, sauces, vegetables, cream and custard desserts, and jellies.

TURMERIC—The root of a ginger family plant, turmeric is an essential ingredient in Indian cooking. It comes ground for coloring and flavoring curry powder blends, prepared mustard, dressings and salads, pickling, relishes, creamed eggs and seafood. The turmeric root has a mild aroma and a mustard-like bitter taste when it is washed, cooked and then dried.
Uses: It comes ground for coloring and flavoring curry powder blends, prepared mustard, dressings and salads, pickling, relishes, creamed eggs, seafood and rice dishes.

VANILLA—Vanilla is the large seed pod of a tropical vine of the orchid family. The seed pod has virtually no scent or flavor until dried and cured. Combining chocolate and vanilla has been a favorite since the times of the Aztecs. Native as a crop to the Mexican Indians, a transplanted orchid needs a single species of bee to pollinate it. The bee is native only to Mexico and does not survive in other areas. A French botanist discovered a method of pollination by hand. This slow and painstaking method has made it possible to raise vanilla crops in many areas of the world.
Uses: Comes whole for flavoring sugar, custards, puddings; in extract form for baking, candy, syrups, preserves, ice cream, and other sweets.

VINEGAR—Vinegar is a mixture of acetic acid and water probably discovered by ancient people accidentally along with wine. It is theorized that the everpresent yeasts and bacteria floated through the air and fell into uncovered earthenware jugs of fruit juice, causing the juice to ferment and become wine. Then, with the addition of a different bacteria to the juice, the wine soured and transformed into the acetic acid and water, or vinegar. There are a number of types of vinegar available. Vinegar is produced from the fermentation of apples (cider vinegar), grapes (wine vinegar), malted barley and oats (malt vinegar), and industrial alcohol (white distilled vinegar).
Uses: Pickling, preserving, tenderizing tough meats and fowl, and adding sour pungency to dishes ranging from vinegar pie to tomato catsup and salad dressings. Can be used as a household cleaner and as a hygienic douche.

Commercial Seasonings With Salt

Don't use any of the following or any that contain salt:

A-1 Sauce	MSG (Monosodium Glutamate)
Accent	Onion Salt
Beau Monde	Pepper Seasoning with Bacon
Bon Appétit	Season-All
Chili Powder (with salt)	Seasoned Salt or Seasoning Salt
Garlic Pepper Seasoning	Spaghetti Sauce Seasoning
Garlic Salt	Soy Sauce
Herb Seasoning	Tomato Seasoning
Lawrey's Seasoning Salt	Vegetable Delight
Lemon Herb Garni	Worcestershire Sprinkle
Lemon-Pepper Marinade	Worcestershire Sauce

Constantly check these and other labels. Salt content may be changed by the manufacturers at any time.

Appetizers

When you are concerned about and aware of sodium, entertaining takes on a new challenge. Because of this, the recipes for many foods and some beverages are offered in this section.

If you are invited to someone's home for dinner, you might offer to bring an appetizer so that you can control the amount of sodium. When eating out or when you are in a situation where you have no control over the appetizers, choose those which are lower in sodium such as fresh vegetables or fruits. This is also a good way to cut down on calorie intake.

Have fun before dinner! Relaxing is a wonderful way to begin each mealtime and to keep the blood pressure from rising.

Cheese Crackers

Great taste, many uses—however, quantity will vary.

⅓	cup skim milk
1	tablespoon cider vinegar
1¼	cups whole wheat flour
¼	teaspoon baking soda substitute
½	cup wheat germ
½	cup unsalted margarine
½	cup unsalted cheddar cheese, grated
½	teaspoon salt substitute
1	egg white plus 2 tablespoons water

Sesame seeds

Combine milk with vinegar and set aside. Combine the flour, baking soda substitute, wheat germ, margarine, cheese, and salt substitute with mixer in large mixing bowl and mix until it resembles coarse meal. Add milk mixture and mix only enough to combine.

Turn out on a floured board and knead briefly. Roll out to ⅓-inch thickness and cut into desired shapes. Place on cookie sheets and prick several times with fork. Bake at 375° F. for 15 minutes. Remove from oven and allow to cool.

When cooled, brush cracker tops with 1 egg white beaten with 2 tablespoons water. Sprinkle with sesame seeds and bake again at 375° F. for 8 minutes.

Makes approximately 3 dozen crackers—the number of crackers will vary with the size and shape selected.

Judy's Apricot Dip

1	12-ounce can apricot nectar
4	teaspoons corn starch
2	tablespoons honey
1	teaspoon shredded orange peel
1	cup plain yogurt
⅔	cup non-dairy topping or whipped whipping cream

Fresh fruits*

Put nectar and corn starch in saucepan. Stir; add honey and orange peel. Stir over medium heat until thick and bubbly. Reduce heat and cook for one minute. Cool. Add yogurt and non-dairy topping or whipping cream. Mix thoroughly and chill.

4 to 6 servings.

*Apples, peaches, oranges, banana spears, or pear slices. Dip those fruits that have a tendency to darken in lemon juice.

Chili Con Queso

Fun to dip! Good for summer barbeques or cold winter evenings.

1   medium onion, finely chopped
3   tablespoons unsalted margarine
3   tablespoons unbleached flour
¼   teaspoon seasoned salt substitute
1   cup skim milk
1   can (1 pound) unsalted whole tomatoes, drained and coarsely chopped
1   can (4 ounces) unsalted green chilies, chopped
8   ounces unsalted Monterey Jack cheese, cubed
4   ounces unsalted cheddar cheese, cubed
½   teaspoon cumin
Unsalted corn chips

In a deep 3-quart saucepan, sauté onions in margarine until tender. Stir in flour and salt substitute. Cook, stirring constantly, just until bubbly. Remove from heat. Stir in milk slowly. Return to heat and continue cooking and stirring until sauce thickens and begins to bubble. Stir in tomatoes, and chilies; cook one minute. Add cheeses and cumin, stirring constantly until melted.

Serve hot. Best served in a chafing dish or crock pot kept at a low heat. If you don't have a chafing dish, use any heavy pottery dish or pot that will hold the warmth. Also, try wrapping a tea towel around the pot to help keep warm.

Serve with unsalted corn chips to scoop the dip.

8 to 10 servings.

Party Snack

4   cups mini-shredded wheat (bite size)
2   cups unsalted pretzels
1   cup unsalted whole raw almonds or pecans
⅓   cup unsalted margarine
½   teaspoon garlic powder
¾   teaspoon seasoned salt substitute

Place wheat, pretzels and nuts on a cookie sheet. Melt the margarine in a saucepan; add garlic powder and seasoned salt substitute to the melted margarine. Drizzle mixture over the ingredients on cookie sheet. Stir well. Bake at 350° F. for about 15 to 20 minutes. Serve warm or cold.

Store in an airtight container. Keeps about one week at room temperature, or up to 3 weeks in the refrigerator. Heat for 10 minutes at 350° F. if stored in refrigerator.

Makes 7 cups.

Cheese Chili Cubes

Good for breakfast, too! (See note below.)

8	eggs
½	cup unbleached flour
1½	teaspoons baking powder substitute (See Helpful Hints, pg. 20) (1 teaspoon above 4,000 ft.)
¼	teaspoon seasoned salt substitute
3	cups unsalted Monterey Jack cheese (12 ounces), shredded
1½	cups (12 ounces) unsalted dry curd cottage cheese
2	tablespoons skim milk or sour cream
2	4-ounce cans unsalted green chilies, drained and chopped

In large mixing bowl, beat the eggs with an electric mixer until light (4-5 minutes). Stir together flour, baking powder substitute and salt substitute. Add to eggs and mix well. Fold in cheeses, milk, and chilies. Turn into greased 9x9x2-inch baking pan. Bake in 350° F. oven for 40 minutes, or until set. Remove from oven; let stand 10 minutes. Cut in small squares. Serve hot. Makes about 3 to 4 dozen appetizers.

NOTE: May be used as a breakfast dish also.

Bake in a greased 9"x13" pan and cut into 6 or 8 squares. Serve topped with heated taco sauce (unsalted) and grated unsalted cheddar cheese. A tall glass of orange juice is a tasty complement to this dish.

Canape Spread or Dip

1	pound dry curd salt-free cottage cheese
2 to 3	tablespoons sour cream or plain skim milk yogurt
1	7-ounce can unsalted diced green chilies
¼	teaspoon pepper
¼	teaspoon powdered onion, or to taste
⅛	teaspoon powdered garlic, or to taste

Unsalted bread cut into desired shapes or unsalted crackers
Unsalted cheddar cheese
Tomato slices
Avocado, skins removed and slices dipped in lemon juice to prevent darkening

Put first six ingredients in blender; mix until well blended. Chill thoroughly. Spread on bread shapes or crackers and top with cheese, tomato slices and avocado.

8 to 10 servings.

Salmon Ball

This is a simple yet elegant spread.

1   8-ounce package Neufchâtel cheese, softened
1   (7¾ ounce) can unsalted salmon
½   teaspoon powdered unsalted seasoning or 1 beef bouillon cube mixed with 1 tablespoon warm water
1   teaspoon lemon juice
½   teaspoon dehydrated minced onions
⅛   teaspoon garlic powder
⅛   teaspoon onion powder
⅛   teaspoon black pepper
½   teaspoon unsalted horseradish (see Helpful Hints, pg. 20)
¾   cup chopped parsley or unsalted chopped nuts
Unsalted crackers

In a medium-sized mixing bowl, cream the cheese until smooth. Add remaining ingredients, except for the parsley, nuts or crackers. Mix well after each addition. Form into a ball and roll in parsley or nuts. Cover with plastic wrap. Chill to firm up in refrigerator overnight or at least a few hours before serving.

Serve with unsalted crackers.

6 to 8 servings.

Sensational Dip

This dip acquired its name from the comments of guests eating this creation. When asked their opinion of this dip, the resounding reply was, "It's sensational!"

1   pint sour cream or yogurt
2   tablespoons unsalted horseradish (see Helpful Hints, pg. 20)
3   large green onions with tops, chopped
1   teaspoon dried chervil*
2   teaspoons fresh parsley, diced
¼   teaspoon seasoned pepper
¼   teaspoon seasoned salt substitute
¼   teaspoon garlic powder
Vegetables

In a medium-sized bowl, mix all ingredients except for vegetables. Cover with plastic wrap and let flavors blend in the refrigerator at least one hour before serving.

Serve with raw vegetables such as carrots, broccoli, zucchini, cauliflower.

8 to 10 servings.

*If this spice is unavailable, use 1 teaspoon parsley flakes and ⅛ teaspoon ground anise seed.

Bombay Dip

This makes a very attractive dish when served.

½   cup dairy sour cream or plain skim milk yogurt
1   8-ounce package Neufchâtal cream cheese
1   tablespoon lemon juice
1   tablespoon grated onion or chopped green
        onion
1   teaspoon curry powder
½   teaspoon dill weed
½   teaspoon dry mustard
Vegetables*

Mix all ingredients in blender, except for vegetables. Cover and refrigerate at least one hour. Serve with fresh vegetables washed and cut into bite size pieces.

*Broccoli, mushrooms, carrots, cherry tomatoes, cucumber spears, cauliflower, and zucchini are good. If desired when using broccoli, blanch and then quickly put in ice water to cease cooking process. This makes the broccoli a rich, deep, attractive green color.

8 to 10 servings.

Idaho Dip

This is a very respectable substitute for the old California Dip which uses the onion soup mix.

2   tablespoons dried minced onion
2   teaspoons unsalted beef soup base or
        2 unsalted beef bouillon cubes
Water
½   teaspoon seasoned salt substitute
¼   teaspoon honey
¼   teaspoon garlic powder
¼   teaspoon Italian seasoning
½   teaspoon chives, chopped
1   pint sour cream or yogurt
Unsalted potato chips or unsalted corn chips

In a one-quart saucepan, cook the onion, beef soup base or bouillon cubes, and honey in a scant amount of water. When the beef soup base or bouillon cubes dissolve, allow to cool completely. Add seasonings, chives, and sour cream. Thin with milk, if necessary.

Serve with unsalted potato chips or unsalted corn chips.

8 to 10 servings.

Guacamole Dip

1   ripe tomato
2   soft avocadoes, skins and pits removed
¼   cup sour cream or skim milk yogurt
1   green onion, finely chopped
½   teaspoon seasoned salt substitute
Freshly ground pepper
3   tablespoons lemon juice
2   tablespoons unsalted green chilies,
        chopped, or 2 tablespoons Basic Hot
        Sauce (see Index)
Unsalted corn chips *or* sliced tomatoes

Either combine first eight ingredients in blender or mash in a small bowl with a fork until smooth. Place avocado pit in serving bowl and spoon guacamole over top. (This prevents dip from darkening. Avocadoes darken when exposed to air. This affects only appearance and can be reduced by keeping the pit in the bottom of the bowl and sprinkling the top of the dip lightly with lemon juice.)

Serve as a dip with the unsalted corn chips or spoon onto sliced tomatoes.

6 servings.

Grape Punch

1   can (6 ounces) frozen grape juice
1   can (6 ounces) frozen lemonade concentrate
1   16-ounce bottle lemon-lime soda

Dilute the grape juice and lemonade according to directions on the cans. Mix in soda. Serve chilled.

Makes 2 quarts.

Hot Cocoa Mix

¾   cup unsweetened cocoa
¾   cup granulated sugar
2⅔ cups instant nonfat milk

Mix cocoa, sugar and instant milk together in a large mixing bowl. Store in air-tight container at room temperature.

To serve, measure ⅓ cup of mix into an 8-ounce cup and add boiling water. Stir thoroughly.

Hot Cranberry- Orange Drink

2⅔   cups cranberry juice
¾   cup orange juice
3   tablespoons raisins
3   teaspoons brown sugar
4   whole cinnamon sticks or ½ teaspoon
        ground cinnamon
12   whole cloves or ¼ teaspoon ground cloves
4   orange wedges

Combine above ingredients, except for orange wedges, in large saucepan. (Whole cinnamon sticks and whole cloves may be tied in a piece of cheesecloth.) Heat to simmering. Pour into hot mugs and garnish each mug with an orange wedge.
Serves 4

Hot Herbal Drink

1   teaspoon rosemary, cumin, fennel or
        verbena, or a mixture of any of these.
1   sprig of mint
1   cup boiling water

Add herbs and mint to boiling water. Remove from heat and allow to steep for 5 to 10 minutes. Strain and sip. Honey may be added for sweetness. Drink a cup of this herbal tea twice a day, morning and evening, for four days. This is a natural diuretic which has been used by Europeans to flush excess water from their tissues.

Hot Spiced Lemonade

2⅔   cups water
½   cup frozen lemonade concentrate*
2 to 3 tablespoons slivered candied ginger
4   lemon slices

In a large saucepan, combine above ingredients, except for lemon slices. Heat to simmering. Pour into hot mugs and garnish each with a lemon slice.
Serves 4

*Read the label as some brands have sodium preservatives and additives.

Soy "Coffee"

Dry roast one pound whole unsoaked soybeans in a 200° F. oven 4-5 hours or until beans are lightly browned all the way through. Watch carefully and stir frequently the last hour to keep from burning. Cool the beans. Then grind in a blender, food grinder, or coffee grinder, using either the coarse or fine grind, as preferred.

The beans may be roasted and stored in an airtight container for a week or two at a time, but for the best flavor grind only enough for one batch at a time. This is most flavorful when freshly ground.

Brew as you would coffee, in a coffee pot, or in a saucepan. This can be mixed half and half with decaffeinated coffee, if desired.

Sore Throat Soother

¼   teaspoon ground cayenne pepper
2   tablespoons honey
¼   cup hot water

Mix above ingredients in a mug. Stir until honey is dissolved. Drink for sore throat relief.
Serves 1.

Debi's Coffee Cooler

4   cups decaffeinated coffee, brewed double strength
½   cup powdered sugar, sifted
2½   teaspoons vanilla
½   cup whipping cream
2   tablespoons powdered sugar
⅛   teaspoon nutmeg
⅛   teaspoon cinnamon
Ice cubes made from double-strength coffee

To hot coffee, add ½ cup powdered sugar. Chill thoroughly. Just before serving, add vanilla to chilled coffee.

In a small mixing bowl, whip cream. Add sugar, nutmeg, and cinnamon; mix well.

Put 2 or 3 ice cubes in sherbet glasses. Pour chilled coffee mixture over cubes and top with a heaping tablespoon of whipping cream mixture.

For an elegant service, put glasses on small plates and serve with a spoon.
4 servings.

Quick Snacks

Here are a dozen quick snacks for your enjoyment.

Coconut: Can be eaten raw or used in recipes.

Dried fruits: Many dried fruits are acceptable snacks. Be sure to check label for sodium preservatives.

Dry roasted peanuts: Unsalted dry roasted peanuts are available in most grocery stores. These peanuts are an excellent and nutritious snack when eaten alone or mixed with raisins. Also, expand upon this mixture of peanuts and raisins and add other unsalted "goodies" like sunflower seeds, coconut, pretzels, or Party Snack (see recipe this section).

Fresh fruit: Keep prepared fresh fruits such as sectioned oranges, grapefruit, and apples in bags or air-tight containers in the refrigerator. Bananas are a very tasty snack and contain potassium which is needed in a low-sodium diet.

Popcorn: Cook any desired amount according to package directions, omitting salt and butter. This is low in calories. Unsalted margarine or butter may be melted and drizzled over the popped corn.

Raisins: Can be eaten raw or used in recipes.

Raw nuts of any kind: If desired, may be roasted (see directions under roasted raw peanuts below).

Raw vegetables: Peel fresh vegetables (except for celery) and keep in a plastic bag, airtight container, or pitcher of water in the refrigerator.

Roasted raw peanuts: Buy raw peanuts, place on a cookie sheet (ungreased) and bake at 325° F. for about 25 minutes, stirring occasionally until lightly browned. Store cooled nuts in an airtight jar or container.

Sunflower seeds or "Sunshine Mix": Sold in health food stores—eat from bag or cook in a favorite recipe.

Unsalted cheeses and unsalted crackers: A delightful combination.

Unsalted potato chips, unsalted corn chips, and unsalted pretzels: All are available in health food stores to satisfy that "junk food" craving.

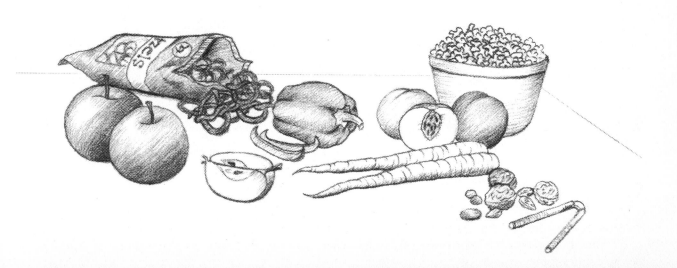

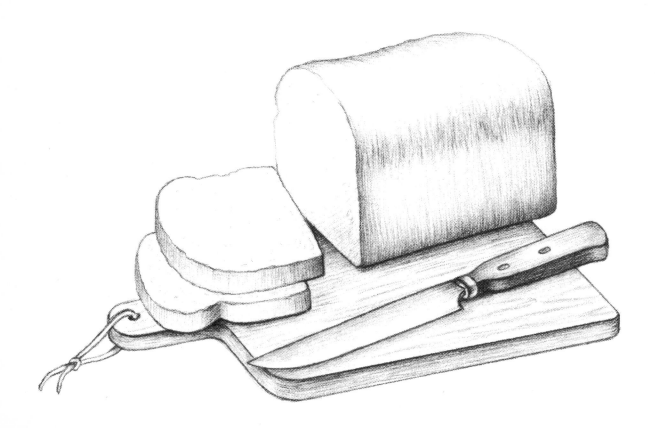

Breads

Often it has been said to us, "Well, I guess you can't have bread because it won't rise without salt." This could not be further from the truth, but it does seem to be a superstition that persists. Bread rises very well without any salt or sodium products. In fact, salt retards the formation of gases, thus slowing the rising process.

Some breads without salt, however, can have a very flat taste. White bread especially can come very close to tasting like cardboard. With this in mind, we discovered ways to enhance the natural flavor of bread.

If you have not made bread in the past, don't panic. It really is quite easy and produces a very satisfying feeling both to those who eat it and to the one who produces it! Two things to remember: 1) Yeast needs to be a "comfortable" temperature (110° to 115° F.). Water should feel just a tiny bit warm when dropped on the inside of the wrist—in fact, it should almost not "feel" at all because it is just a little warmer than body temperature. 2) Ingredients added to the yeast mixtures (such as eggs, milk, flour, or butter) should also be a "comfortable" temperature. Too much heat or too much cold will kill the yeast action. Especially at high altitudes (4,000 ft. and above) be careful of allowing the bread to rise too much—bread rises in the oven at the beginning of baking until the heat of the baking process halts the rising action.

Making your own yeast breads does not take much actual time, but does require "being around." That is, it only takes a minute to punch it down and reshape it, then an hour or so is required to let it rise between mixing, then shaping, and finally baking.

Yeast breads freeze well, so if you cannot bake Monday through Friday, the weekends serve this purpose nicely. When in a pinch, go to the market. Many store bakeries carry salt-free bread. It does not keep well on the shelf, so you might have to ask for it at the bakery, or look in the frozen food section. Actually, this store-bought bread seems to produce the best consistency for poultry stuffing. Do not expect, however, this frozen salt-free bread to be moist and flavorful!

All breads should be baked in a *pre-heated oven*. This "sets" the bread quickly. If you do not preheat your oven, you will have problems as the rising action will not be halted as quickly as it needs to be.

Eggs may be listed as an optional ingredient. This is to give you, the cook, the opportunity to lower the sodium content, as well as the cholesterol level, by leaving the eggs out. Eggs, however, add more protein, keep the bread from drying out, and make the loaf slice more easily with less crumbling.

Warm water—it is best to use unsoftened, cold water heated to the correct temperature. This avoids the introduction of unwanted properties from the softening and heating processes.

Bread crumbs—use the pieces that do not slice well, heels or older bread. Roll with a rolling pin or crumble between fingers. Freeze in one-cup portions until needed.

Croutons—see mixed salad suggestions in Salad Section. Use or freeze until ready to use. Crisp croutons briefly in oven at 400° F. for 5-10 minutes after freezing.

Salt substitute—a dash or ¼-½ teaspoon will make the dough rise more slowly as it controls the yeast action by slowing its rate of gas formation. This can be helpful particularly in recipes calling for mostly unbleached flours. Salt substitute used in small quantities will also help bring out flavors.

Good luck and happy breadmaking!

Timmie's Onion Bread

This bread is sure to please many!

½   cup skim milk or water
3   tablespoons honey
4   tablespoons unsalted margarine
1½ cups water
1   tablespoon (1 package) yeast
5-6 cups unbleached flour
2   large raw onions, chopped
2   eggs

In a 3-quart saucepan, heat the milk (or water) with the honey, margarine and water until the temperature is 115°-120° F. In a large bowl, mix yeast with 3 cups of the flour. Gradually add the heated liquid mixture. Beat until smooth. Add onions and eggs and mix until blended. Add enough flour to make a soft dough. Knead on a floured board until smooth and elastic (about 10 minutes). Place in a greased bowl. Cover; let rise until doubled in bulk, about one hour. Punch down. Divide dough in half and shape into two loaves and place in two greased 9 x 5 x 3-inch bread pans. Cover; let rise again, about one hour. Bake at 400° F. for 40 minutes or until loaf sounds hollow when tapped. Rub the tops with unsalted margarine if you like soft crusts, or brush with skim milk for harder, shiny crusts. Remove from pans and cool on racks.
Makes two loaves.

Biscuits

Good old-fashioned biscuits like Grandma used to make!

1¾ cups unbleached flour
4½ teaspoons baking powder substitute (3¼ teaspoons in altitudes above 4,000 ft.)
¼ teaspoon salt substitute
¼ cup wheat germ
1   tablespoon granulated sugar
¼ cup (½ stick) unsalted margarine or ¼ cup shortening
1   cup skim milk

In a medium-sized mixing bowl, sift together flour, baking powder substitute, and salt substitute. Add wheat germ and sugar; mix. Cut in margarine until mixture resembles coarse meal. Add milk and mix just to combine ingredients. Pat out dough on a floured board to ½-inch thickness. Cut into 2-inch circles. Bake on ungreased cookie sheet at 425° F. until lightly browned (about 12 minutes).
Makes 12-16 biscuits.

Aunt Jenny's Potato Refrigerator Rolls

Aunt Jenny lived well into her 80's. She always made these rolls for special occasions. So special times and Potato Refrigerator Rolls go hand in hand. She usually served these rolls with Pear Preserves.

1   cup mashed potatoes
1   tablespoon (1 package) yeast
1   cup very warm (110°-115° F.) potato water
⅔   cup shortening
½   cup granulated sugar
2   eggs
½   cup skim milk
6 to 8 cups unbleached flour

In a 2-quart saucepan, cook and mash potatoes. Reserve one cup liquid (add water as needed to make one cup liquid). Dissolve yeast in warm potato water. In a large mixing bowl, cream shortening, sugar and eggs. Heat milk and mashed potatoes to lukewarm temperature; add yeast mixture. Then, add sugar and egg mixture. Add flour to make stiff dough. Toss on a lightly floured board and knead until smooth and elastic. Put in a large greased bowl. Grease top of dough. Cover with towel and let rise in a warm place free of drafts until doubled in bulk. Punch down.

Grease top lightly. Place in covered bowl and refrigerate until ready to use. May be refrigerated up to three days.

About 1½ hours before baking, roll out and shape as desired.* Place on greased cookie sheets or greased muffin tins and let rise until doubled (about 45 minutes) and bake at 350° F. for 10-15 minutes or until lightly browned.

Makes approximately 36 rolls.

*For a pretty shape: Roll out dough in two parts. Make a large circle of one part; cut into wedges as for pie. Start rolling at largest part of wedge. Brush with melted unsalted margarine or unsalted butter before shaping, if desired.

This recipe also makes great sweet rolls! Take one-half of the dough and roll into rectangular shape. Spread with ¼ stick melted unsalted margarine. Sprinkle with approximately ½ cup firmly packed brown sugar, 2 teaspoons ground cinnamon, and ⅓ cup unsalted nuts. Drizzle with about 3 tablespoons honey. Roll into a long roll and slice off into about 12 pieces. Place in a greased 9x15-inch pan and allow to rise until almost doubled in size and bake for 20 minutes at 350° F. Frost with a powdered sugar glaze (see Toppings and Frostings—Dessert Section) that has been thinned with orange juice.

Any-Fruit-Goes Bread

1 cup unbleached flour
½ cup whole wheat flour
1 teaspoon baking soda substitute (¾
      teaspoon in altitudes above 4,000 ft.)
1 teaspoon baking powder substitute (¾
      teaspoon in altitudes above 4,000 ft.)
½ cup granulated sugar
¼ cup unsalted margarine
½ cup chopped nuts
2 eggs
½ cup prune juice*
⅔ cup raw prunes, cut up*

Sift the unbleached flour into a large mixing bowl. Add the whole wheat flour, baking soda, baking powder and sugar to the flour and mix well. Cut in the margarine with a pastry blender until mixture looks like coarse meal. Mix in nuts.

In a smaller bowl beat eggs until foamy. Add prune juice and prunes and blend. Add egg and prune mixture to flour and shortening mixture. Mix until just blended—no more. Pour batter into a 9x4x3-inch bread loaf pan that has been well greased on the bottom, and lined with waxed paper that has been greased. Bake at 350° F. (375° F. at altitudes above 4,000 ft.) for 50-60 minutes or until a toothpick inserted in the center comes out almost clean.

Remove from oven. Immediately loosen bread from pan, turn out onto wire rack to cool and lift off waxed paper.

Cover tightly or wrap the cooled bread to prevent drying.

Makes one loaf.

*Variations that will make this "Any-Fruit-Goes" bread:

Cranberry Bread: Omit prunes and prune juice and add ½ cup orange juice and ⅔ cup halved fresh cranberries.

Apricot Bread: Omit prunes and prune juice and add ½ cup apricot nectar and ⅔ cup diced dried apricots.

Date Bread: Omit prunes and prune juice and add ½ cup orange juice and ⅔ cup dried dates.

Fig Bread: Omit prunes and prune juice and add ½ cup fig juice and ⅔ cup diced dried figs.

Apple Bread: Omit prunes and prune juice and add ½ cup apple juice and ⅔ cup diced, tart, fresh apples.

Christmas Coffee Cake

Traditional Christmas "birthday" coffee cake. Make your own mix option ahead of time by mixing some of the ingredients together and storing in the refrigerator. Breakfast is a breeze!

½   cup (1 stick) unsalted margarine
1   cup granulated sugar
2   eggs
2   cups unbleached flour
1   teaspoon baking soda substitute
1   teaspoon baking powder substitute (¾ teaspoon in altitudes above 4,000 ft.)
1   cup sour cream (plus 2 tablespoons in altitudes above 4,000 ft.) or plain non-fat yogurt
½   teaspoon lemon juice
1   teaspoon vanilla
Topping

In a large mixer bowl, cream the margarine, sugar and eggs. In a small bowl, mix dry ingredients and add alternately with the sour cream to the egg mixture, beginning and ending with dry ingredients. Add lemon juice and vanilla; mix until just blended. Pour ½ of the batter into a greased 9x13-inch pan. Sprinkle with half of the topping mixture. Pour remaining batter over this layer, then sprinkle remaining topping mixture on top of batter. Bake at 325° F. for 30-35 minutes (or at 350° F. for 35-40 minutes in altitudes above 4,000 ft.).

Topping: ⅔ cup brown sugar, ½ cup granulated sugar, 2 teaspoons ground cinnamon, and 1 cup pecans. Mix well.
Makes 12 servings.

To make as a mix ahead, place the following ingredients in a medium-sized mixing bowl:

½   cup unsalted margarine
1   cup granulated sugar
2   cups unbleached flour
1   teaspoon baking soda substitute
1   teaspoon baking powder substitute

Beat ingredients together until the margarine is in very tiny particles. Place in a freezer bag, label, and store in freezer. Make topping ahead also and freeze in a separate container. To cook with mix, preheat oven to 325° F. (350° F. above 4,000 ft.). Beat ½ the mix and eggs together in a large mixing bowl until well blended. Alternately add the sour cream or yogurt to the mixing bowl with the remaining mix. Add lemon juice and vanilla. Mix just until blended. Follow directions as for making the cake above. Using frozen mix may increase necessary baking time by 5-8 minutes.

Wheat Berry Bread

Wheat berries are made by cooking kernels of wheat. The berries add texture and extra bursts of flavor!

½ cup whole kernels of wheat, simmered for 2½ to 3 hours in about 2 cups water (more water may be added as needed); drain
1⅔ cups skim milk, scalded and cooled
1 tablespoon (1 package) yeast
⅓ cup honey
2 tablespoons unsalted margarine, melted
1 teaspoon salt substitute
5½ to 6⅓ cups whole wheat flour
½ cup toasted wheat germ

In ¼ cup warm water, dissolve yeast. Put into large mixing bowl and add milk, honey, margarine and salt substitute. Stir in 4 cups of the flour and beat well until dough is smooth. Add another 1½ cups flour and the wheat germ.

Knead dough on lightly floured board and add more flour if necessary. When satiny smooth, put in large greased bowl and cover. Let rise until doubled in bulk (about 1½ hours). Punch down and turn out onto board and knead in cooked wheat berries. Divide dough in half, form into loaves, and place in two greased 9x5x3-inch loaf pans. Cover with a towel and let rise in warm oven until top of bread dough and pan are even. Bake in preheated oven for 45 minutes at 375° F. Turn out onto wire racks and cool.

Makes two loaves.

Basic Biscuit Mix

Who needs boxed mixes?—We can make our own in a snap!

5 cups whole wheat flour
5 cups unbleached flour
½ cup baking powder substitute (¼ cup plus 2 tablespoons in altitudes above 4,000 ft.)
¼ cup granulated sugar
2 cups shortening
1½ cups instant nonfat milk (optional)

In large mixing bowl, thoroughly stir together dry ingredients. Cut in shortening until mixture resembles coarse meal. Store covered in refrigerator or freeze. Makes about 12 cups of mix. To measure mix, spoon into measuring cup and level with knife. This mix can be used in recipes in the same proportions as a prepared biscuit mix.

Cornbread

The dry ingredients can be mixed and stored in an airtight container and kept in the freezer for later use.

1	cup unbleached flour
¼	cup whole wheat flour
¾	cup yellow cornmeal
2	tablespoons granulated sugar or honey
5½	teaspoons baking powder substitute (4½ teaspoons in altitudes above 4,000 ft.)
¼	teaspoon salt substitute
1	egg
⅔	cup skim milk
⅓	cup vegetable oil

Mix the flours, cornmeal, sugar, baking powder substitute and salt substitute in a large mixing bowl. At this point, ingredients can be stored in an airtight container and kept in the freezer for later use. In a small mixing bowl, beat the egg. Add the milk and oil to the beaten egg. Pour the egg mixture into the flour. Stir with a fork until *just* moistened. Immediately pour mixture into a greased 8x8x2-inch metal pan. Spread evenly with a spatula or the back of a spoon.

Bake at 400°-425° F. for 20-25 minutes or until a toothpick inserted in the center comes out clean. Frozen mix may require a few extra minutes baking time. Cut into 9 squares. Serve hot. Good with honey-butter. (See page 86.)

Makes nine squares.

Variation: To above recipe, add one 8½-ounce can unsalted whole kernel corn and 2 tablespoons dehydrated minced onions (which have been softened in a small amount of water). Bake in a greased 9x9x2-inch metal pan. When finished baking, sprinkle with ½ cup grated unsalted cheddar cheese. Allow cheese to melt (return to warm oven if necessary) and then cut into 9 squares for serving.

Dropped Biscuits

2	cups Basic Biscuit Mix (pg. 61)
⅔	cup skim milk
2	tablespoons wheat germ

Combine ingredients in mixing bowl and stir with fork until just blended. Drop by rounded teaspoonfuls on greased cookie sheet. Bake in 425° F. oven for 12-15 minutes. Remove from oven and cool. Makes about 10 or 12. Good served with honey or jam.

Grandma's Yummy Doughnuts

These doughnuts bring visions of heaping plates of hot, tender doughnuts and happy childhood moments.

1   cup granulated sugar
2   eggs, beaten
½   cup sour cream or plain skim milk yogurt
½   cup skim milk
1   teaspoon vanilla
3   teaspoons baking powder substitute (2 teaspoons in altitudes over 4,000 ft.)
½   teaspoon baking soda substitute
3   cups unbleached flour, sifted (plus 4 tablespoons in altitudes over 4,000 ft.)
1   cup whole wheat flour
1   teaspoon ground cinnamon
½   teaspoon ground nutmeg

In a large mixing bowl, cream the sugar and eggs. Add sour cream, milk and vanilla. Sift the dry ingredients and spices together and add to ingredients in mixing bowl. Mix until just blended; do not overmix! Let sit in refrigerator at least 20 minutes or up to overnight. When ready to fry, knead 10 to 12 times on well-floured board. Roll out to about ½-inch thickness. Cut with doughnut cutter. Fry in hot vegetable oil at 375° F. (use thermometer) for 2-3 minutes on each side. Drain on paper towel and roll in a sugar-cinnamon mixture.

Sugar-cinnamon mixture: Mix 1 cup granulated sugar and ½ teaspoon ground cinnamon.

Makes 18-20 doughnuts.

Banana Bread

½   cup (1 stick) unsalted butter or unsalted margarine
1   cup granulated sugar
3   ripe bananas, crushed
1   tablespoon sour cream or skim milk
2   eggs, well beaten
1   teaspoon baking soda substitute
1   cup unbleached flour
1   cup whole wheat flour
¾   teaspoon baking powder substitute (½ teaspoon in altitudes above 4,000 ft.)

In a large mixing bowl, cream together butter or margarine and sugar. Add bananas. Mix well. Add eggs; mix thoroughly. Add remaining ingredients and mix thoroughly. Bake in greased 9x5x3-inch loaf pan at 375° F. for 45 minutes.

Makes one loaf.

Russian Rye Bread

4	cups unbleached flour
4	cups rye flour
2	cups unsalted whole grain instant cereal
1	cup whole wheat flour
2	tablespoons (2 packages) yeast
2	tablespoons instant decaffeinated coffee
2	tablespoons caraway seeds
2	tablespoons honey
1½	teaspoons fennel seeds
2½	cups water
⅓	cup light molasses
⅓	cup unsalted margarine
1	ounce (1 square) unsweetened chocolate
2	tablespoons white vinegar
2	tablespoons cornmeal

In a large mixing bowl, combine 3 cups of the unbleached flour, 1 cup of the rye flour, cereal, yeast, whole wheat flour, coffee, caraway seeds, honey and fennel seeds. In a saucepan, heat water, molasses, margarine, chocolate and vinegar until warm (110°-115° F.). Stir constantly. Add this liquid to the dry ingredients in the mixing bowl. Beat for one minute at low speed and three minutes at high speed. Stir in remaining rye flour and enough of the remaining unbleached flour to make a moderately stiff dough. Knead until smooth and elastic. (This dough may be a bit sticky but that is all right.) Place in large greased bowl and let rise about 1½ hours or until almost doubled. Punch down and divide dough in half. Shape each into a ball. Place on a well-greased cookie sheet that has been sprinkled with the cornmeal. Flatten slightly and cover with a towel. Let rise in a warm place for 45 minutes to one hour, or until almost doubled. Bake at 350° F. for 40-45 minutes. (375° F. for 50 minutes in altitudes above 4,000 ft.) Brush the hot bread with a few tablespoons of skim milk. Cool on wire rack.

Makes 2 loaves.

Muffins

3	cups Basic Biscuit Mix (pg. 61)
3	tablespoons honey
1	egg, beaten
1	cup skim milk
½	cup blueberries or other fruit (optional)
½	cup nuts, chopped (optional)

Combine Mix and honey in mixing bowl. Combine egg and milk; make a well in dry ingredients. Pour in liquid. Add fruit or nuts if desired. Stir just until moistened. Divide into 12 greased muffin cups. Bake in 400° F. oven for 20-25 minutes.

Makes 12 muffins.

Pennsylvania Cinnamon Flop

No eggs — low in cholesterol. When this is removed from the oven the "cake" sinks in the middle and looks like it "flopped."

1   cup granulated sugar
1   tablespoon unsalted margarine
1   cup skim milk
2   teaspoons baking powder substitute
2   cups unbleached flour

Topping

⅔   cup packed brown sugar
1½ teaspoons ground cinnamon
2   tablespoons unbleached flour
½   stick (4 tablespoons) unsalted margarine
        cut in 12 pieces

In a large mixer bowl, cream the sugar and the margarine. Gradually add the milk, mixing well after each addition. Add the baking powder and flour. Mix. Grease and dust with flour two 9-inch pie plates.

In a small mixing bowl, make the topping by mixing all the ingredients together, except the margarine. Sprinkle half of the mixture onto the top of each of the cake batters.

With a knife handle or finger, poke six holes evenly in the batter of each cake. Fill each hole with a piece of unsalted margarine.

Bake at 375° F. for 20-25 minutes. Remove from oven and cut into pie-shaped wedges and serve hot!

Two 9″ cakes equal 12 servings.

Hamburger Buns, Hot Dog Buns

Prepare the Whole Wheat Bread dough recipe, pg. 68. Roll out ¼ of the dough on a greased counter top to about ⅓ thickness. Butter or grease top of dough generously and fold greased sides together.

For hamburger buns: cut with a tin can to the size that you desire.

For hot dog buns: cut with a knife or bend a can (such as a sardine can) into the desired shape and cut.

Place buns on greased cookie sheet about ¾-inch apart. Let rise until doubled in size. Bake at 350° F. for 25-30 minutes. Remove from oven and cool on wire racks.

Makes about a dozen buns for each fourth of whole wheat bread recipe.

Angel Rolls

These are light, airy, quick rolls. No kneading is required and they are made in a mixer!

1	tablespoon (1 package) yeast
1	cup very warm water (110° F.-115° F.)
2	tablespoons granulated sugar
1¼	cups unbleached flour, sifted
¼	teaspoon salt substitute
1	egg
2	tablespoons unsalted margarine, melted
1	cup whole wheat flour

Sprinkle yeast over very warm water in a large mixer bowl. The water should be cold water heated to very warm. (Very warm should feel comfortably warm when dropped on wrist. See introduction to Breads.)

Stir in the sugar, the unbleached flour and the salt substitute. Beat with electric mixer at medium speed until smooth.

Add the egg, margarine and whole wheat flour. Beat until smooth. Scrape down sides of the bowl; cover and let rise in a warm place until almost double; about 30 minutes. Mix batter down vigorously; spoon into 12 to 16 well-greased muffin cups, filling two-thirds full.* Cover with a towel. Let rise until almost double in size, about 15 minutes or until the dough reaches the top of the muffin pan cups.

Bake at 400° F. for 25 minutes or until golden brown. Cool on wire rack after removing from pans.

Makes 12-16 rolls. This recipe doubles easily and the rolls freeze well.

*Delicious variation: brush the tops with beaten egg and sprinkle with sesame seed, poppy seed, caraway seeds or minced onion.

Lynn's Poppy Seed Loaf

2	eggs
1½	cups granulated sugar
⅓	cup vegetable oil
1½	teaspoons vanilla*
¼	cup poppy seeds (2 ounces)
2	cups unbleached flour
2¾	teaspoons baking powder substitute (2¼ teaspoons in altitudes over 4,000 ft.)
1	cup skim milk
1	teaspoon lemon juice

In a large mixer bowl, beat eggs; add sugar and oil. Mix well. Add vanilla and poppy seed. In another bowl, sift together flour and baking powder substitute. Add these dry ingredients to egg mixture alternately with milk and lemon juice, mixing thoroughly after each addition.

Pour into a very *well-greased* 9x5x3-inch loaf pan. Be sure pan is generously greased (not oiled) as this bread has a tendency to stick.

Bake for one hour at 350° F. Remove from oven; cool in baking pan for 5 minutes and turn out on wire rack. Cool and slice about ¼-inch thick.

This recipe doubles easily and freezes well. Makes one loaf.

Variations: use ¾ teaspoon orange or lemon extract instead of vanilla.

Herb Bread

½   cup skim milk or water*
3   tablespoons honey
4   tablespoons unsalted margarine
1½   cups water
1   tablespoon (1 package) yeast
4-5 cups unbleached flour
2   teaspoons dill seed
1   teaspoon dill weed
½   teaspoon celery seed
½   teaspoon fennel seed
2   tablespoons dehydrated onions
2   tablespoons dehydrated parsley flakes
1   cup whole wheat flour
2   eggs

In a medium-sized saucepan, heat the milk (or water) with the honey, margarine and water until the temperature is 110°-115° F. In a large bowl, mix yeast and 3 cups of the flour. Add liquid mixture to the large bowl and beat until smooth. Add herbs, whole wheat flour and eggs, and mix until blended. Add enough unbleached flour to make a soft dough. Knead on a floured board until smooth and elastic (about 10 minutes). Place in a large greased bowl. Cover. Let rise until doubled in bulk; about 1 hour. Punch down. Divide dough in half and shape into two loaves and place in greased 9x5x3-inch bread pans. Cover; let rise again, about one hour. Bake at 400° F. for 40 minutes or until loaf sounds hollow when tapped. Rub the tops with unsalted margarine if you like soft crusts, or brush with skim milk for harder, shiny crusts. Remove from pans and cool on racks.

Makes 2 loaves.

*As a variety, use water from boiled potatoes and ½ cup warm mashed potatoes.

Whole Wheat Bread

This recipe makes loaves of nutritious, satisfying bread. Great for sandwiches, toast, or served as a complement to meals.

4   tablespoons (4 packages) yeast
½   cup very warm (110°-115° F.) water
1   tablespoon honey
5   cups very warm (110°-115° F.) water
11 to 12 cups (freshly ground) whole wheat flour
⅔   cup vegetable oil
⅔   cup honey
4   eggs (optional)

Sprinkle yeast on ½ cup warm water and one tablespoon honey. Set aside to rise. Combine 5 cups warm water and 7 cups of the flour in a very large mixing bowl and mix until moistened. Add oil, honey, yeast mixture, and eggs (optional). *For raisin bread, add ingredients below at this point.* Mix to blend. Add 3 cups more flour and mix well. Beat well for at least 5 minutes, adding more flour until sides of bowl are completely clean.

Remove from bowl and put on floured board. Add more flour as necessary and knead until the dough is no longer sticky. Divide dough into four equal parts and mold into generously greased 9x5x3-inch bread pans. Preheat oven to 250° F.

with a pan of water in the bottom of the oven. Turn off oven and place bread on rack in the middle of oven to rise for about 20 minutes or until raised so that the top of the bread is about even with the top of the pans.

Adjust oven temperature to 350° F. and bake bread for 40 minutes. Remove pans from oven and turn out onto cooling racks. When completely cooled, store in airtight containers. This bread freezes well.

Makes 4 loaves

*Raisin Bread

Add ¼ cup ground cinnamon, 4 eggs (if not added previously), 1 cup raisins, 1 cup unsalted nuts, and 1 cup flour to the recipe above at the *.

South Seas Coffee Cake

A delicious combination of ginger and pine-apple!

Cake

1	20-ounce can crushed pineapple in juice
3	tablespoons lemon juice
1½	tablespoons crystallized ginger, chopped
¾	cup golden raisins
½	cup (1 stick) unsalted margarine
1	cup granulated sugar
2	eggs
2½	cups unbleached flour
½	cup whole wheat flour
3½	teaspoons baking powder substitute (2¾ teaspoons in altitudes above 4,000 ft.)
1½	teaspoons ground cinnamon
¾	teaspoons baking soda substitute
⅔	cup pecans, chopped

Topping

¾	cup brown sugar, firmly packed
3	tablespoons unbleached flour
3	tablespoons unsalted margarine
1½	teaspoons ground cinnamon
¼	cup wheat germ
¼	cup pecans, chopped

Drain pineapple; save juice. In a small sauce-pan, combine pineapple juice, lemon juice and ginger; heat to boiling. Remove pan from heat; add pineapple and raisins. Let stand at room temperature for 15 minutes to cool the mixture.

In a large mixing bowl, cream margarine, sugar and eggs until fluffy. In another bowl, mix flours, baking powder substitute, cinnamon, and baking soda substitute together. To creamed mixture, alternately add dry ingredients and pineapple mixture, mixing well after each addition. Fold in pecans.

Spread half the batter in a greased, 9x13x2-inch baking pan.

Prepare topping in a small mixing bowl. Combine brown sugar, flour, margarine, cinnamon and wheat germ. Mix ingredients together until mixture resembles coarse meal. Stir in pecans.

Spread half of the topping mixture over batter in pan. Spread remaining batter in pan and top with remaining topping.

Bake in 350° F. oven for 30-35 minutes. Remove from oven. May be served warm or cold. Cut into 12 squares. May be topped with non-dairy whipped topping, whipped cream, milk, or crushed pineapple just before serving.

12 servings

Cinnamon Rolls

1	cup skim milk
1	cup cold water
2	tablespoons (2 packages) yeast
1	tablespoon honey
5	cups unbleached flour
1½	cups whole wheat flour
6	tablespoons shortening or unsalted margarine
½	cup granulated sugar
3	eggs, beaten
½	cup (1 stick) unsalted margarine, melted

Cinnamon
Brown sugar

In a one-quart saucepan, scald milk; add cold water. Transfer to large mixing bowl. When cooled to lukewarm, add yeast, honey, and 3 cups of the flour. Beat until smooth. Cream in a small mixing bowl the shortening and sugar; add beaten eggs. Beat into ingredients in large mixing bowl. Add remaining 2 cups flour and the wheat flour. Add more wheat flour, if needed, until dough becomes smooth. Let rise in large greased bowl until doubled.

Divide dough into thirds and roll out into thin rectangles. Spread each with melted unsalted margarine; sprinkle with cinnamon and brown sugar as desired. (Plumped raisins and/or nuts may be added here if desired.) Roll up jelly-roll fashion and cut crosswise about every 1½-inches. Put in greased 9x13-inch pans, cut side down, and let rise until doubled. Bake 20 minutes at 375° F.

Yields about 3 dozen rolls.

French Bread

The trick with this bread is to add the flour gradually and stir until dough is still slightly sticky. Putting a pan of hot water in the oven during baking is the secret to a crusty loaf of bread. This bread is quick to prepare!

2	cups warm water
2	tablespoons (2 packages) yeast
¾	teaspoon salt substitute
1	tablespoon vegetable oil
1½	tablespoons honey
4-6	cups unsifted unbleached flour (1 cup of this may be whole wheat flour)

Cornmeal

Measure warm water into large, warm mixing bowl. Sprinkle the yeast over the water and stir until dissolved. Add the salt substitute, oil and honey. Add flour and stir until well blended.

Dough may be sticky. Knead for a few minutes on floured board until smooth. Place in greased bowl. Cover, let rise about one hour or until doubled.

Turn dough onto lightly floured board. Divide into two equal portions. Roll each into an oblong 15x10-inches. Beginning at the wide side, roll up tightly; seal edges by pinching together. Taper ends. Place loaves on greased baking sheets sprinkled with cornmeal. Cover; let rise in warm place about 1 hour or until doubled in bulk. With a razor, make 4 diagonal cuts on top of each loaf.

Place a pan of hot water on the lowest rack in the oven. Bake in 450° oven for about 25 minutes or until loaves sound hollow when tapped. Turn out of pans and cool on wire racks.

Makes two loaves.

Dilly Bread

Great for company or every day eating!

¼ cup very warm water (110°-115° F.)
½ tablespoon honey
2 tablespoons (2 packages) yeast
1 cup warm unsalted, dry curd cottage cheese*
½ cup sour cream or plain skim milk yogurt

¼ teaspoon salt substitute
¼ teaspoon baking soda substitute
1 egg
2 tablespoons granulated sugar or honey
1 tablespoon vegetable oil
3 cups unbleached flour
½ teaspoon dill weed
1 tablespoon dry onion, minced
2 teaspoons dill seed

In a small bowl, mix warm water, honey and yeast. Set aside to rise. Combine cottage cheese, sour cream, salt substitute, baking soda substitute, egg, sugar, and oil in mixer. Mix well and add 1½ cups of the flour; mix for 5 minutes on medium speed. Add the yeast mixture and dill weed, onion, and dill seed. Mix well and add remaining flour. Let rise one hour (optional in altitudes over 4,000 ft.). Punch down and place in a greased one-quart casserole dish. Let rise for 30 minutes or until doubled. Bake at 350° F. for 40-50 minutes. Put unsalted margarine on top and, if desired, sprinkle with onion powder. Turn out of pan on wire rack to cool. Also delicious served hot.

Makes one loaf.

*If unable to obtain unsalted cottage cheese, use one cup sour cream or yogurt and two eggs as a substitute.

Susan's Fennel Bread

1   tablespoon (1 package) yeast
1   teaspoon granulated sugar
1   cup cold water heated to very warm
         (110°-115° F.)
1   teaspoon salt substitute
2   tablespoons melted unsalted butter or
         vegetable oil
1   tablespoon fennel seeds
3   cups unbleached flour
1   egg yolk
1   teaspoon skim milk
2   teaspoons fennel seeds
Cornmeal

In a large mixer bowl, dissolve the yeast with sugar in ½ cup of the lukewarm water. Let stand until bubbly. Stir in remaining water, salt substitute, unsalted butter, fennel seeds and enough flour to make a stiff dough. Knead for 10 minutes. Place in a greased bowl. Cover; let rise until doubled (1½ to 2 hours). Punch down. Shape into a round loaf. Place on greased baking sheet sprinkled with cornmeal. Cover and let rise until doubled (one hour). After dough has risen 30 minutes, slash across top of loaf criss-cross fashion with sharp knife. Heat oven to 375° F. Brush loaf with one egg yolk beaten with one teaspoon skim milk. Sprinkle with 2 teaspoons fennel seeds. Bake 30 minutes or until browned. Makes one loaf.

Zucchini Bread

This is so moist and sweet that it could be used as a dessert.

3   eggs
1   cup vegetable oil
1   cup granulated sugar
1   cup brown sugar
2   cups ground zucchini
1   cup whole wheat flour
1   cup unbleached flour (plus 4 tablespoons
         in altitudes over 4,000 ft.)
1½   teaspoons baking soda substitute
¾   teaspoon baking powder substitute (½ tea-
         spoon in altitudes over 4,000 ft.)
3   teaspoons ground cinnamon
3   teaspoons vanilla
½   cup chopped nuts

In a large mixing bowl, mix all ingredients thoroughly. Grease a 9x5x3-inch loaf pan; put waxed paper on bottom of pan and grease the waxed paper. Pour batter into pan. Bake for 15 minutes at 350° F. (375° F. in altitudes above 4,000 ft.) then reduce oven temperatures to 325° F. and bake for 50 minutes more or until toothpick inserted in center comes out clean.

Makes one loaf.

This recipe can be doubled. Bake in three 8½ x 4½ x 3-inch pans prepared as directed above. Bake about 10 minutes less than required above.

Makes three small loaves.

Eva's Scones

3   tablespoons (3 packages) yeast
½   cup very warm water (110°-115° F.)
2   cups skim milk
¼   teaspoon salt substitute (optional)
½   cup granulated sugar
½   cup shortening
3   eggs
2   cups whole wheat flour
4   cups unbleached flour
⅛ - ¼ teaspoon ground cinnamon

Dissolve yeast in water using a medium-sized mixing bowl; set aside to rise. Scald milk in saucepan; add salt substitute (if used), sugar and shortening. Cool to lukewarm.

In a small mixing bowl, beat eggs. Gradually add to lukewarm milk mixture, beating constantly during addition. In a large mixing bowl or bread mixer, mix liquids with flours and cinnamon. Use bread mixer, or if no bread mixer is available, knead by hand until ingredients are thoroughly mixed. (Dough should be soft and sticky.) Chill in bowl for at least 30 minutes.

Roll out on lightly floured surface to less than ½-inch thickness. Cut into 2-inch squares.

Drop into hot fat until lightly browned. Remove from fat and quickly drain on paper towels to eliminate excess grease. Serve immediately with a honey-butter spread (See Toppings for Pancakes, Waffles, page 86).

Makes 3 to 4 dozen scones.

Raisin Loaf

2   cups raisins
1   cup water
4   cups whole wheat flour
3   tablespoons unbleached flour
1   tablespoon baking soda substitute
1   teaspoon ground cinnamon
2   cups honey
¼   cup vegetable oil
4   eggs
2   teaspoons vanilla
1   cup mashed bananas or 1 cup firm
       applesauce
2   cups coarsely chopped walnuts

Combine raisins and water in medium sauce-pan; bring to boil; turn off heat and cool at room temperature to plump raisins. Combine flours, baking soda substitute and cinnamon in a medium-sized bowl. In another bowl, beat honey, oil, eggs and vanilla. Add raisins with water, bananas and nuts to honey mixture. Add flour mixture, stirring just to blend all ingredients. Divide equally into two greased 9x5x3-inch baking pans (bread size). Bake in 325° F. oven for one hour. Lower oven temperature to 250° F. and continue to bake for an additional 30 minutes or until wooden toothpick inserted in center comes out clean. Turn out of pans after 5 minutes and cool on wire racks. Store in airtight container.

Makes two loaves.

Breakfasts—
Cereals, Pancakes, Waffles

It has often been said that breakfast is the most important meal of the day. Every meal is important. However, breakfast to someone on a low-sodium diet may be quite a change from the "bacon and eggs" routine!

Breakfast meats are particularly high in sodium content. We have included one "traditional-tasting" sausage recipe. You may also consider cooking plain hamburger patties. Basically, however, it is best to change your dietary habits and think of replacing meats for breakfast with whole grains, nuts, cereals and dairy products. This is for several reasons: meat is high in cholesterol, harder to digest, used less efficiently in the body and is higher in sodium content than whole grains, nuts, cereals, milk and eggs.

Breakfast may also become a time to eat non-traditional foods. We know of people who enjoy melted unsalted cheese on unsalted toast; unsalted peanut butter on unsalted wheat toast; or skim milk yogurt on unsalted wheat toast. Some have Cheese Chili Cubes and/or any leftovers from the previous night's dinner. Microwave ovens are very helpful with leftovers.

Fresh fruit is a great "wake-up the system" food. A glass of skim milk served with breakfast is also another source of protein.

Cereal Suggestions

Always use skim milk on your cereals. Keep the amount of milk used to a minimum, though, as one cup of skim milk has about 130 milligrams of sodium. Be sure to check the labels for ingredients when purchasing commercially prepared cereals. Many delicious hot and cold cereals are available which are low in sodium. Many commercially prepared cereals, however, do contain sodium so it is necessary to read labels carefully. A few suggestions follow.

Creamed wheat: Quick! Just leave out the salt while cooking.

Granola: Make your own—it's easy, nutritious and adds bulk and fiber to the diet. There is a recipe in this section.

Oatmeal: Cook the quick (not instant) variety of oatmeal according to directions, leaving out the salt. Low in sodium, oatmeal makes a quick, hot breakfast. Add raisins, chopped apple, brown sugar and cinnamon for variety.

Shredded wheat: High in nutrition and low in sodium, shredded wheat comes in bite-size as well as large biscuits for a quick breakfast treat.

Puffed rice: This provides a quick breakfast and is available at the grocery stores and health food stores. If the product available in the grocery stores tastes a little bland to you, try the varieties found in the health food stores which contain whole grains.

Puffed wheat: This low sodium cold cereal, like the puffed rice, is great for those "in-a-hurry" breakfasts.

Whole grain cereals: Instant as well as long-cooking varieties are available without added salt. When cooking cereals, refrain from adding the salt called for in the cooking instructions—the cereal is just as good without the salt added!

Swedish Pancakes

Company good, yet easy enough to serve for everyday. These are quite easy and fast to prepare. These also make a great dessert.

1   cup unbleached flour (1¼ cups in altitudes above 4,000 ft.)*
1   teaspoon granulated sugar (optional)
2   cups skim milk
5   eggs
See below for filling/topping options

Mix all the ingredients in a blender or in a bowl with a beater or wire whisk until well blended. The flour may look a little lumpy, but mix until large lumps are gone. Heat a 10-12-inch skillet over medium-high heat and lightly grease with unsalted margarine or vegetable oil. Pour ¼ cup of the mixture in a 10-inch skillet and ⅓ cup in a 12-inch skillet. The pan should be rotated so the mixture will cover the entire bottom of the pan. Cook pancake on each side until lightly browned, about 2-3 minutes total time. Place on a warmed plate.

*Use half whole wheat flour for variety, more nutrition, and added taste.

Filling/Topping options:
    Roll and sprinkle lemon juice and powdered sugar on the top.
    Line center with jelly, roll and sprinkle with powdered sugar.
    Place several tablespoons fresh or frozen fruit down center, roll and top with whipped cream or non-dairy topping
    Place 2-3 tablespoons unflavored or flavored yogurt in center, and roll. Top with another dollop of yogurt and/or fruit.
    Line the center with ½ sliced banana. Roll, top with lemon juice.
    Spread center of pancake with applesauce or apple butter. Roll and sprinkle the top with cinnamon or nutmeg.
    Use your imagination!

For two people: Cut the ingredients in half using 3 eggs. Makes about 10 10-inch pancakes.
To store: Cook all pancakes and freeze or keep batter in the refrigerator and cook as for fresh the next day.
    Makes approximately 15 12-inch pancakes.

Whole Wheat Pancakes

Make your own mix as an option for very quick morning preparations!

1   cup whole wheat flour
3½   teaspoons baking powder substitute (1
        tablespoon in altitudes above 4,000 ft.)
1½   cups sweet or soured skim milk, or plain
        yogurt
2   eggs
2   tablespoons vegetable oil
½   cup untoasted wheat germ

Combine ingredients in a large mixing bowl. Mix, using no more than 50 strokes (pancakes get "tough" with too much mixing). Drop by table-spoonfuls onto moderately hot griddle or skillet (a drop of water should "dance" when dropped on the hot surface) which has been lightly greased with vegetable oil.

Cook until lightly browned and surface bubbles break. Turn and cook other side of pancake until lightly browned.

Serve with blueberries, strawberries, peaches, or other fresh fruit folded into batter. Pancakes may also be topped with fresh fruit if desired.

Makes about 15 pancakes.

This can be made into a mix and kept in the freezer until ready to use. This way, you have your own "packaged" mix!

Mix:
6   cups whole wheat flour
½   cup (scant) baking powder sutstitute
        (⅓ cup in altitudes above 4,000 ft.)
3   cups wheat germ

Mix ingredients together and store in an air-tight container in the freezer. When ready to use, mix as directed above for pancakes adding:
¾   cup mix
¾ to 1 cup skim milk
1   egg
1   tablespoon vegetable oil

Makes about 8 to 10 pancakes.

Vegetable Omelet

¼ green bell pepper, seeded and diced, or ¼
   cup diced zucchini, skins left on
2 mushroom caps, diced
2 tablespoons unsalted margarine
4-5 eggs, beaten well
3 tablespoons unsalted cheddar cheese,
   grated (optional)
1 small tomato, chopped
1 green onion, chopped
1 tablespoon alfalfa sprouts (optional)

Melt one tablespoon margarine in a 10-12-inch skillet. Gently sauté over a low heat the green pepper and mushrooms just until slightly tender, about 2-3 minutes. Remove from skillet.

Melt the remaining one tablespoon margarine in the skillet. When it bubbles, add the beaten eggs and cover skillet with a lid. Cook until just set.

Mix the pepper, mushrooms, cheese, tomato, onion and sprouts. Spoon down the center of the omelet and fold one side toward the middle. Then fold the second side over that. Slip out onto serving plate. Garnish with additional grated cheese, if desired.

Serves 2-3. When this omelet is served with Quick Fried Potatoes (pg. 84) and unsalted toast, it makes a festive company meal.

Onion Omelet

Unusual and festive, yet so simple to do.

1 small sweet Spanish or white onion
2 tablespoons unsalted margarine
3 tablespoons sour cream or plain skim milk
   yogurt
¼ teaspoon dill weed
Ground black pepper
3 eggs, beaten well
Tomato slices
Parsley sprigs

Peel and thinly slice onion. Separate into rings. Melt one tablespoon margarine in a small skillet. Add onion rings and cook over low heat until tender. Stir in sour cream, dill and pepper to taste. Keep warm.

Heat a 6-8-inch skillet. Add the remaining one tablespoon margarine, coating the entire bottom of the pan. When the margarine bubbles, pour in the egg mixture all at once. Cook with a lid on until mixture is just barely set. Spoon onion mixture onto the center of the omelet. Fold both sides over the onions. Slip out onto serving plate. Garnish with fresh chopped parsley and tomato slices. Serve with unsalted muffins or unsalted toast.

Serves 2

Potato Pancakes

Different but quite tasty!

4　　large raw potatoes, peeled
1　　small onion
½　　cup skim milk
½　　teaspoon salt substitute
1　　egg, beaten
2　　tablespoons unbleached flour
Shortening for frying
Sour cream or unsalted butter or plain skim milk
　　yogurt

In a large bowl, grate potatoes and onion; add milk; mix with remaining ingredients except for shortening and sour cream. *OR*—cut potatoes into approximately ⅓-inch cubes and chop onion; place in blender with remaining ingredients (except for shortening and sour cream) and blend until potato and onion are well mixed. (Potatoes have a tendency to darken, but this will not be noticeable when cooked.)

Heat skillet or griddle to a medium-hot temperature. Drop by tablespoonfuls into skillet or on griddle that has been lightly greased with shortening or vegetable oil. Brown on both sides, cooking about 3-4 minutes per side. Serve at once. May be topped with sour cream, unsalted butter, served plain or with yogurt.

Six servings.

Spiced Sausage Patties

These are really good!

1½　pounds unseasoned ground lean pork
⅛　　teaspoon ground red pepper
¾　　teaspoon ground black pepper
¾　　teaspoon ground sage
¼　　teaspoon seasoned salt substitute

Mix all ingredients in medium-sized mixing bowl. Shape into small patties or into one-inch balls. Fry in a large frying pan* about 20 minutes or until done. Drain grease from pan after 10 minutes of cooking and again when sausages are thoroughly cooked. Drain on paper toweling and serve.

4-6 servings.

*Optional method of cooking: Place sausage patties or balls on rack of broiler pan. Bake for 20 minutes at 350° F.

Pancake and Waffle Recipe

1   cup of Pancake and Waffle Mix Deluxe
        (see recipe opposite)
¾   cup water or skim milk

     Mix until lump-free and add:
¼   cup oil
1   egg

(You may need to add more water or milk to get a thinner batter for pancakes as a thick batter is desired for waffles.) Heat skillet or waffle iron to 350° F. and drop batter onto oiled surface. Turn pancakes when bubbles break.

Pancake and Waffle Mix Deluxe

Mix together the following grains:
3   cups whole wheat grain*
                OR
4½   cups whole wheat flour**
1   cup rolled oats or whole oats*
                OR
1   cup rolled oats ground in blender**
1   cup frozen whole soybeans*
                OR
1   cup soy flour**
1   cup popcorn or corn*
                OR
1   cup cornmeal**

Grind these* grains in mill or buy these** ingredients at supermarket or health food store. Sift into large bowl and add the following:
    4½ tablespoons low-sodium baking powder
        (4 tablespoons in altitudes above 4,000 ft.)
    ½ cup whey powder or instant dried milk
        (available at health food store)
Mix thoroughly and store in a tight container in the refrigerator or freezer.

French Toast

4	slices low-sodium bread (whole wheat is good!)
2	eggs, beaten
1	teaspoon skim milk
⅛	teaspoon ground cinnamon
2	tablespoons unsalted margarine

In a small mixing bowl, beat the eggs. Add milk. Add the cinnamon to egg mixture. Melt the margarine in a skillet. Dip the bread in the egg mixture and cook on both sides until lightly browned. This should take about 3-4 minutes per side.

2 servings.

Baked French Toast

2	eggs
½	cup skim milk
½	teaspoon vanilla
6	slices low-sodium bread
1	cup bran flakes
¼	cup melted unsalted butter or margarine

In a shallow dish combine eggs, milk and vanilla. Dip bread slices in egg mixture turning once and allowing both sides to absorb liquid. Coat each dipped piece with bran flakes. Place in a single layer on a well-greased baking sheet. Drizzle melted butter over top. Bake in 450° oven for 10 minutes or until browned.

3 servings.

Apple Pancakes

Nice and fancy, yet easy to do.

½	cup raisins
Boiling water	
2	eggs, lightly beaten
1	cup skim milk
1	cup whole wheat flour
½	cup cornmeal
3	tablespoons granulated sugar or honey
1	tablespoon ground cinnamon
1½	tablespoons baking powder substitute
2	tart, juicy apples, sliced thin

In a small saucepan, plump raisins for 10 minutes in boiling water to cover. Drain thoroughly. In a mixing bowl, beat eggs and milk together.

Stir in flour, cornmeal, sugar or honey, cinnamon and baking powder substitute. Add apples and raisins and fold into batter.

Drop by heaping tablespoonfuls onto a hot griddle or into a large skillet that has been lightly greased with vegetable oil. To test for a hot griddle, a drop of water should "dance" or sizzle vigorously when dropped upon the griddle. Allow space between each cake so there is room for expansion.

Cook about 5 minutes on each side; turn when browned. Serve immediately.

Makes 16 pancakes.

Cooked Cracked Wheat Cereal

Healthy; easy; hot.

1 cup cracked wheat
3 cups water

Combine cracked wheat and water in 3-quart saucepan. Cook over medium heat for 20 minutes, stirring frequently. Water may be reduced to 2 cups and the cereal cooked in top of double boiler for about 45 minutes.

For serving variety, add skim milk and sugar; brown sugar and unsalted butter; honey and unsalted butter; pure maple syrup or light molasses, or whatever you may like. Serve with skim milk.

Makes 2 to 4 servings.

Whole Kernel Cooked Cereal

Start cooking the night before and breakfast is ready when you get up in the morning!

1 cup whole kernel wheat
2 cups water

In a 3-quart saucepan, place wheat and water. Cook over low heat, starting the night before. Serve with skim milk.

May also be cooked in a slow-cooker set on low heat overnight, or baked for about 5 hours or overnight in a covered pan at 150-200° F. Yet another way is to put wheat and boiling water the night before in a quart-sized thermos, top tightly secured, and serve in the morning.

2 servings.

Mexican Eggs

Perfect for breakfast, brunch, lunch or dinner!

1	tablespoon unsalted butter or unsalted margarine
1	medium-sized onion, chopped
2	green onions, chopped
1	green pepper, chopped
2	8½-ounce cans unsalted tomatoes or 4 fresh tomatoes, chopped
½	teaspoon crushed hot chili peppers (optional)
¼	teaspoon ground cumin
1	cup unsalted cheddar cheese, grated
4	eggs, beaten
2	heaping tablespoons sour cream
2	unsalted flour tortillas, heated and "buttered" (unsalted, that is!)

In small saucepan, sauté onions in unsalted butter until tender. Add green pepper, tomatoes, chilies and cumin. Gently simmer while preparing remaining ingredients. Grate cheese. Heat 10-inch skillet and grease lightly with unsalted butter or oil. Pour eggs into skillet and cook, stirring occasionally, until set. Place eggs on warm plates. Top with hot tomato sauce, cheese, and a heaping tablespoon sour cream. Serve immediately with hot flour tortillas which have been lightly spread with unsalted butter or unsalted margarine.

2 servings.

Quick Fried Potatoes

3	already-baked potatoes
⅛	cup vegetable oil
1	small onion, sliced
½	teaspoon paprika
¼	teaspoon garlic powder
¼	teaspoon salt substitute

Slice the potatoes, leaving the skin on. In a 10-inch skillet heat the oil over medium heat. Add the onion and sliced potatoes. Sprinkle the remaining seasonings over the onions and potatoes. Cook 10 minutes or until the desired brownness.

Serves 2-3

Granola

A batch can be made anytime and stored at room temperature for several weeks. This freezes well, too!

10 cups rolled oats
1   cup sesame seeds
1   cup untoasted wheat germ
1   cup sunflower seeds
1   cup chopped almonds or cashews
1   cup coconut (optional)
1   cup honey
1   cup brown sugar
1   cup unsalted margarine
1   teaspoon vanilla

In a very large bowl or container, mix the oats, sesame seeds, wheat germ, sunflower seeds, nuts and coconut (if desired). In a 2-quart saucepan, melt the honey, sugar and margarine. Remove from heat; add vanilla. Pour the melted mixture over the top of the dry ingredients and mix very well. This may take a bit of time, as the honey mixture tends to bunch up. Keep at it and continue stirring as the ingredients will all mix together.

Put in two 9x13x3-inch pans. Bake in oven at 275° to 300° F. for about 40 minutes, stirring occasionally, until ingredients are evenly light brown.

Remove from oven and allow to cool, stirring often.

Store in an airtight container. This looks pretty in a large glass jar with a tight-fitting lid.

To serve: Add fruit (berries, bananas, melon) and raisins, if desired. Serve with skim milk.

Makes approximately 4 quarts.

Toppings for Pancakes, Waffles and French Toast

Maple Syrup: Purchase the "real thing" as your pocketbook allows.

Maple Flavored Syrup: Combine 1½ cups liquid brown sugar with ½ cup water; heat and stir, but do not boil. Add a few drops (3-4) of maple flavoring and 1 tablespoon unsalted margarine.

Whipped "Butter": Cream ½ cup (¼ pound) unsalted margarine and 2 tablespoons unsalted butter until fluffy.

Honey "Butter": Gradually add ¼ cup honey to Whipped "Butter" (above), beating until smooth. Grated orange peel or lemon peel may be added if desired (add about 2 teaspoons).

Cranberry-Orange "Butter": Put 1 small unpeeled, diced orange, ¼ cup raw cranberries, and ¼ cup sugar (or ⅛ cup honey) in blender. When blended, fold into Whipped "Butter" (above).

Jams, Jellies, and Preserves: Check label to see that salt has *not* been added.

Fresh or Frozen Fruits

Honey: Comes in many flavors and textures. Be adventuresome.

Plain Yogurt: Mix with fruits (fresh or frozen) and/or 1 teaspoon frozen orange juice concentrate. Fruit flavored yogurts may have sugars, stabilizers, preservatives added. Check the labels. Of course, skim milk yogurt is lower in cholesterol and calories!

Salads, Salad Dressings, Sauces and Seasonings

In our age of "quick foods," many of us have come to depend upon mixes, bottled dressings and sauces. Starting from "scratch" can sound like a big task. This is just not so! Many dressings and sauces are just as easy to make as cooking with packaged mixes. The flavor seems so much improved once pure, natural ingredients are used, and the sodium and preservatives are eliminated.

Most of the dressings and sauces included here are "basics." Then you, as the chef, can add other seasonings or spices to change the flavor or add variety. However, these dressings and sauces are fine just as they are.

A Few Hints

1. Keep all salads, sauces, and dressings refrigerated until ready to use or keep the ingredients refrigerated until ready to mix.

2. Most salad dressings benefit by being made at least a few hours ahead of serving time. This allows the flavors to mingle and become less harsh.

3. When dressings and sauces are served in an attractive pitcher or bowl with a ladle they appear more appetizing, and are less messy.

4. Salads provide vitamins, roughage, bulk and nutrition to any diet. Dressings are not only a complement, but add the needed unsaturated oil for daily consumption. Sauces can add protein as well as sparking up the taste of foods.

5. Dressings and sauces make excellent gifts when attractively "packaged." They are also fun to make. Salads make relatively simple potluck meals. Think about that!

6. When eating out, oil and vinegar or oil and lemon juice make a very respectable tasting low-sodium dressing. If that is not available, Thousand Island dressing tends generally to be lower in sodium than Italian, Ranch, Blue Cheese, or Green Goddess. The "yes and no's" of a salad bar:

YES	NO
Lettuce	Croutons
Sprouts	Cheese
Sunflower seeds (unsalted raw)	Toasted wheat berries
Ground black pepper	Pickles
Sesame seeds	Beets
Fruit	Garbanzo beans
Cucumbers	Mixed beans (green, kidney, etc.)
Cauliflower	Bacon bits
Green peppers	Pickled peppers
Fresh mushrooms	Cottage cheese
Radishes	Blue cheese, Italian, Ranch, and
Broccoli	Green Goddess dressings
Tomatoes	
Onions	
Cruets of oil and vinegar (mix yourself)	
Lemon juice or wedges (you may have to ask for them)	

Ad-lib Fruit Salad

Let your creativity flow, depending upon what fruits are in season, on sale, or in your cupboard.

1   cup watermelon pieces *or* cantaloupe
         pieces, (optional)
2   bananas, sliced
1   20-ounce can pineapple chunks, drained, *or*
         2 cups fresh pineapple, chopped
1   pound fresh cherries, *or* a 16-ounce can of
         cherries or plums, drained
3   ripe peaches, peeled and sliced *or*
         16-ounce can sliced peaches, drained
1   apple, cored and sliced
½   cup coconut *or* ½ cup chopped nuts
         (walnuts, pecans—you choose)
         (optional)
1   cup grapes (optional)
1   cup sour cream or plain yogurt (optional)

About an hour before serving time, prepare fruit (juice can be saved—and mixed together if desired—for breakfast). Place all ingredients in a large salad bowl. Mix well.

Cover and refrigerate, stirring occasionally, until serving time.

8 servings.

Bean Salad

Good pot-luck or picnic dish as it travels and keeps well.

2   one-pound cans unsalted green beans
2   cups cooked kidney beans
2   cups cooked garbanzo beans
1   cup sliced fresh mushrooms (optional)
1   cup sliced asparagus (optional), cooked
         until just barely tender
1   large onion, sliced
1   cup white vinegar
⅓   cup vegetable oil
⅔   cup honey

Cook kidney and garbanzo beans according to instructions in the introduction to the Ethnic Foods section, pg. 141.

Place drained green beans, kidney beans, garbanzo beans, mushrooms, and asparagus in a large ceramic bowl. In a one-quart saucepan, heat the onion, vinegar, oil and honey until the mixture comes to a boil. Pour the heated mixture over the bean mixture. Stir well. Cover and refrigerate at least 6 hours, but flavors mingle better when marinated overnight.

Serves 6 to 8

Blender Mayonnaise

Familiarize yourself with this recipe as it is a "staple" in many recipes. Preparation is easy and quick.

1   egg
2   tablespoons vinegar
½   teaspoon dry mustard
½   clove garlic
¼   teaspoon paprika
⅛   teaspoon pepper
Dash of cayenne pepper
1   cup oil

Put egg, one tablespoon vinegar and spices in blender. Run on low while *gradually* adding ½ cup oil. As mixture become thick, more power is required, so turn blender on high speed. Add remaining vinegar, then slowly add remaining oil.

Adding the oil gradually is what gives the mayonnaise the light fluffy texture, so this is a *very* important procedure. The slower the addition of oil, the better!

This recipe does *not* double well. It is better to make two batches.

Store in a pint jar, covered, in the refrigerator. Makes about 2½ cups.

Tuna Salad

Lunch, dinner, sandwich—whichever meal you choose—this is fast to make.

2   6½-ounce cans salt-free tuna, drained
½   teaspoon celery seed
½   teaspoon paprika
1   teaspoon low-sodium pickle relish
2   large green onions, chopped
2   tablespoons chopped fresh parsley
⅓-½ cup Blender Mayonnaise or low-sodium
        mayonnaise
2   tablespoons lemon juice
2   hard cooked eggs, finely chopped
¼   teaspoon seasoned salt substitute
¼   teaspoon seasoned pepper

Mix all of the above ingredients in a medium-sized bowl. Refrigerate until ready to use. This may be used as a filling for a sandwich or served on a bed of lettuce and garnished with fresh sliced tomatoes, unsalted canned beets, small pieces of carrots, or any desired vegetable. When served this way it makes an attractive dinner salad.

This filling can be spread on whole wheat bread slices, sprinkled with unsalted cheddar cheese, and placed under the broiler for 2-3 minutes or until the cheese melts and bubbles. Garnish with tomato slices and alfalfa sprouts, if desired. This makes a great cold weather dish with a steaming bowl of soup.

4 salad servings or 6 to 8 sandwich servings.

Spinach Salad

2   bunches spinach leaves
4-6 eggs, hard cooked, diced
1   cup jícama, peeled, diced (optional) or
     ½ cup raw sunflower seeds
1   cup vegetable oil
¼-½ cup granulated sugar
⅓   cup unsalted catsup
¼   cup vinegar
1   tablespoon dehydrated minced onion
2   unsalted beef bouillon cubes,
     finely crushed (optional)

Wash and remove stems of spinach leaves; drain. Cook and prepare eggs. Prepare jícama. Mix remaining ingredients in a 4-cup measure; beat with a wire whisk; set aside.

Tear spinach leaves into a large salad serving bowl. Sprinkle eggs and jícama or sunflower seeds on top of spinach. Just before serving, add dressing and toss thoroughly.

4 servings.

Zucchini Salad

½   cup vegetable oil
3   tablespoons wine vinegar
1   clove garlic, minced
¼   teaspoon chervil (may substitute parsley
     and anise for chervil)
¼   teaspoon seasoned salt substitute
¼   teaspoon ground black pepper
1   pound zucchini sliced thinly
     (about 3 medium)
¼   cup thinly sliced green onions with tops
     (about 3 large ones)
Lettuce cups
Diced tomatoes

With a wire whisk, mix the oil, vinegar, garlic, chervil, seasoned salt substitute and pepper in a pint jar. Pour over the zucchini and onion which have been mixed in a medium-sized bowl. Cover and chill at least one hour. Serve in lettuce cups, spooning on any remaining dressing. Garnish with diced tomatoes.

Serves 4.

Tossed Salad with Oranges

Excellent with Mexican dishes, but great with American dishes also. It's quite colorful and tasty!

2   medium heads crisp, broken pieces of
            Romaine lettuce
1   medium-sized orange, peeled and thinly
            sliced
½   cucumber, thinly sliced
½   sweet onion, slivered
½   bell pepper, diced
½-1   cup raw, peeled and chopped jícama *or*
            ¼ cup raw sunflower seeds
⅓   cup slivered almonds (unsalted)
Small inner Romaine leaves
½   cup salad oil or olive oil
⅓   cup wine vinegar

Place Romaine lettuce in a salad bowl. On the greens, arrange the orange, cucumber, onion, green pepper and jícama (if available) or sunflower seeds and almonds. Garnish rim of the salad with tips of inner Romaine leaves, if desired.

In a quart jar, blend oil with wine vinegar. Pour dressing over salad and mix lightly to serve.

Makes 8 servings.

Emerald Isle Mold

Truly an elegant looking, as well as tasting, salad.

1   envelope (1 tablespoon) unflavored gelatin
2   tablespoons granulated sugar
½   cup boiling water
¼   cup limeade
¼   cup cold water
1   cup sweet white wine or lemon-lime soda
2   cups green grapes, whole or sliced

In a medium-sized bowl mix the gelatin and sugar. Add the boiling water and stir until gelatin is dissolved. Stir in the limeade, water, and white wine or soda. Chill until mixture begins to thicken. Fold in the grapes. Pour into a 4-cup mold, or leave in the mixing bowl as it also makes a nice shaped mold. Chill until firm by quickly heating the bottom of the mold in a slightly larger bowl of hot water. Turn out onto plate.

Serves 4-6.

Orange Gel-ohs!

1   envelope (1 tablespoon) unflavored gelatin
½   cup boiling water
1   cup chopped oranges
1   tablespoon granulated sugar
2   tablespoons lemon juice
1   cup cold lemon-lime soda (not "diet")
        or 1 cup cold orange juice

In a small bowl, mix the gelatin and boiling water. Stir until the gelatin is completely dissolved. In a 4-cup salad mold or bowl, combine the gelatin and remaining ingredients. Stir until mixed. Cover with a plastic wrap or lid and refrigerate until well set.
Serves 4.

Jiffy Fruit Gelatin

1   envelope (1 tablespoon) unflavored gelatin
½   cup boiling water
1   tablespoon lemon juice
1½   cups apricot, peach, or pear nectar
1   16-ounce can fruit cocktail, undrained

In a medium-sized bowl combine the gelatin and boiling water. Stir until the gelatin is dissolved. Add the lemon juice, nectar and fruit cocktail. Stir until well mixed. Pour into a 4-cup mold, if desired. Chill until firm.
Serves 4-6.

Raspberry Ripple

1   envelope (1 tablespoon) unflavored gelatin
2   tablespoons granulated sugar
¾   cup boiling water
¼   cup cranberry juice cocktail
¾   cup cold water
2   cups frozen raspberries, with juice
¼   cup chopped walnuts or pecans (optional)
1½   ounces (½ of a 3-ounce package) Neufchâtal cream cheese, finely diced (optional)

In a medium-sized mixing bowl combine the gelatin and sugar. Add the boiling water and stir until the gelatin is dissolved. Add the cranberry juice, cold water, and frozen raspberries in their juice. Stir well. Pour into a 4-cup mold and chill until the mixture is partially set. Fold in the nuts and cream cheese. Chill until firm. Turn out mold onto a lettuce-lined plate.
Serves 4-6.

Rosey Salad Mold

1   envelope (1 tablespoon) unflavored gelatin
2   tablespoons granulated sugar
¾   cup boiling water
1¼   cups rosé wine *or* cherry juice *or* cranberry
         juice
1   small banana, thinly sliced
½   cup finely diced cantaloupe
1   cup thinly sliced strawberries or peaches

In a medium-sized bowl mix the unflavored gelatin and sugar. Add the boiling water and stir until the gelatin is completely dissolved. Stir in the wine or juice, and fruits. Pour into a 4-cup mold or 6 individual serving dishes. Chill until firm.

Serves 4-6.

Homemade Cranberry-Orange Relish

1   pound fresh cranberries (4 cups)
2   small oranges, quartered, skins on
1½   cups granulated sugar

Put the cranberries and oranges into a blender and mix until just blended or put through a food grinder. Stir in the sugar.

Store, covered, in the refrigerator or freezer. Makes 3 cups.

Cranberry-Orange Relish Mold

Making gelatin is as easy as opening a box mix when made like this.

1   envelope (1 tablespoon) unflavored gelatin
1   cup cranberry juice cocktail
1   8½-ounce can pineapple chunks
1¼   cups homemade Cranberry-Orange Relish
¼   cup walnuts, chopped

In a saucepan, soften gelatin in cranberry juice. Cook over medium heat and stir until gelatin is dissolved. Drain pineapple, reserving syrup. If necessary, add water to pineapple syrup to make ½ cup liquid; add to gelatin along with relish. Chill in saucepan until partially set. Fold in pineapple and nuts. Turn into 4 cup mold; chill until firm.

4 servings.

Citrus-Plus Salad

1   large grapefruit, peeled, sectioned
          and diced
2   large oranges, peeled, sectioned and diced
1   medium avocado, halved, peeled
          and diced
1   sour apple, unpeeled and diced
1   small banana, diced (optional)
1   small head escarole or romaine lettuce
          torn into bite-sized pieces

Toss all ingredients in a medium sized salad bowl. Pass Honey Dressing and serve at once.

Cucumber Salad Dressing

1   cup (8 ounces) plain yogurt
3   tablespoons lemon juice
¼   cup minced green onions (about 4)
2   tablespoons grated Parmesan cheese
2   teaspoons dried dill weed *or* 2 tablespoons
          finely snipped fresh dill *or* 1 teaspoon
          garlic powder
¼   teaspoon white pepper
⅓   cup very finely chopped cucumber,
          leave on peeling
3   tablespoons vegetable oil

In a quart jar, combine all the above ingredients. Stir until very well blended. Refrigerate, covered, 2 hours or longer to blend flavors. Stir before serving. Pour over lettuce salad or other greens.
Approximately 2 cups.

Creamy Herb Dressing

1   egg
1   small onion, quartered
1   clove garlic
2   teaspoons prepared unsalted mustard
½   teaspoon seasoned salt substitute
¼   teaspoon black pepper
1   teaspoon leaf tarragon
½   teaspoon sweet basil
¼   cup tarragon vinegar
1   cup vegetable oil
1   tablespoon fresh parsley, minced

Place all of the above ingredients, except for oil and parsley, in a blender and mix one minute. With blender running very slowly, add oil until all oil is added and the dressing is thick and creamy. Stir in parsley. Pour dressing into a quart jar. Cover. Refrigerate. Makes about 1¾ cups dressing. Serve on lettuce salads.

Quick Salad Dressing

½   cup wine vinegar
1   cup vegetable oil
½   teaspoon granulated sugar
1   teaspoon Salad Herbes

Mix salad dressing ingredients together in a pint jar with a lid and shake vigorously just before adding to salad ingredients.

Honey Dressing

In a pint jar, beat with a wire whisk:

3   tablespoons lime juice
3   tablespoons lemon juice
3   tablespoons honey
½   cup oil
1   teaspoon poppy seed
½   teaspoon dry mustard
½   teaspoon paprika
⅛   teaspoon ground black pepper

Makes about ¾ cup dressing. Store in the refrigerator.
4 servings.

Mixed Salad Suggestions

Let your imagination run rampant when making salad combinations.

Lettuce—all kinds!
Spinach
Jícama
Tomatoes—cherry or
   big boys
Sprouts—alfalfa,
   radish, bean, etc.
Sesame Seeds
Peppers—green
   and/or red

Onions—green, red,
   sweet yellow
Red Cabbage
Oranges
Avocado
Salt-free croutons*
Mushrooms
Carrots
Radishes
Cucumbers

Mixed green salads offer variety and nutrition to your meals. With fresh, cleaned lettuce as the basis for the salad, build a salad using any of the ingredients above—maybe you can think of some more, too! Put lettuce and other selected ingredients into salad bowl and toss with salad dressing just before serving. When adding salad dressing, be careful to add only enough to coat the salad ingredients as too much dressing creates a soggy, oily salad.

*To make salt-free croutons
   Cube unsalted bread. Melt margarine and add

garlic powder, dried parsley, onion powder, dill, and/or other seasonings desired. Bake in 350° F. oven for 25 minutes, or until croutons are browned. Remove from oven and allow to cool before use. Store unused croutons in air-tight container in refrigerator.

Snappy Salad Dressing

Try this flavorful dressing as a vegetable marinade, too!

2	7¼-ounce cans ready-to-serve low-sodium tomato soup
½	cup oil
⅓	cup wine vinegar
2	cloves garlic, minced
2	tablespoons lemon juice
2	tablespoons snipped chives
2	tablespoons snipped parsley
2	teaspoons granulated sugar
1	teaspoon dried tarragon, crushed
¼	teaspoon marjoram

In screw-top quart jar, combine all ingredients; cover and shake well. Chill. Shake well before using. Serve with tossed salads. Makes about 2½ cups dressing.

French Dressing

Better than commercial French dressings available in markets or restaurants, but similar in taste, color, and texture.

2	cups oil
1	cup cider vinegar
½	teaspoon seasoned salt substitute
4	teaspoons sugar
4	teaspoons brown sugar
4-6	teaspoons dry mustard (to taste)
½	teaspoon black pepper
2	teaspoons paprika
½-1	teaspoon dehydrated onion flakes
⅛	teaspoon ground cloves
1	6-ounce can unsalted tomato paste
2	teaspoons garlic powder
½	cup unsalted chili sauce
⅓	cup water (optional)

Place all ingredients, except water, in a 2-quart container and mix with a wire whip or blend in a blender. If a less thick dressing is desired add water.

This must stand to let flavors mingle—24 hours is ideal, but at least 6 hours.
Makes approximately 1½ quarts.

Mustard Salad Dressing

There is a distinct continental flavor about this dressing. This may also be used as a dip for fresh vegetables.

1   cup Blender Mayonnaise or unsalted
        mayonnaise
2   tablespoons unsalted prepared mustard
½   teaspoon Salad Herbes
½   teaspoon unsalted fresh horseradish
        (refrigerated section of grocery store)
⅓   cup white wine or white vinegar

Mix ingredients in a quart jar with a wire whisk. Refrigerate covered until ready to use. Best when a few tablespoons are served over individual salad portions, rather than tossed with the greens.
Makes approximately 1½ cups.

Variation:
⅔   cup vegetable oil
2   tablespoons unsalted prepared mustard
½   teaspoon Salad Herbes
½   teaspoon unsalted horseradish
⅓   cup cider vinegar

Mix ingredients as instructed above.

Homestead Dressing

This is a fairly close version of the packaged "Ranch-Style" dressings that use buttermilk. In some restaurants this is called "White French."

1   recipe Blender Mayonnaise
¼   cup skim milk
¼   cup dehydrated parsley
1   cup plain yogurt (8-ounce carton)
½   teaspoon garlic powder
½   teaspoon onion powder
⅛   teaspoon white pepper
½-¾ teaspoon fines herbes
¼   cup sour cream
1   green onion, chopped

After making the Blender Mayonnaise, keep it in the blender. Add all the ingredients except for the sour cream. Whirl 20-30 seconds to completely blend all ingredients. Pour into a quart jar. Stir in the sour cream. Store covered in the refrigerator. As with most salad dressings, the flavor is better after this is mixed a few hours, or overnight.
Makes approximately 1 quart.

Milligram Island Dressing

A fine version of Thousand Island dressing. Enjoy!

1	hard boiled egg, finely chopped
1	cup unsalted mayonnaise or Blender Mayonnaise
⅓	cup unsalted catsup
1	tablespoon lemon juice
3	tablespoons unsalted pickle or cucumber relish
1	teaspoon granulated sugar
1	tablespoon green onion, finely chopped
2-3	tablespoons skim milk or enough to thin to desired pouring consistency

Mix ingredients in a quart jar. Store covered in refrigerator. Serve over lettuce wedges or torn greens.

Makes approximately 2 cups.

Vinaigrette Salad Dressing

Or . . . what to do when you can't use the capers and anchovy paste?

1	cup red wine vinegar
2	teaspoons granulated sugar
2	cups vegetable oil
1	teaspoon fines herbes
2	teaspoons dried parsley flakes
½	teaspoon garlic powder
1	whole clove
2	green onions, finely chopped

In a quart jar, beat the first six ingredients with a wire whisk. Add the clove and green onions. Store in a covered quart jar in the refrigerator until ready to use. It is best to let these flavors blend a few hours before serving. Excellent on any green salad.

Makes approximately one quart.

Italian Dressing

This tastes almost like bottled or packaged Italian dressing.

½   cup white vinegar
1   cup vegetable oil
⅓   cup water
½   teaspoon dried garlic
¼   teaspoon red ground pepper
½   teaspoon dry mustard
1   teaspoon dehydrated onion
1   teaspoon dehydrated green pepper
¼   teaspoon crushed red pepper flakes
        (optional)
1   teaspoon Italian seasonings
1   teaspoon granulated sugar

Mix in a quart jar with a wire whisk. Store covered in the refrigerator. Let flavors mingle at least one hour before serving. Best served cold.
Makes approximately a pint.

Zippy Dressing

2   cups vegetable oil
1   cup cider vinegar
2   tablespoons unsalted catsup
6   dashes tabasco sauce
2   tablespoons unsalted chili powder
1   tablespoon Italian seasonings
¼   teaspoon garlic powder
¼   teaspoon ground cumin
¼   teaspoon ground oregano
½   teaspoon paprika

Put all ingredients in a quart jar. Mix well with a wire whisk. Store, covered, in the refrigerator.
Makes approximately 1½ quarts.

Lemon Sauce

Serve warm or cold over gingerbread or cake.

½   cup sugar
3   tablespoons cornstarch
2   cups water
¼   cup unsalted margarine
1   tablespoon grated lemon rind
3   tablespoons lemon juice

Measure sugar and cornstarch into a 1-quart saucepan. Mix well. Stir in water. Cook and stir over medium heat until thick and clear. Blend in margarine, lemon rind, and lemon juice.
Makes 2¼ cups.

Lemony Herb Sauce

¼ cup green onion, chopped
2 tablespoons unsalted butter or
   unsalted margarine
1 tablespoon unbleached flour
1 low-sodium chicken bouillon cube, crushed
¼ teaspoon crushed thyme
¼ teaspoon ground marjoram
¾ cup water
¼ teaspoon lemon peel, grated
1 tablespoon lemon juice

In a 1-quart saucepan, cook onion in butter until tender. Stir in flour, crushed bouillon cube, and herbs. Add water. Cook and stir until thickened and bubbly. Stir in lemon peel and juice. Serve over vegetables or use as a sauce over cooked fish.
Makes approximately one cup.

Marinade for Meats and Chicken

This gives a flavor quite reminiscent of bottled barbecue sauce.

1 12-ounce can unsalted tomato paste
3 cups water
1 fresh lemon, sliced thinly
2 teaspoons dehydrated onion, minced
¾ teaspoon garlic powder
¾ cup brown sugar
½ teaspoon seasoned salt substitute
Dash of tobasco sauce

Mix all of the above ingredients together in a large bowl or 6-quart kettle. Add washed meat or chicken and marinate in refrigerator, covered, for at least 6 hours or up to 2 days.
This is great for barbecue or baking. Spare ribs of pork, cut country style, are good baked in this marinade. If used, be sure to pre-bake the pork for ½ hour, drain off all the fat, and cut off all fat.

Makes enough to marinade approximately 6 pounds of meat.

Herbed Marinade

For you to use to prepare meat for barbecuing or broiling.

1	cup olive oil or salad oil
½	cup lemon juice
1	teaspoon seasoning powder (e.g., Vegit or Jensen's)
2	teaspoons crushed thyme
2	teaspoons ground marjoram
1	teaspoon black pepper
2	cloves garlic, minced
1	cup onion, chopped
½	cup fresh parsley, chopped

Combine ingredients in bowl or plastic bag large enough to hold meat during marinating process. Mix well. If time allows, let marinade set at room temperature for 24 hours before adding meat.

Add meat (lamb or chicken) as desired, and mix to coat meat thoroughly with marinade. Cover bowl or seal plastic bag and marinate in refrigerator for several hours. About every hour, remove marinating meat and stir to recoat meat with marinade.

Enough marinade for 3-4 pounds meat.

Tomato Catsup

5	pounds ripe or canned unsalted tomatoes
2	small or 1½ medium onions
1	sweet red pepper
½	teaspoon whole allspice
½	teaspoon whole cloves
2	sticks cinnamon
½	teaspoon dry mustard
½	teaspoon celery seed
¼	cup *plus* 2 tablespoons granulated sugar
1	teaspoon lemon juice
½	cup red wine vinegar
1	teaspoon paprika

If using fresh tomatoes, wash, remove stems, peel, cut into quarters. Peel onions. Remove stems, seeds, and white portion from pepper. Chop onion and pepper. Put tomatoes, onions and pepper in a large saucepan. Heat slowly, until tomato juice runs freely; then boil, stirring frequently, for 30 minutes. Rub through a fine sieve. Return sieved pulp to saucepan; boil rapidly for 30 minutes or until slightly thick. Tie allspice, cloves and cinnamon in cheesecloth; add to the thickened pulp along with mustard, celery seed, sugar, vinegar and lemon juice. Boil mixture until there is no free liquid, stirring frequently; add paprika and blend well.

Pour into quart jar and store in refrigerator for up to three months.

"Bottled" Chili Sauce

7	pounds ripe or canned unsalted tomatoes, chopped
½	pound sweet green peppers, chopped
½	pound sweet red peppers, chopped
¼	cup onions, chopped
½	cup granulated sugar
1½	tablespoons lemon juice
1½	cups red wine vinegar
½	teaspoon ground cloves
½	teaspoon ground allspice
½	teaspoon ground cinnamon

Wash vegetables, remove stems from tomatoes and peppers. Remove seeds and white portion from peppers. Peel onions. Chop vegetables; in a large saucepan put sugar and lemon juice; simmer until mixture begins to thicken. Add vinegar and spices; continue cooking until thick (about one hour), stirring occasionally. Pour sauce in quart jars and store in refrigerator up to three months.

Basic Tomato Sauce

4	pounds fresh ripe tomatoes
3	tablespoons olive oil
3-4	cloves garlic, minced
3	onions, chopped
2	tablespoons sweet basil
2	bay leaves
¼	teaspoon fennel seed, crushed
1	teaspoon freshly ground black pepper

Juice of half a lemon

Put the tomatoes into the blender and liquefy. In a large frying pan, sauté the garlic and onions in the olive oil. Add the tomatoes, basil, bay leaves, fennel seeds, black pepper and lemon juice. Let the sauce simmer until it thickens and the flavors have blended. This takes 30-45 minutes.

Makes about 6½ cups of sauce.

Soy Sauce

¾   cup low-sodium beef broth or stock (2 tea-
       spoons low-sodium beef base flavor or
       2 low-sodium beef bouillon cubes
       diluted in ¾ cup water)
4   teaspoons lemon juice
5   teaspoons Kikkoman Milder Soy Sauce
½   teaspoon lemon peel
1   tablespoon cocktail sherry

Mix all ingredients in pint jar. May be stored in tightly-covered jar in refrigerator for up to 2 weeks. May be frozen in ice cube trays, stored in plastic bags and used one cube per 1½ tablespoons.

Under 100 mg of sodium per tablespoon of this soy sauce. Use sparingly!

Cheese Sauce

2   tablespoons (¼ stick) unsalted margarine
       or unsalted butter
3   tablespoons unbleached flour
2   cups skim milk
¼   teaspoon seasoned salt substitute
¼   teaspoon paprika
¼   teaspoon white pepper
¼   pound unsalted cheddar cheese, grated

Melt the butter in a 2-quart saucepan; add flour and stir. Add milk to flour gradually with a wire whisk and stir until sauce thickens. Add the seasonings. Stir in cheese until it melts.

The cheese sauce may be served over a variety of cooked vegetables (such as broccoli, cauliflower, peas, etc.) or may be used as a topping for baked potatoes.

Makes approximately 3 cups sauce.

Tartar Sauce

The perfect companion to any fish meal!

1   recipe Blender Mayonnaise
2   green onions, whole, chopped
1   teaspoon lemon juice
4   teaspoons unsalted cucumber relish
¼   teaspoon seasoned salt substitute
1   tablespoon fresh parsley, chopped
2   tablespoons sour cream
¼   teaspoon onion powder
¼   teaspoon dill weed
½   teaspoon sugar

Mix together in a quart jar and refrigerate, covered, for several hours before serving. This allows flavors to blend.

Curry Powder and Curries

Curry powder is thought possibly to be the world's first spice blend. Native to India, curries vary from one region to another in ingredients and in the amount of added chili peppers. Curries need to be served over a base that will absorb the sauce such as rice. Curry dishes need to include an acid such as the tamarind juice which is used in India, or lemon, lime, or tomato juice which can be substituted. Yogurt is commonly used in India as an acid.

In India, the curry powder blend is ground as needed with a handy mortar or curry stone. As mentioned before, curry powders and curries vary greatly and the cook can devise the preferred blend.

Curried Dressing

4 teaspoons paprika
1 teaspoon dry mustard
2 teaspoons curry powder
1 teaspoon black pepper
¼ teaspoon red or cayenne pepper
½ teaspoon tarragon leaves
1 cup vegetable oil
¼ cup white vinegar

Mix all ingredients together with wire whisk.
Store in quart jar, covered, in the refrigerator.
Use on salad greens.
Makes approximately 1½ cups.

Mild Curry Powder

1 tablespoon black peppercorns
1 tablespoon cumin seeds
3 inches of stick cinnamon
1½ teaspoons coriander seeds
4 whole cloves
1 teaspoon cardamom seeds
2 teaspoons turmeric
¾ teaspoon dried chili pepper *seeds*
Pinch of fenugreek

Pulverize above ingredients in a blender, electric grinder or with a mortar. Store in an air-tight container.

Hot Curry Powder

1½   teaspoons cumin seeds
1   teaspoon coriander seeds
1   teaspoon turmeric
1   teaspoon black peppercorns
1   teaspoon dried chili peppers
¾   teaspoon ground ginger
½   teaspoon cayenne pepper

Pulverize above ingredients in a blender, electric grinder, or with a mortar. Store in an air-tight container.

Bouquet Garni for Soups

½   teaspoon ground marjoram
½   teaspoon ground thyme
½   teaspoon parsley flakes
¼   teaspoon ground savory
⅛   teaspoon ground sage
⅛   teaspoon crumbled bay leaf
¾   teaspoon finely chopped parsley

Place all ingredients in the center of a piece of cheesecloth. Tie securely with string. Add to soup at the end of cooking (never leave in soup over one hour). Will season 2 quarts of liquid.

Chinese Five-Spice Powder

Use sparingly with meat and poultry; never more than ½ teaspoon per pound of meat.

15   whole cloves
6   inches whole stick cinnamon
6   whole star anise
3   teaspoons cracked black peppercorns
3   teaspoons fennel seeds

Pulverize above ingredients in a blender or electric grinder or with a mortar. Continue processing until ingredients have become a powder. Store in an air-tight container. Keeps well for over a year.

Or try this combination. It's a little different and makes a smaller quantity.

1   teaspoon crushed anise seed
1   teaspoon ground cinnamon
¼   teaspoon crushed fennel seed
¼   teaspoon ground black pepper
⅛   teaspoon ground cloves

Mix above ingredients in the container with a spoon. Store air-tight.

Bouquet Garni for Bouillon

1	bay leaf
1	whole clove
1	tablespoon finely chopped celery or celery flakes
½	teaspoon ground marjoram
2	teaspoons parsley flakes
2	peppercorns
¼	teaspoon ground savory
2	teaspoons ground thyme

Place all ingredients in the center of a piece of cheesecloth. Tie securely with string and use for flavoring stews. Flavors 2 quarts of liquid.

Pumpkin Pie Spice Blend

Great for pumpkin pie, squash dishes, sweet potato pie, gingerbread and spice cookies. Using the proportions below, the preground spices can be used or you can grind your own in a blender, electric grinder or with a mortar.

4	teaspoons ground cinnamon
1	teaspoon ground ginger
½	teaspoon ground cloves

Mix all ingredients together and store in an airtight container.

Fines Herbes

A French term meaning "fine herbs"

Fines herbes is a blend of two or more mild herbs, usually including parsley. These herbs, finely minced, can include equal parts of parsley, chives, tarragon and chervil. Other herbs can be substituted, according to the desires of the cook. These herbs can be grown at home easily to obtain maximum freshness. Mix up more than you need, dry, and keep on hand in a tightly sealed jar for future use. All herbs used in the fines herbes blend are mild enough to use in quantity to flavor otherwise bland foods such as egg and cheese dishes, delicate sauces, soups, fish, or green salads and salad dressings. One to three teaspoons of fines herbes blend is sufficient to flavor each serving (approximately 1-2 cups in size).

1 teaspoon dried parsley
1 teaspoon dried chives
1 teaspoon dried tarragon
1 teaspoon dried chervil

For tarragon and chervil you may substitute sweet basil, summer savory, dill, sweet marjoram, mint or thyme.

Fines herbes combination suggestions:

—Beef or other red meats: thyme, chervil and basil; or chives, basil and parsley.
—Chicken, Meat, Eggs or Salads: chervil, parsley, and chives.
—Fish, Chicken, or Veal: parsley, rosemary, and tarragon.

Vegetables and Side Dishes

Fresh vegetables, raw or cooked, taste better than amost any other foods without the addition of salt. When cooking a fresh vegetable (many people term it "plain vegetables"), add a tablespoon of lemon juice to the water for every 10-16 ounces of vegetables. This helps the vegetable maintain its bright color and adds a flavor boost. The prettiest and most flavorful vegetable dishes will be produced when fresh vegetables are used.

Fresh frozen vegetables are the next best alternative to fresh vegetables. However, read labels carefully as some frozen vegetables have salt added. *Beware of* frozen:

lima beans
green peas
mixed vegetables
brussel sprouts
specialty vegetables frozen in sauces
potato products (i.e., french fries, tater tots, etc.)

Peas and lima beans are sorted for the freezing process by soaking in a salt brine. A few recipes in this book call for frozen peas. The amount of peas per serving would be small in these recipes. Of course, fresh would be preferred, if available. To eat peas as a side dish would give each serving about 200 mg of sodium. Use fresh or specially "no-salt added" canned peas for side dishes.

Celery is very high in sodium per stalk. Therefore, use celery sparingly as a seasoning, never as a side dish. Some sources also consider carrots to be rather high in sodium for the low-sodium diet. However, used sparingly in a total low-sodium diet, carrots should not be harmful.

Potatoes are often accused of being fattening. Not so! Potatoes are high in vitamin C and low in calories. The accompaniments are the troublemakers! However, here are some low-sodium suggestions to put on your potatoes, either at home or in a restaurant: (*Note:* these are not all low-calorie!)

sour cream	unsalted cheddar cheese, grated
grated onion	fresh mushrooms (can be sautéed with
black pepper, ground	onions in unsalted butter
paprika	green peppers, chopped
seasoned salt substitute	unsalted butter or unsalted margarine

Rice is also low in sodium, provided it is cooked in cold water (be careful of softened water). Rice has much more nutrition and flavor if long grain brown rice is used instead of white in any recipe calling for rice. Many noodle or pasta products have no salt added. Read labels! Again, it is the way rice or pasta is cooked that helps keep it low in sodium.

Of course, rice, potatoes, vegetables and noodles cooked "just plain" with no salt added *can* become pleasing to your palate and be a perfect accompaniment to many meals. When looking for something special or for a taste variety, try one of the following recipes. You'll be sure to enjoy the compliments!

Asparagus-Cashew au Gratin

2   14½-ounce cans unsalted asparagus spears,
       with liquid or 20-ounce package frozen
       asparagus plus ¼ cup water
1   tablespoon unsalted margarine or unsalted
       butter
½   cup whipping cream
2   eggs
2   tablespoons unbleached flour
¼   teaspoon seasoned salt substitute
¼   teaspoon black pepper
½   pound unsalted cheddar cheese, grated
¼   pound cashews, unsalted, coarsely chopped
Paprika

   Simmer asparagus in a 3-quart saucepan with
liquid and margarine or butter until liquid has
evaporated. Set aside. In a deep mixing bowl,
whip cream, eggs, flour, salt substitute and pepper with mixer until foamy. Set aside. In 2-quart
greased casserole, layer ⅓ of the cheese, then all
asparagus, next another ⅓ of the cheese, then the
cashews, and then the cream mixture. Let stand
about 30 minutes. Top with remaining ⅓ cheese.
Sprinkle with paprika and bake in 300° F. oven for
35 minutes or until set.

Serve immediately.
   Variations: Unsalted french green beans or
unsalted peas may be substituted for the
asparagus. Also, you may wish to use slivered
almonds instead of cashews. Fresh, sliced mushrooms may be added, if desired.
   4 to 6 servings.

Asparagus Chinese Style

1   pound fresh asparagus
2   tablespoons vegetable oil
2   tablespoons fresh gingerroot, minced
1   teaspoon brown sugar
1   tablespoon water
2   tablespoons lemon juice
1   teaspoon cornstarch
1   tablespoon water
1   8-ounce can sliced water chestnuts, drained

   Wash asparagus, removing tough part of stalk.
Cut diagonally in thin slices. Put oil in a large
heavy skillet. Add gingerroot, sugar, water and
lemon juice, stirring until tender and crisp. Add
cornstarch mixed in one tablespoon of water and
stir until clear. Add water chestnuts and stir until
just heated through.
   4 servings.

Polish Noodles and Cabbage

4   ounces fine egg noodles
4   tablespoons unsalted margarine or
       unsalted butter
1   large onion, cut in fine strips (1 cup)
1   tablespoon caraway seeds
1   pound green cabbage, thinly shredded (3
       to 4 cups tightly packed)
¼   teaspoon salt substitute
½   teaspoon black pepper

In a 5-quart kettle, cook the noodles according to package directions, omitting salt. Drain the noodles and rinse in cold water, drain again. Set aside.

In a large skillet, cook the onion and caraway seeds in 2 tablespoons of the margarine until the onions are golden brown. Add the noodles and keep warm.

In the same 5-quart kettle used to cook noodles, cook the cabbage in the remaining 2 tablespoons margarine, stirring to mix the margarine with the cabbage. Continue cooking tightly covered until cabbage is tender-crisp. Add the noodle-onion mixture and salt substitute and pepper. Mix thoroughly.
4 servings.

Baked Potato Casserole

This is sure to attract great company reviews! A good way to use leftover baked potatoes.

8   potatoes, cooked
2   7¼-ounce cans low-sodium cream of
       mushroom soup
1   cup sour cream
1   stick (½ cup) unsalted butter or unsalted
       margarine
½   cup onion, chopped
2   cups unsalted cheddar cheese, shredded
Low-sodium corn flakes, crumbled

Bake potatoes until tender; cool. Remove peels. Dice and set aside.

Heat together, but *do not boil,* soup, sour cream, butter or margarine, onion and cheese. Mix with potatoes and place in a 2½-quart casserole dish. Top with corn flakes. Bake at 350° F. for 20 minutes, or until sauce bubbles and mixture is steaming hot.

6 to 8 servings.

Dilled Zucchini

2	zucchini

Boiling water

2	tablespoons unsalted margarine
1	tablespoon lemon juice
¼	teaspoon dill weed

Cut unpared zucchini lengthwise in half. Cook covered in a 2-quart saucepan in one inch of boiling water until barely tender. Drain; brush with melted margarine, sprinkle with lemon juice, then dill weed, and serve.

4 servings.

Green Beans

1	pound frozen unsalted green beans
1	tablespoon onion, minced
½	teaspoon dill weed
½	teaspoon lemon juice

Slivered almonds

In a 3-quart saucepan, cook green beans (according to directions on package, omitting salt). Add onion, dill weed and lemon juice. Put in a one-quart casserole dish. Top with almonds. Bake for 20 minutes at 350° F. or until heated through.

Variations: Add one 6-ounce can low-sodium vegetable-tomato juice and one teaspoon minced fresh mint.

Add one 7¼-ounce can low-sodium mushroom soup and 2 chopped green onions. Omit dill weed and almonds. Top with crushed low-sodium corn flakes.

4 servings.

Sweet-Sour Red Cabbage

1	large head red cabbage
1	large onion, chopped
4	tablespoons vegetable oil
2	tart apples, pared and chopped
¼	teaspoon pepper
2	tablespoons bottled grenadine syrup
¼	cup cider vinegar

Trim cabbage and shred. In a large 5-quart kettle, sauté onion in oil until soft; stir in cabbage, apples, pepper and grenadine syrup. Heat slowly to boiling; cover. Simmer 25 minutes or until cabbage is crisply tender; remove from heat. Drizzle vinegar over cabbage; toss to mix. Spoon into heated serving bowl.

Serve with Sauerbraten (pg. 156).

8 servings.

Vienna Rice

This version for rice is a colorful addition to this meal.

1　small onion, minced
1　cup raw brown rice
1　tablespoon unsalted margarine
1　tablespoon unsalted, vegetable seasoning
　　　powder
¼　teaspoon black pepper
1　tablespoon paprika
3　cups water
3　unsalted beef bouillon cubes
1　cup unsalted peas, cooked without salt
2　tablespoons unsalted margarine

In a large skillet, sauté onion and rice in margarine for 5 minutes; add seasoning powder and pepper, bouillon cubes and water. Bring to a boil, stir once, cover and simmer for 40 minutes or until rice is tender. Add cooked peas and remaining margarine and toss lightly. Heat through.
Sprinkle paprika on top and serve.

Rice with Nuts

This rice is an excellent accompaniment to poultry dishes.

1　pound (about 3 cups) wild rice and
　　　long grain rice, mixed
2　7¼-ounce cans low-sodium cream of
　　　mushroom soup
12　small fresh mushrooms, sliced
½　cup unsalted margarine
2½　cups water
1　cup green onions, minced with tops
1　green pepper, chopped
1　cup blanched, slivered almonds
2　8-ounce cans water chestnuts, drained,
　　　sliced

In a large mixing bowl, combine all ingredients; put in a 9x13-inch pan and cover with aluminum foil. Cook in 325° F. oven, stirring every 20 minutes. After the butter melts, the heat may be reduced to 300° F. Cook for a total of 2-2½ hours.

German Potato Pancakes

Serve these pancakes with Sweet-Sour Red Cabbage (pg. 113) and Sauerbraten (pg. 156).

2	tablespoons unbleached flour
¼	teaspoon baking powder substitute
½	teaspoon salt substitute
½	teaspoon black pepper
6	medium potatoes
2	eggs, beaten
1	tablespoon onion, grated
1	tablespoon fresh parsley, chopped
¼	cup vegetable oil for frying

In a large bowl, combine flour, baking powder substitute, salt substitute and pepper. Set aside. Wash, pare, and grate potatoes. Drain well. Combine flour mixture, grated potatoes, eggs, onion and parsley.

Heat oil in a large skillet. Drop batter into skillet, using approximately ¼ cup per pancake. Cook until edges are brown; turn.

Keep warm to serve.

Vegetable Casserole

The cooking time can be reduced if the fresh vegetables are sautéed before baking.

1	1-pound can unsalted green beans, drained
1	1-pound can unsalted whole tomatoes
½	cup celery, chopped
¾	cup onion, sliced
1	cup carrot strips
1	green pepper, cut into strips
2	tablespoons tapioca
2	teaspoons granulated sugar
½	teaspoon seasoned salt substitute
2	tablespoons unsalted margarine

In a large bowl, mix ingredients together and put in a 3-quart greased casserole dish. Bake uncovered in a 325° F. oven for 1½ hours.

Variation: The baking time can be reduced by first sautéing the onion, celery and carrot strips in a small skillet. Mix ingredients, put in a 3-quart casserole dish, and bake for 40 minutes at 325° F.

Frittata

Frittata is a wonderful main course, snack, side dish—or cut into small pieces as an appetizer.

3   tablespoons olive oil
1   clove garlic, minced
1   large onion, thinly sliced
1   large green pepper, thinly sliced
2   zucchini, thinly sliced
1   carrot, cut julienne
8   eggs, beaten
¼   cup unsalted cheddar cheese
½   teaspoon crushed dried oregano
¼   teaspoon freshly ground black pepper
½   teaspoon sweet basil
¼   teaspoon crushed fennel seed

In a large frying pan, heat the oil and sauté the garlic, onion and green pepper for approximately one minute. Add the zucchini and carrot, and sauté for another minute. In a large bowl, beat the eggs with the cheese, oregano, black pepper, basil and fennel seed. Pour the eggs over the vegetables and cook at medium heat, lifting the sides to allow the liquid to run under the frittata. Cook about 5 minutes. Cover the frying pan with a plate and turn the frittata out onto the plate. Slide it back into the frying pan again to cook the other side—about 5 minutes.

Cut into wedges and serve.

Variation: In place of zucchini, try broccoli, eggplant, other kinds of squash, cabbage, turnips, etc. Prepare the vegetables ahead of time and you'll be ready to put the frittata together when you want. It is just as good cold as hot.

6 to 8 servings.

Lemon Glazed Carrots

6   large carrots, pared and thinly sliced
Boiling water
¼   cup unsalted margarine
¼   cup brown sugar
1   teaspoon grated lemon peel
1   tablespoon lemon juice
Chopped fresh parsley

In a 2-quart casserole dish, cook carrots in one inch of boiling water for about 10 minutes, or until carrots are tender. Drain and set carrots aside. Melt margarine in 10-inch skillet over moderate heat. Add sugar and stir until dissolved. Stir in lemon peel and lemon juice. Add carrots and cook, stirring frequently, until carrots are glazed and margarine is cooked down. Turn carrots into serving dish and sprinkle with parsley.

6 servings.

Main Dish Soups

Soups without salt can be tricky. Compensating for salt in soups can be done, so do give soups your attention . . . and patience. We have given you a selection of meat and vegetarian soups. When possible, be alert to soups without meat.

Soups should never be ordered in restaurants, as soups are traditionally "loaded" with salt. Canned soups, unless specifically labeled "low-sodium," are also too high in sodium for use. Canned soups labeled "low-sodium" or for "salt restricted diets" make a good base for your creativity. To eat these low-sodium soups, just as they are out of the can, may leave you wondering what you just ate! They need a little TLC and an imaginative use of seasonings.

A big kettle of steaming, home-made soup is a joy all day, in both the aroma and the eating. Soups feed many people economically, freeze well, and can be cooked ahead. With salad and bread or crackers (yes, low-sodium crackers are made), soups are a marvelous main dish, in any season.

As the saying goes, "When you put on a pot of soup, you put on a kettle of love."

Beef Bean Soup

2   beef shanks
1   cup unbleached flour
¼   cup (½ stick) unsalted margarine
Water
1   large onion, sliced
½   head cabbage, shredded
1   bay leaf
¼   cup parsley, chopped
1   teaspoon paprika
½   teaspoon seasoned salt substitute
1   12-ounce can unsalted tomato paste
1   1-pound can unsalted tomatoes
1   12-ounce can unsalted tomato juice
2   potatoes, peeled and chopped
1   1-pound can unsalted green beans,
      undrained
½   cup port wine or grape juice

Remove fat from beef shanks.

Dredge beef shanks in flour. In 6-quart kettle, melt margarine. Add beef shanks to kettle and brown. Add water to cover beef shanks. Add remaining ingredients and simmer 3-4 hours, or until the meat falls off the bones. Add wine or grape juice about ½ hour before serving.

4 servings.

Cabbage Soup

2   pounds beef bones
1   cup onion, chopped
3   carrots, pared and coarsely chopped
2   cloves garlic, chopped
1   bay leaf
2   pounds beef short ribs, trimmed of fat
1   teaspoon dried thyme
½   teaspoon paprika
8   cups water
8   cups (1 medium head) cabbage, coarsely
      chopped
2   1-pound cans unsalted whole tomatoes
1   teaspoon seasoned salt substitute
½-¾ teaspoon tabasco sauce
3   tablespoons lemon juice
3   tablespoons granulated sugar
Sour cream or yogurt
¼   cup fresh parsley, chopped

In a 9x13x2-inch roasting pan, mix beef bones, onion, carrots, garlic, bay leaf, short ribs, thyme and paprika. Bake at 450° F., uncovered, until meat browns (about 20 minutes). Drain grease. Transfer baked ingredients to a 6-quart kettle. Add water, cabbage, tomatoes, salt substitute and tobasco sauce. Bring to a boil and simmer for 1½ hours. Skim off fat. Add lemon juice and sugar; simmer uncovered for one hour. Remove meat, bones and short ribs from kettle. Remove meat from bones; cube and return meat to soup, remove all fat. Cook 5 minutes longer. Ladle into bowls.

Serve each portion with one tablespoon sour cream in center and sprinkle with the parsley.

Makes 10 to 12 servings.

Meatball Soup

2	tablespoons vegetable oil
1	medium-sized onion, minced
1	clove garlic, minced or pressed
2	teaspoons unsalted chili powder
24	ounces unsalted tomato juice
4	cups water
4	teaspoons unsalted chicken broth concentrate or 2 unsalted chicken bouillon cubes
1	large carrot, diced
1	large broccoli stalk, diced
Meatballs (recipe below)	
1	cup fresh or frozen unsalted peas

Heat oil in a 6-quart kettle over medium heat; add onion, garlic and chili powder. Sauté until onion is translucent and tender; do not brown.

Add tomato juice, water, chicken broth or bouillon cubes, carrot, and broccoli. Simmer, covered, while preparing meatballs. Add browned meatballs to broth; cover and simmer 20 minutes. Skim fat from broth. Add peas and cook 10 minutes more.

Meatballs

1	egg
2	tablespoons uncooked brown long-grain rice
½	pound lean ground beef
2	teaspoons parsley, finely chopped
⅛	teaspoon mint extract or ¼ teaspoon dried mint
½	teaspoon black pepper

Combine ingredients in medium-sized mixing bowl. Form into ½-inch diameter balls. Place meatballs on broiler pan rack and bake in 350° F. oven for 20 minutes, allowing drippings to fall into pan. Add meatballs to broth.

3 to 4 servings.

Variations: A mixture of ¼ pound lean ground beef and ¼ pound lean pork may be used instead of ½ pound beef.

A mixture of ¼ pound lean ground beef and ¼ cup dried, unsalted soy granules, reconstituted, may be used instead of ½ pound beef.

Corn Chowder

2   onions, chopped
2   tablespoons unsalted margarine
2   15-ounce cans unsalted sweet corn,
        do not drain
1   cup water
2   cups skim milk
1   unsalted chicken or vegetable bouillon
        cube
½   teaspoon paprika
1   tablespoon lemon juice
½   teaspoon white or black pepper
½   teaspoon seasoned salt substitute
1   stalk celery, finely chopped
2   raw potatoes, chopped
1   cup yellow unsalted cheese, grated
1   green pepper, sliced
3   green onions, chopped

In 6-quart kettle, sauté onion in margarine until onion is tender. In a blender, liquidize 1½ cans of the corn. Place all of the corn with liquid and water in the kettle. Simmer for 30 minutes. Stir in milk, bouillon, paprika, lemon juice and pepper. Add seasoned salt substitute, celery and potatoes. Simmer until potatoes are cooked. Garnish each served bowl of soup with cheese, green peppers and green onions.   4 servings.

Bouillabaisse

Bouillabaisse is a special dish and the ingredients will vary depending upon the seafood available in your locale.

We suggest that you prepare all the ingredients ahead of time before guests arrive. Make fish stock ahead of time. Put prepared ingredients in separate containers and refrigerate those foods requiring refrigeration.

Then, after guests arrive, and about 30-40 minutes before desired serving time, you can start "building the bouillabaisse." Guests can join you around the kettle and watch this appetizing and wonderful smelling process.

Fish stock or water
5   pounds mixed fish (snapper, scallops,
        halibut, etc.)
2   pounds lobster or crab legs (in shell)
4   dozen clams (razor, butter, etc.)
5   leeks *or* 2 bunches green onions
3   large onions
5   garlic cloves
6   ripe tomatoes
⅓   cup olive oil
Bouquet Garni—(1 teaspoon thyme, 3 bay leaves,
        1 tablespoon parsley, 2 stalks chopped
        celery and 1 teaspoon rosemary tied up in

cheesecloth)
¼ teaspoon saffron
¼ teaspoon salt substitute
½ teaspoon black pepper
¼ teaspoon cayenne pepper
1 pound uncooked, deveined, shelled shrimp

If making fish stock, use fish head and/or bones. Place fish in 6-quart kettle. Cover with water and simmer gently for about one hour.

Cut fish into bite-sized pieces, keeping heavy meated fish separated from the more delicate fish. If using lobster, split lobster down middle from head to tail, on the underside; remove intestines. Break off claws and crack them. Cut body and tail into pieces.

If using crab, wash. Remove intestines. Remove claws and crack them. Cut body into pieces.

Wash and clean clams.

Carefully wash leeks or onions. Cut into small pieces.

Peel and chop onions and garlic.

Cut tomatoes into wedges.

Prepare shrimp.

Make Bouquet Garni.

Heat olive oil in a 6 or 8-quart kettle and add leeks, onions, garlic and tomatoes. Cook for a few minutes. Add Bouquet Garni.

Arrange heavier meated fish on top of the vegetables and cook for about 8 minutes. Add more delicate fish, lobster or crab, and saffron. Add seasonings. Cover with fish stock or water.

Bring to a boil and immediately reduce heat to low. Gently simmer for 15 minutes. Add clams and shrimp and cook just until the clam shells open.

Spoon fish meat and some of each of the ingredients out into large bowls and add broth.

Good served with French bread and a tossed salad.

8 servings.

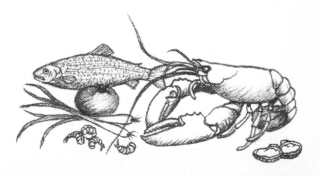

Split Pea Soup

Vegetarian Style

2   tablespoons unsalted margarine
2   large onions, peeled and chopped
1   teaspoon celery seed
16   ounces (1 pound) dried split green peas
8   cups water
1   tablespoon unsalted chicken broth concentrate *or* 2 unsalted chicken bouillon cubes *or* unsalted vegetable broth cubes
¼   teaspoon ground cloves
2   bay leaves
Pepper and seasoned salt substitute to taste
1   teaspoon dried marjoram
2   carrots, chopped finely
Sour cream

Melt margarine in soup kettle. Fry the onions with the celery seed until onions are tender and clear colored. Add remaining ingredients, except for sour cream, and cook for one hour, covered, or until peas are tender. Take out bay leaves. Beat with a wire whisk or potato masher to liquidize the peas.

When serving, top each bowl with a dollop of sour cream.

8 servings.

Potato Soup

4   large raw potatoes, peeled and diced
1   large stalk celery, diced
2   large onions, diced, *or* leeks
2   cups water
⅓   cup vegetable oil *or* unsalted margarine
¼   cup minced fresh parsley
¾   teaspoon seasoned salt substitute
Dash cayenne pepper
¼   teaspoon white pepper
2   cups skim milk
1   cup grated unsalted cheddar cheese
Paprika

Place all ingredients, except for cheese, milk and paprika, into a 5-quart kettle. Simmer, uncovered, over moderate heat for 40-45 minutes, or until potatoes are soft; stirring occasionally. Add the milk and stir. With wooden spoon, press some potatoes against the sides and bottom of pan to break into small pieces. Heat just until boiling. May be thinned with more milk, if a thinner soup is desired. Ladle into bowls. Sprinkle the top of each serving with some cheese and paprika to taste.

4 servings.

Garden Soup

1   cup dry pinto or pink beans
2   tablespoons vegetable oil
1   large onion, diced
3   cloves garlic, minced
4   large tomatoes, peeled, seeded and diced
½   pound fresh green beans, diced
1   small zucchini, diced
1   medium-sized raw potato, unpeeled and
       diced
1   cup leeks, diced
¼   pound fresh spinach, chopped
1½ quarts water
½   teaspoon seasoned salt substitute
2½ teaspoons leaf basil, crumbled
½   teaspoon leaf thyme, crumbled
½   teaspoon pepper
8   ounces spaghettini noodles
1   cup grated unsalted Monterey Jack cheese
       or unsalted Swiss cheese
6   slices unsalted French bread, toasted

Cook beans as directed in the introduction to
Ethnic Dishes section. Set aside.

Heat oil in 6-quart kettle; add onion and garlic
and sauté until tender. Stir in tomatoes, green
beans, zucchini, potato, leeks and spinach. Add
water, seasoned salt substitute, basil, thyme and
pepper. Heat to boiling; lower heat and cover.
Simmer 30 minutes.

Break spaghettini into 2-inch pieces; add to
soup. Add cooked beans and simmer until spaghettini is tender but firm, about 10 minutes.
Serve soup topped with unsalted grated cheese
and toasted French bread slices. Great with a
green salad.

Makes about 6 two-cup servings.

Turkey Soup

This soup is a good way to use the turkey leftovers. The leftovers determine the soup consistency and appearance.

1	meaty turkey carcass; trimmed of fat, skin and small bones

Water
6	unsalted chicken bouillon cubes
2	stalks of celery with leaves, chopped
½	cup chopped fresh parsley
2	large carrots, peeled and chopped finely
2	large onions, chopped finely
1	tablespoon sweet basil
2	teaspoons paprika
1	teaspoon seasoned salt substitute
1	teaspoon celery seed
1	cup white wine, white port, or water

Turkey dressing*
Turkey gravy*
Leftover vegetables*
½	cup raw brown rice
2	teaspoons black pepper

Place the turkey carcass into a 6-8 quart kettle. Cover with water. Bring to a boil. Lower the heat and simmer for 2 hours. Add the remaining ingredients and simmer for 2-4 hours or until the carcass starts falling apart. Remove the carcass and all bones.

10 servings.

*Add these ingredients in whatever proportions are left from the turkey dinner prepared.

Cauliflower Soup

This soup is good with whole wheat unsalted bread topped with melted unsalted cheddar cheese, or a bean salad with lettuce.

1   small onion, chopped
2   tablespoons unsalted margarine
1   medium head fresh cauliflower *or*
         1 medium head fresh broccoli; wash
         and chop into bite size pieces
4   tablespoons unbleached flour
¼   teaspoon black pepper
1   teaspoon dill weed
3   cups water
2   unsalted chicken bouillon cubes
1   large raw potato, diced
2   tablespoons lemon juice
1   tablespoon dried parsley flakes
¼   teaspoon paprika
2   cups skim milk

In a 6-quart kettle, sauté onion in margarine until tender. Stir in flour, pepper and dill weed. Cook until bubbly. Stir in cauliflower or broccoli and remaining ingredients except the milk. Heat to boiling. Reduce heat and simmer, covered, for 15 minutes or until vegetables are crisply tender. Uncover, add milk, heat thoroughly.

Serves 4

Vegetarian Lentil Soup

Freeze leftovers for another meal of this delicious, hearty soup.

1   pound lentils (2 cups), rinsed and sorted
2½   quarts water (approximately)
1   cup pearled barley
1   large onion, chopped (1 cup)
2   large stalks celery with leaves, chopped
1   large carrot, diced
1   large potato, finely diced
3   tablespoons dried parsley flakes
2   16-ounce cans unsalted tomatoes, cut up
2   12-ounce cans unsalted tomato juice
1½   teaspoons seasoned salt substitute
1   teaspoon ground black pepper

Place all ingredients in a 6-8 quart kettle; bring to boil. Reduce heat; cover and simmer 1½ hours or more until lentils and barley are tender; stirring occasionally. Add more water if soup appears too thick. This soup can be put on early in the day and cooked slowly over low heat until dinner time.

Makes 8 quarts.

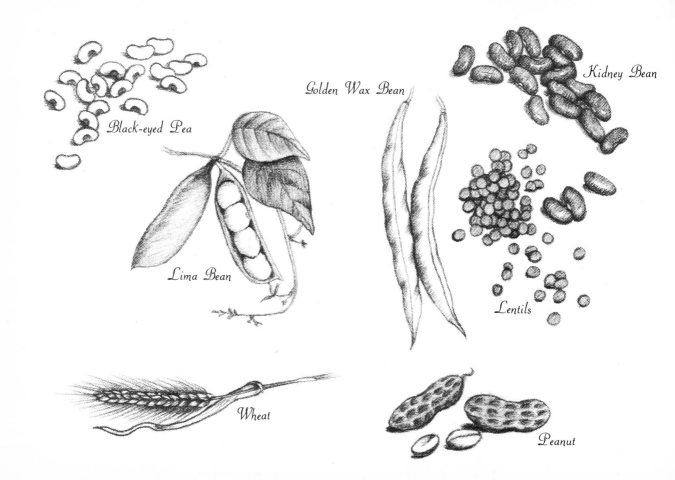

Black-eyed Pea

Golden Wax Bean

Kidney Bean

Lima Bean

Lentils

Wheat

Peanut

Meatless Main Dishes

Eating no meat at all should be an ideal dietary goal since there are many benefits. The benefits to the budget are also tremendous. In order to gain the maximum nutritional and protein value from a vegetarian meal, one should be aware of the following facts:

1) *Brown rice* supplies complete proteins when combined with:

wheat
soybeans
peanuts
black-eyed peas
kidney beans
lentils

chick peas
navy beans
pinto beans
fresh or dried lima beans
red chili beans

2) *Whole wheat* supplies complete proteins when combined with:

soybeans
peanuts
black-eyed peas
kidney beans
chick peas
sesame seeds and soybeans

navy beans
pinto beans
dried or fresh lima beans
red chili beans
lentils
rice and soybeans

3) *Legumes** supply complete proteins when combined with:

rice	sesame seeds
corn	barley
wheat	oats

Reduce your reliance on animal proteins and increase your intake of protein-rich vegetables. For instance, did you know that a cup of kidney beans has the same amount of protein as a two-ounce pork chop or piece of fish?

*Legumes include soybeans, peanuts, black-eyed peas, kidney beans, chick peas, navy beans, pinto beans, dried or fresh lima beans and lentils.

A few ideas on how to use food complements

1) Unsalted peanut butter on unsalted wheat bread.
2) Unsalted corn tortilla with Mexican-Style Beans (see recipe pg. 144).
3) Melted unsalted cheddar cheese on an unsalted corn tortilla.
4) Cooked cracked wheat cereal with some skim milk poured over top.
5) Rice and bean casserole.
6) Grilled unsalted cheese on unsalted wheat bread.
7) Fried egg sandwich on unsalted wheat bread garnished with sprouts and tomatoes.

Try your own combinations to make complete proteins; but, by all means, try some of the following vegetarian dishes and other vegetarian dishes you can adapt to your low-sodium diet.

Broccoli Quiche

This is a very attractive dish when served. It is so good, it could be served for breakfast, lunch, or dinner.

1	10-ounce package frozen chopped broccoli, thawed and drained well. (Or you may substitute a 15-ounce can of unsalted spinach, drained and chopped.)
1	tablespoon unsalted margarine
½	cup onion, chopped
¾	cup skim milk
2	eggs
½	teaspoon salt substitute
¼	teaspoon basil leaves, crumbled
⅛	teaspoon ground nutmeg
⅛	teaspoon ground black pepper
5	fresh mushrooms, sliced
1	cup unsalted cheddar cheese, grated
1	cup dry curd unsalted cottage cheese (or ricotta cheese)
½	cup unsalted Monterey Jack cheese, grated
¼	cup blanched almonds, slivered
1	tomato, cut into 8 wedges
1	tablespoon Parmesan cheese
1	10-inch whole wheat Pastry Shell (pg. 197) baked for 10 minutes in a 425° oven

Drain the broccoli or spinach *well*. Set aside.

In a small skillet, heat the margarine. Add the onion and cook until transparent. Add the milk and heat until scalded.

In a medium bowl, beat the eggs with the salt substitute, basil, nutmeg, and pepper. Beat until blended. Add the mushrooms and the cheeses. Mix in broccoli or spinach. Slowly add the hot milk mixture and blend well. Pour into the partially baked pastry shell.

Cook about 30 minutes at 375° F. or until pie is just set. Arrange tomato wedges and almonds on top of pie, sprinkle with Parmesan cheese and bake 4 minutes longer. Cool to lukewarm before cutting.

This is good served with a lettuce salad and crusty French Bread (pg. 70).

6 servings.

Baked Lentils with Cheese

A nice dish for making ahead.

1¾   cup lentils, rinsed
2½   quarts water
1   bay leaf
2   large onions, finely chopped
2   cloves garlic, minced
2   tablespoons vegetable oil
2   large carrots (1 cup), thinly sliced
½   cup celery, thinly sliced
½   cup green pepper, thinly sliced
1   16-ounce can unsalted tomatoes
½   teaspoon salt substitute
½   teaspoon pepper
¼   teaspoon leaf marjoram, crumbled
¼   teaspoon ground sage
¼   teaspoon leaf thyme, crumbled
1½   cups unsalted cheddar cheese, grated

Combine the lentils, water and bay leaf into a 6-quart saucepan and bring to a boil. Lower heat, cover and simmer 30 minutes or until lentils are tender. Drain, reserving the liquid for soups.

Sauté the onions and garlic in oil in a small skillet until soft. Add this to the lentils along with the carrots, celery, green pepper, tomatoes, salt substitute, pepper, marjoram, sage and thyme and stir to mix. Put the mixture in a greased 13x9x2-inch baking dish. Cover with aluminum foil and bake in a 375° F. oven for one hour. Uncover and sprinkle the cheese on top. Bake for 5 minutes more or until cheese melts. Remove from oven. Let stand 15 minutes before serving. Cut into squares to serve. This is attractive served with cooked corn, green beans or broccoli.

9-12 servings.

Cheese Soufflé

Soufflés take a little extra work, but the end result is an elegant, puffy creation.

2   tablespoons unsalted margarine
2   heaping tablespoons unbleached flour
1   cup skim milk
6   heaping tablespoons unsalted cheddar
          cheese, grated
4   large eggs, separated
½   teaspoon dry mustard
¼   teaspoon seasoned salt substitute
¼   teaspoon white pepper

In a 3-quart saucepan, melt the margarine and

add the flour with a wire whisk. Over medium high heat, stir until the mixture thickens. Remove from heat and gradually stir in the milk. Return to heat, stirring until the mixture thickens. Remove from heat again and add the grated cheese. Allow to cool slightly. Mix in the egg yolks, mustard, seasoning salt substitute and pepper. Whisk the egg whites until they are very stiff and then fold into cheese mixture. Turn into a greased 2-pint soufflé dish or deep greased quart casserole dish and bake in a 400° F. oven for 40 minutes until risen up to or above dish top and is golden brown.

Remove from oven and serve immediately. If not served quickly the soufflé has a tendency to fall. This will not affect the quality, just the looks.

Good served with Cheese Sauce (page 104) spooned over each serving.

4 servings.

Corn "Pie"

Quick preparation and low cost, too! If this recipe is cut in half it can be cooked in a pie plate, hence, the name "corn pie."

2   tablespoons unsalted margarine
1   4-ounce can unsalted diced green chilies, drained*
1   large onion, chopped
2   8½-ounce cans low-sodium cream-style corn
1   16-ounce can unsalted corn, undrained
1   tablespoon granulated sugar or 1 teaspoon honey
1   cup cornmeal
2½ cups unsalted cheddar cheese, shredded
½   cup skim milk
¼   teaspoon seasoned salt substitute
5   dashes tabasco sauce
2   eggs, beaten
Low-sodium crackers

Grease a 6-quart casserole dish. In a small skillet melt the margarine and sauté the chilies and onion until onion is transparent. In a bowl, combine remaining ingredients except the crackers. Stir well. Add the onions and chilies. Pour into the casserole. Crumble the crackers on top of the mixture. Bake at 375° F. for 50-60 minutes or until center is set.

Excellent served with a lettuce salad garnished with chopped raw vegetables and a bowl of fresh fruit.

6 servings.

*May substitute one fresh green pepper, finely diced if the chili flavor is not desired.

Cheesed Vegetables

Quick, easy and economical!

4   tablespoons (½ stick) unsalted butter or
       unsalted margarine
¼   cup unbleached flour
2   cups skim milk
¼   teaspoon seasoned salt substitute
¼   teaspoon seasoned black pepper
3   cups grated unsalted cheddar or unsalted
       jack cheese
1   10-ounce frozen package french cut green
       beans *or* 1½ cups fresh green peas
1   large head cauliflower, cut into bite size
       pieces
4   fresh carrots, peeled and cut into ½-inch
       chunks
2   cups raw brown rice, cooked according to
       package directions, omitting salt

Melt the butter in a 2-quart saucepan; add the flour and stir. With a wire whisk, stir the flour mixture while adding the milk gradually. Stir until the mixture is smooth and thickened. Add the seasonings and cheese. Stir until all are blended and cheese is melted. Set aside.

In a 6-quart kettle, cook the vegetables* in a scant amount of water. Cook only until *just barely* tender. (A steamer or microwave works very well here.) If there is any liquid left in the vegetables, pour into the cheese mixture and stir well over low heat until mixture thickens again.

Pour cheese mixture over vegetables. Stir well. Spoon over the cooked rice onto the individual serving plates. Excellent served with muffins and a tossed green salad.

4 servings.

*Any combination of colored vegetables may be used here such as:

broccoli	green beans
corn	summer squash
turnips	zucchini

Green Rice

Very colorful!

1   cup brown rice
1   cup unsalted Monterey Jack cheese, grated
⅓   cup dehydrated, chopped parsley
1   15-ounce can low-sodium spinach, drained,
       chopped
2   eggs, beaten well
1   cup skim milk
¼   cup unsalted margarine

1   tablespoon unsalted broth or seasoning
            powder
¼   cup dehydrated, minced onion
1   tablespoon Parmesan cheese

Cook rice in 3-quart saucepan, according to package directions, omitting salt.

In a large mixing bowl, combine all of the above ingredients, except for the Parmesan cheese, and mix well. Place in an ungreased 2-quart casserole dish. Sprinkle with the Parmesan cheese and bake at 325° F. for 45 minutes or until jack cheese is melted and bubbly.

Serve with a green salad that is sprinkled with sesame or sunflower seeds.

4 servings.

Vegetable Roll-ups

A relatively quick, easy dish to prepare that has a mild mysterious flavor.

2   tablespoons vegetable oil
1   large onion, thinly sliced
2   cloves garlic, minced
½   pound fresh mushrooms, sliced
1½   large green peppers, cut into chunks
3-4   carrots, thinly sliced
2   medium zucchini, cut in ½-inch slices
3   large tomatoes, peeled, cut in ½-inch
            chunks
1   teaspoon unsalted chili powder
½   teaspoon ground cumin
1   teaspoon oregano leaves *or* ½ teaspoon
            ground oregano
1½   cups unsalted jack cheese, shredded
12   unsalted flour tortillas
4   tablespoons sour cream
2   cups shredded lettuce
1   cup unsalted cheddar cheese, shredded

In a 12-inch skillet heat the oil and sauté the onion and garlic until the onion is limp. Add the mushrooms, green peppers, carrots, zucchini, tomatoes, chili powder, cumin and oregano. Bring to a boil, stirring gently, until vegetables are just *barely* tender. (If there is too much liquid, thicken slightly with one tablespoon cornstarch.) Stir in shredded jack cheese until melted. Warm the flour tortillas. Spoon several tablespoons filling down the center of each tortilla. Roll into a thin cylinder. Place on a dinner plate. Use two roll-ups per serving. Top each with a dollop of sour cream and a handful of shredded lettuce. Top each portion with grated cheddar cheese.

6 servings.

Vegetables and Pasta

1   8-ounce package spinach egg noodles or thin spaghetti noodles
1   small bunch broccoli, cut in flowerettes with 1-inch stems or 2 fresh medium-sized zucchini or fresh green beans (about 2 cups of cut 1-inch sized pieces)*
10   cauliflowerettes
½   pound asparagus, washed, stems removed, tender portion chopped into pieces or 4 carrots, peeled and diced
Water
¼   pound fresh mushrooms, chopped or 2 large fresh tomatoes, diced
2   tablespoons minced fresh parsley or 1 tablespoon dried parsley
2   teaspoons dried basil or 8 fresh basil leaves, minced
½   teaspoon nutmeg
5   tablespoons unsalted margarine
½   cup skim milk
⅓   cup grated Romano cheese (preferably fresh, not bottled)
½   teaspoon seasoned black pepper or regular black pepper
1   green onion, chopped
¼   cup toasted, slivered almonds (optional)

In a large 5- or 6-quart kettle, cook spinach noodles according to package directions, omitting salt. Drain. Set aside.

In a large saucepan or skillet, cook broccoli, cauliflower and asparagus in boiling unsalted water for 3-5 minutes. Drain, then stop vegetables from cooking by running under cold water until vegetables are cool. Drain.

In a large skillet, cook mushrooms, parsley, basil and nutmeg in margarine. Cook over low heat about 5 minutes. Add vegetables; cook 3 minutes longer, stirring. Return pasta to kettle. Add vegetable mixture, milk, Romano cheese, pepper. Toss to coat noodles. Serve immediately. Sprinkle with green onions and nuts, if desired.

Serves 6.

*Any in-season fresh vegetable may be used here.

Lentil Strawstacks

4   cups dried lentils
10   cups water
1   large onion, sliced
1   bay leaf
3   garlic cloves, minced
1   1-pound can unsalted tomatoes

1   12-ounce can unsalted tomato juice
3   tablespoons Chili Con Carne seasoning
2   teaspoons ground cumin
1   6-ounce can tomato paste, unsalted
Unsalted corn chips
Shredded lettuce
Green onions, chopped
Green peppers, sliced into rings
Unsalted cheddar or Monterey Jack cheese, shredded

Wash and sort lentils in a colander. Place in a 6-quart kettle. Add water, lentils, onion, bay leaf and garlic. Bring to a boil. Reduce heat and simmer, uncovered, for 30 minutes. Add tomatoes, tomato juice, seasonings and tomato paste; simmer for 1-1½ hours, or longer. This will have a slightly runny texture and lentils should be soft.

To serve, layer on each plate in the following order: corn chips, lettuce, green onions, pepper rings, a ladelful of lentil sauce, and cheese.

The corn chips make this meal one of complete protein—no meat needed!

Good with hot rolled corn tortillas and fresh carrot strips. You may also add sliced avocado, fresh tomatoes and a dollop of sour cream as a variety or addition to the above ingredients.

The lentil sauce can be made ahead and frozen for later use.

Approximately 10 servings.

Sweet Curry

A unique dish that is quite quick to prepare.

¼   cup vegetable oil
2   large sweet onions, finely chopped
1   29-ounce can unsalted tomato pureé
¼   cup brown sugar, packed
2½   teaspoons curry powder, or to taste
2   tablespoons apple juice
3   medium-sized tart apples, cored and finely diced
1½   cups fresh peas
1½   cups finely chopped carrots or cauliflower
½   cup raisins
1½   cups raw brown rice, cooked according to package directions, omitting salt
1   cup roasted unsalted peanuts, chopped

Heat oil in a deep, heavy skillet and sauté onions until tender. Add purée and brown sugar and bring to a boil. Mix curry into the juice; stir into the onion mixture. Cook 2 minutes. Add apples, peas, carrots and raisins. Heat through for about 10 minutes. Serve over brown rice. Sprinkle with chopped peanuts.

When served with a tossed salad and muffins, this dish is something "extra"!

Serves 4.

Egg Fu Yong

This recipe is an adaption of one by the same name found in a delightful vegetarian cookbook called Not Just A Load of Old Lentils, *by Rose Elliot, published by the White Eagle Publishing Trust, England.*

1   pound fresh bean sprouts (1 quart mung
          beans, if sprouting yourself)
6   eggs
2   large onions, finely chopped
¼   teaspoon pepper
¼   teaspoon salt substitute
¼   cup fresh parsley, chopped
Vegetable oil

Wash bean sprouts and drain well. Beat eggs in a medium-sized bowl and add remaining ingredients. Mix well. Pour oil to cover the bottom of a 12-inch skillet; heat oil. Drop a few tablespoons of the egg mixture at a time into the skillet to make each pancake. Cook until edges and bottom of pancake are lightly browned; turn. Remove from skillet and keep warm while cooking remaining pancakes. Add oil as needed.

Serve with boiled or fried rice (pp. 139, 148).
Makes 18 3-inch pancakes.

Quick Macaroni

This recipe is an adaption of one found in Not Just a Load of Old Lentils, *by Rose Elliot, published by the White Eagle Publishing Trust.*

2   onions, chopped
1   tablespoon unsalted margarine
3   cups macaroni (whole wheat or veg-roni)*
2   16-ounce cans (4 cups) low-sodium
          tomatoes
½   green pepper, finely chopped
1   cup water
2   cups unsalted cheddar cheese, shredded
Salt-free bread crumbs or crackers

In a small skillet, fry the onions in margarine until tender. In a deep, greased 3-quart casserole dish layer onions, uncooked macaroni, tomatoes with liquid, green pepper, water and most of the cheese. Top with bread crumbs and the remaining cheese. Bake uncovered at 325° F. for 1-1½ hours.

Serve with a green salad.
6 servings.

*Four cups of macaroni, uncooked, is equal to approximately one pound.

Herbed Linguine

A family favorite!

12	ounces linguine noodles
1	medium-sized bunch broccoli, cut into 1-inch pieces (about 6 cups)
¾	cup walnuts, coarsely chopped
¼	cup (½ stick) unsalted margarine
1	tablespoon oil
1½	pints cherry tomatoes, stems removed*
1	large clove garlic, minced
¼	teaspoon red pepper flakes
1¼	teaspoon sweet basil
1	cup chicken broth (made with 1 unsalted bouillon cube in 1 cup of boiling water)
¼	cup fresh parsley, chopped
¼	cup freshly grated Romano cheese

In a 6-quart kettle, start cooking the pasta in boiling unsalted water, following directions on label. Add the broccoli to the linguine during the last 5 minutes of cooking time. Drain. Rinse with cold water. Toast the walnuts 5 minutes in a 350° oven.

Melt 2 tablespoons margarine and the oil over moderate heat in a medium-sized skillet. Add the tomatoes and cook, stirring often. Cook 2 minutes. Add the garlic, pepper flakes, and basil and cook 2-5 minutes longer, until tomatoes are tender but still hold their shape. Remove from heat; cover, and keep warm.

Melt the remaining 2 tablespoons of margarine in the pasta kettle. Return broccoli and linguine to kettle. Toss to coat with margarine. Add the tomatoes in their sauce, the broth, and parsley. Toss to blend.

Divide pasta among 4-6 plates. Sprinkle the top of each serving with some of the walnuts and some of the grated cheese. Serve immediately.

With French bread and a green tossed salad with sprouts, this is a very filling meal!

4-6 servings.

*If cherry tomatoes are unavailable, use 6-8 medium tomatoes cut into wedges.

Nut Stuffed Cabbage Rolls

This requires a little time to prepare; however, the results are very satisfying!

12-14 large firm cabbage leaves
1½   cups unsalted whole wheat bread crumbs
¼   teaspoon paprika
¼   teaspoon garlic powder
¼   teaspoon seasoned salt substitute
½   teaspoon sage leaves, crumbled
2   tablespoons instant chopped onions
½   cup boiling water
1½   cups chopped, dry-roasted, unsalted
     peanuts, cashews, or sunflower seeds
1   teaspoon celery seed
½   teaspoon dill seed
2   eggs
1   cup unsalted Monterey Jack cheese, grated
2   cans (7¼-ounces) unsalted tomato soup
¼   teaspoon black pepper
½   teaspoon ground oregano
1   small onion, sliced

Cut off the bottom of the cabbage head and place the head in a 3-quart kettle of unsalted boiling water to cover. Remove when limp. This should take about 5 minutes.

Meanwhile, place the bread crumbs with paprika, garlic, salt substitute, sage seasoning and instant onion in a bowl. Add the ½ cup boiling water and let stand 5 minutes to soften bread crumbs. Add the nuts, celery and dill seeds, eggs, and ½ cup cheese to the crumbs. Divide this mixture evenly onto center of cabbage leaves. Fold over the sides of the leaves and roll into a thin cylinder. Place each, folded side down, into a greased 9x9-inch baking dish. Combine soup, pepper, oregano and onion in a small bowl. Pour over cabbage rolls. Sprinkle remaining ½ cup cheese on top. Bake covered at 325° F. for 1 hour.
Serves 6.

Toasty Soybean Casserole

A great make-ahead dish. Stores well cooked or uncooked.

¾   cup dry soybeans, cooked according to
     package directions, omitting salt
1   cup raw brown rice, cooked according to
     package directions, omitting salt

2   cups corn (fresh, frozen, or unsalted
       canned)
2   cups (16-ounce can) low-sodium canned
       tomatoes
1   large onion, chopped
½   cup celery, chopped
½   teaspoon minced dry garlic
1   teaspoon ground thyme
1   teaspoon summer savory
⅛   teaspoon cayenne pepper *or* chili powder
1   6-ounce can unsalted tomato paste
1   tablespoon Brewer's yeast (optional)
2   unsalted chicken bouillon cubes *or* 2
       teaspoons unsalted vegetable powder
½   cup water
1   cup unsalted cheddar cheese, grated
⅓   cup untoasted wheat germ
¼   cup (½ stick) unsalted margarine
1   cup cashews or almonds, chopped

Cook soybeans in deep 3-quart kettle while rice is cooking. Drain; reserve liquid for soups or bread.

In a large mixing bowl, combine the cooked soybeans, corn, tomatoes, onion, celery, garlic and herbs. In another bowl, combine the tomato paste, Brewer's yeast, bouillon or seasoning and water.

Place half of the cooked rice on the bottom of a greased 9x13-inch pan. Cover with the soybean mixture. Spread the tomato paste mixture over the soybean and vegetable mixture and cover all with the remaining rice. Sprinkle with grated cheese and wheat germ. Dot with unsalted margarine. Sprinkle nuts on top. Bake, uncovered for 30 minutes at 350° F. or until edges of casserole bubble and mixture is hot.

Cut into squares and serve. This freezes well. Serves 6 to 8.

Fast Fried Rice

¼   cup oil for frying
1   egg, beaten
4   large green onions, chopped
2   carrots, peeled and chopped
¼   teaspoon seasoned salt substitute
1   cup raw brown rice, cooked according to
       package directions, omitting salt

Cover bottom of deep 12-inch skillet with oil. In skillet, mix together egg, onions, carrots, and salt substitute. Fry over medium high heat, stirring constantly for 2 minutes. Add rice and heat thoroughly. Remove from heat and serve.

Wheat Salad

A meal for anytime of year; lunch or dinner and a great dish to take to a "potluck."

Salad Dressing

1	recipe Blender Mayonnaise (pg. 90)
4	tablespoons oil
3	tablespoons lemon juice
1	teaspoon basil
1	teaspoon oregano
½	teaspoon black pepper
½	teaspoon dehydrated minced garlic
1	teaspoon dry mustard

Salad

2	cups water
1	cup bulgar *or* cracked wheat sifted of all loose flour
1	unsalted chicken bouillon cube
1	cup carrots, shredded
1	green pepper, seeded and diced
½	cup fresh parsley, chopped
½	cup green onions, chopped with tops
3	hard-cooked eggs, sliced

About 5 cups mixed lettuce greens, torn into bite-size pieces

1	cup unsalted cheddar cheese, shredded

Make Blender Mayonnaise. Put Mayonnaise and remaining salad dressing ingredients in mixing bowl. Mix. Cover and put in refrigerator.

In a 2-quart saucepan, cook the wheat in water with bouillon cube for 15 minutes. Put the hot wheat in a large bowl. Put 1 cup of the salad dressing on the hot wheat. Cover and place in refrigerator at least two hours. About 1-2 hours before serving, add the carrots, pepper, parsley and green onions. Mix thoroughly. Return to refrigerator. When serving, place refrigerated mixture on lettuce. Garnish with sliced eggs and cheese.

May be topped with more salad dressing, if desired.

If you desire to make this non-vegetarian, add chopped chicken, beef, or tuna chunks.

6 servings.

Ethnic Dishes

Ethnic dishes provide unusual flavor experiences. Many "typical American foods" have their origins in other countries. In this section, you will find some old favorites and some new taste treats. Try something new and provide menu variety—something a low-sodium diet may appear initially to lack. Eating ethnic foods, such as Italian and Mexican, while still maintaining a low-sodium diet, will provide you with pleasure as well as maintained health.

Some Notes About Preparing Beans

A complement to and frequent ingredients in ethnic dishes are beans. A very ordinary item in diets, beans, properly prepared, provide essential nutrition.

No longer can you open a can of commercially-prepared beans, for salt has been added. All recipes calling for beans will require the cook to wash, sort, soak and cook dry beans. To do this, wash the beans and remove any dirt clumps, rocks, grasses, etc. Then follow any of these three cooking methods:

1. The night before, put beans in a large kettle and cover with water. (Use 2½-3 cups of water for each cup of beans.) Cover the kettle and let soak overnight. In the morning, drain soaking water from the beans and cover beans again with fresh water. Cover. Bring to a boil. (Boil beans very gently; rapid boiling and constant stirring cause the skins to break which diminishes the flavor as well as the nutritional value.) Reduce heat and simmer until beans are tender. Cooking time will vary with the type of bean. The following are approximate cooking times (for cooking at sea level-2,500 foot elevations):

Black beans—about 2½ hours
Black-eyed beans (black-eyed peas, cowbeans)—½-¾ hour
Cranberry beans—about 2 hours

Great Northern or small white beans—1-2½ hours
Kidney beans—about 2 hours
Lima beans—1 hour for large and 45 minutes for small
Navy or pea beans—1½-2½ hours
Pinto beans—2-3 hours
Garbanzo beans—about 1 hour (check at 45 minutes)
Soy beans—about 1-2 hours
Small red beans—about 2 hours

2. Early in the day of cooking, put beans in a large kettle and cover with water. Keeping kettle covered, bring water to a full boil. Turn off heat and allow beans to stand, covered, for one hour. Add more water, if necessary, to cover beans. Bring to a full boil again; reduce heat and simmer, covered, adding water as needed, until beans are tender (cooking times vary with the type of bean). A crock pot can also be used here after the beans have been brought to a full boil. Use the cooking times suggested above.

3. Use a pressure cooker to cook the beans. Follow manufacturer's directions and recommended cooking time.

Hints

Beans are frequently accused of producing inordinate amounts of stomach gas. Beans are a "base" and if combined during the meal with an "acid" this gas does not present such a social problem! So combine the eating of beans with either tomatoes, oranges, limeade (to drink), or vinegar.

Beans, like peas and lentils, are legumes. Beans are so rich in protein that they often can be used as a meat substitute. The United States consumes more meat per capita than any other country in the world, thus typical American dishes contain meat. But dishes typical of other countries feature legumes instead of meat.

The most important bean in the world is the soybean. It is native to Eastern Asia where it has been grown for thousands of years. It is seldom eaten as a vegetable in the Orient. It is used more often as a sauce (soy sauce), soy cakes (tofu), as curdled beans, or ground for flour to augment wheat.

In the United States, soybeans are used more for industrial purposes than dietary. Yet, soybeans used in cooking "take on" the flavor of seasonings well, especially when chopped, minced or ground. Consider making soybeans a greater part of your diet, thus making your eating more economical and healthful!

So . . . no more opening cans of prepared specialty items! You may feel like "you're on your own," but with a bit of planning and cooking ahead of time, you will soon create your own specialty items. To save time and energy, double your recipes and freeze a complete dish, or double the amount of dried beans called for in the recipe and freeze the remainder.

Be adventuresome and take a taste trip into the world of ethnic foods. You'll be *glad* you are on a low-sodium journey!

Chili Rellenos

1   27-ounce can unsalted whole green chilies; washed and seeds removed*
½   pound unsalted Monterey Jack cheese, sliced to ¼ " thickness, 3-inch strips
1   12-ounce can unsalted tomato paste
1½ cups skim milk
4   eggs, beaten
¼   cup plus 1 tablespoon unbleached flour

Place chilies in greased 9x13x2-inch pan; insert cheese strips into each chili. Spread tomato paste over the chilies. In a small bowl mix remaining ingredients and pour over chilies. Bake in 350° F. oven for 45 minutes. Remove from oven. Eggs should be set and the edges bubbling.

Cut into 12 pieces and serve.

To divide recipe in half to serve 4 to 6:

3   4-ounce cans of unsalted green chilies, diced or whole*
¼   pound unsalted Monterey Jack cheese, sliced to ¼ " thickness, 3-inch strips
1   6-ounce can unsalted tomato paste
¾   cup skim milk
2   eggs, beaten
2   heaping tablespoons unbleached flour

Layer ingredients as for recipe above. Use a 9x9-inch square pan. Bake for approximately 35 minutes or until egg mixture is set.

*If whole chilies are hard to find, use diced chilies. Spoon onto the bottom of the pan until the bottom is entirely covered. Cut cheese into cubes and cover the chilies with cheese cubes. Follow remaining directions.

Mexican-Style Beans

2   pounds pinto beans, soaked overnight
1   bay leaf
1   7-ounce can unsalted green chilies, diced
3   garlic cloves, minced
2   tablespoons unsalted Chili Con Carne
        seasoning powder or chili powder
2   tablespoons dehydrated minced onion
1   teaspoon seasoned salt substitute
2   cups unsalted cheddar cheese, grated
        (optional)
2   dozen 10-inch unsalted flour tortillas

The night before, wash and soak beans. (See introduction to this section for further preparation instructions.) Cook beans with one bay leaf.

About 3 hours before serving, add chilies, garlic, chili powder, onion, and salt substitute to the cooked beans. Cook uncovered about 2-3 hours or until the liquid and beans are of a moist but not runny consistency. Mash with a potato masher or wooden spoon. If adding cheese, blend until all is melted. Beans are ready to serve or freeze.

For Burritos: Place several spoonfuls of bean mixture down the center of a warmed flour tortilla. Roll up and place on an ovenproof plate. Place in a 250° F. oven until ready to serve.

These burritos make a complete meal when topped with grated unsalted cheese, shredded lettuce, and diced tomatoes.

Makes about 24 burritos.

Green Chili Beef Burritos

2   pounds beef or pork roast
1¼   cups unsalted broth, saved from cooked
         meat
¼   cup whole wheat flour
1   medium onion, finely chopped
1   7-ounce can unsalted green chilies, diced
1   tomato, chopped
½   teaspoon black pepper
¼   teaspoon garlic powder
12   unsalted flour tortillas (about 10-12 inches
         in diameter)

Early in the day or night before, place meat in a 5-quart kettle and cover with water. Simmer, covered, until meat is tender (about 2 hours). Put kettle in refrigerator until fat is chilled.

About 2 hours before serving, remove kettle from refrigerator. Remove meat to chopping block and dice. Set aside.

Skim fat from broth in kettle; discard fat.

Measure broth; add water, if necessary, to make 1¼ cups liquid. Return broth to kettle and simmer over low heat. Add flour, stirring constantly. Broth should thicken slightly.

Put diced meat in kettle and add remaining ingredients, except for flour tortillas, and mix well. Simmer for at least 15 minutes to cook in flavors, stirring frequently.

To Prepare Burritos: Spoon about 4 tablespoons filling down center of heated tortilla. Fold sides of tortilla toward middle and roll into a tube-like shape.

Yields 12 burritos.

South of the Border Rice

This requires planning ahead to cook beans and rice, but actual preparation time is minimal.

2	cups dry black beans (cooked according to directions in introduction to this section)
1	cup raw brown rice, cooked according to directions on package, omitting salt
3	cloves garlic, minced
1	large onion, chopped
1	7-ounce can unsalted green chilies, diced, *or* 1 large green pepper, seeded and diced
¾	pound unsalted Monterey Jack cheese, grated
1	cup ricotta cheese
1	cup unsalted dry curd cottage cheese
2	tablespoons skim milk or yogurt, or juice from beans
½	cup unsalted cheddar cheese, grated

The night before wash and sort beans. See introduction to this section for cooking instructions.

About an hour before serving: In a large bowl, mix cooked rice and cooked beans, garlic, onion and chilies. In a small bowl, mix cheeses and milk. Layer rice-bean mixture alternately in a greased 9x13-inch pan with the cheese mixture. Cover with foil and bake at 350° F. for 30 minutes, or until bubbly around edges. During the last 10 minutes of baking, sprinkle grated cheddar cheese over the top. When cheese has melted, and is bubbly, remove from oven.

Serve with tossed salad, French Bread (pg. 70), and lots of sliced oranges or tomatoes.

This freezes well.

8-10 servings.

Tacos

Easy to prepare. Simmer for 30 minutes or up to several hours.

2   pounds lean ground beef
1   6-ounce can low-sodium vegetable-tomato
         juice
2   teaspoons dehydrated minced onion
½   teaspoon garlic powder
1   teaspoon ground cumin seed
½-1   teaspoon Chili Con Carne seasoning
         powder
12   unsalted prepared corn tortilla taco shells
2   cups unsalted cheddar cheese, grated
½   head Iceberg lettuce, shredded
3   fresh tomatoes, diced
4   green onions, chopped
Sour cream or yogurt
Basic Hot Sauce (optional)

In a large skillet, brown ground beef and drain off all fat. Add juice, onion, garlic powder, cumin seed, and Chili Con Carne powder and simmer for at least 30 minutes.

Spoon meat filling into prepared shells. Top with cheese, lettuce, tomatoes, onions and sour cream.

Add unsalted Hot Sauce as desired.
8-12 servings.

Chicken Tacos

A nice change from the typical hamburger variety.

1   chicken, baked or boiled
½-1   teaspoon comino seeds
½   teaspoon lemon juice
1-2   tablespoons Basic Hot Sauce
1   6-ounce can low-sodium V-8 Juice
½   teaspoon seasoned salt substitute
1 or 2 green onions, minced
1   dozen unsalted prepared taco shells or un-
         salted corn tortillas, fried lightly in
         small amount of oil to taco shape
1   cup unsalted Monterey Jack cheese, grated
½   small head Iceberg lettuce, shredded
2   medium tomatoes, finely chopped
1   cup sour cream (optional)

Skin, bone and chop cooked chicken into bite-size pieces. Put into 3-quart saucepan and add comino seeds, chili sauce, V-8 Juice, seasoned salt substitute and onions. Cover and bring to a boil. Put in refrigerator and let marinate at least a few hours—two days at the most. Divide filling into shells. Sprinkle with cheese and bake in a 9x13-inch greased pan at 350° F. for about 10-20 minutes or until filling is heated through. Remove from oven and top with shredded lettuce, tomatoes and sour cream.

Makes 12 tacos.

Jimmy's "Chimmies"

(Chimichangas)

4   cups (about 3 pounds) boneless beef (chuck or round is good)
2   cups water or liquid from cooking beef
2   onions, chopped
8   ounces Ortega diced green chilies (more for hotter taste)
2   tablespoons unbleached flour
One dozen large 10-12-inch flour tortillas
Oil
Lettuce, finely shredded
Guacamole (recipe follows)
Sour cream
Unsalted cheddar cheese, grated
Tomatoes, chopped
Green onions with tops, chopped
Basic Hot Sauce

Trim beef of all fat. Cut into large chunks. In a 6-quart kettle, cook beef covered with water, until it falls apart (this is a good place to use a pressure cooker). Drain and save liquid from meat; add enough water, if necessary, to make 2 cups liquid; set aside. Shred meat into 6-quart kettle and add onions, chilies and liquid. Gently simmer until onions are tender. Add flour to thicken

Heat tortilla in an ungreased hot skillet for a few seconds on each side until tortilla begins to bubble. Place 3-4 heaping tablespoons of filling on each tortilla. Fold over one end, then both sides, and roll up. Do this with remaining filling and tortillas.

Put oil in large frying pan about one-inch deep. Fry Chimichangas in hot oil until brown on one side, turn and fry on other side until browned. Remove to plater covered with paper towels. Keep in warm oven while frying remaining "chimmies."

Makes one dozen.

To serve: Put one chimichanga on plate. Spread with Guacamole (pg. 153), lettuce, 2 dollops sour cream, cheese, tomatoes and onions. Top with Basic Hot Sauce (pg. 149), if desired.

Fried Rice

Good companion to Egg Fu Yong.

3   cups raw brown rice, cooked as directed
      on package, omitting salt
3   blade pork chops, fat removed (optional)
½   cup vegetable oil
1   carrot, finely diced
5   sprigs fresh parsley, chopped fine
¾-1 cup green onions, tops and bottoms,
      chopped
¼   teaspoon seasoned salt substitute
2   teaspoons unsalted beef broth concentrate
      or 2 unsalted beef bouillon cubes
2   eggs, beaten

In a 3-quart saucepan, cook the rice and cool. Cut raw pork, if used, into tiny pieces. In 6-quart kettle, brown pork in oil (use all the oil or rice will stick). If not using pork, heat oil in kettle. Add rice and remaining ingredients, except for eggs. Stir to mix. Make a hole in the center of the rice and add the eggs. Allow eggs to set for one minute, then stir to mix. Continue stirring and add more oil as needed to keep the rice from sticking. Turn off heat when rice is just heated through.
    Serves 6.

Feijoada

(Brazilian Supper)

This recipe can easily be converted for a meatless meal.*

3   cups dried black beans, sorted and washed.
      Soak beans overnight. Cover with water
      and cook in a slow cooker all day with
      1 bay leaf. (See Some Notes About Pre-
      paring Beans in introduction to this
      section.)
3   tablespoons vegetable oil
2   large onions, chopped fine
6   cloves garlic, minced, or 2 to 3 tea-
      spoons dried, minced garlic
1   teaspoon garlic powder
3   blade or loin pork chops, cooked,
      fat removed
1   pound cooked unsalted smoked pork
      (this smoked flavor is important)**
2   cups dry red wine or 2 cups unsalted
      tomato juice mixed with 2 tablespoons
      red wine vinegar
¼   teaspoon seasoned salt substitute
3   teaspoons ground oregano
¼   teaspoon leaf thyme, crumbled
½   teaspoon ground sage

2   cups long-grain brown rice, cooked accord-
        ing to package directions, adding 1
        tablespoon minced dried onion and
        omitting salt
4-6   oranges, peeled and diced

Cook beans according to above directions. (See introduction to this section for further details.) In 6-quart kettle, sauté onion in oil. Add garlic, pork chops, smoked pork, wine or tomato juice, salt substitute, oregano, thyme and sage. Add this mixture to the beans, mashing slightly with a potato masher. Simmer for 1 to 1½ hours or longer to develop flavors. On each serving plate, place a mound of rice. Spoon bean mixture over the rice. This bean mixture should look very dark and be slightly runny or soupy in consistency. Accompany with oranges in a separate dish.

This is excellent served with crusty French Bread (pg. 70), or Dilly Bread (pg. 71), or cornbread, a tossed salad, and cooked greens such as spinach, turnip or collard.

Serves 6.

*Pork shoulder or loin may be smoked in a home cooker with no salt. In some "smoke-house"-type restaurants, they will smoke the meat for you with no salt. It is worth the effort and is truly a great gourmet company meal.

**For meatless meals: Omit pork chops and smoked pork. Substitute one large seeded, chopped green pepper and 1 large chopped tomato. Garnish with toasted sesame seeds to boost the protein in the beans.

Basic Hot Sauce

1   quart canned unsalted tomatoes
1   6-ounce can unsalted tomato paste
1   large onion, peeled
1   green pepper, seeded
1   clove garlic or ½ teaspoon dehydrated
        minced garlic
3   jalapeno peppers, canned or cooked fresh
1   tablespoon granulated sugar
1   tablespoon cider vinegar

Put all ingredients into blender and blend. Store in a covered container in the refrigerator. Use within three days or store unused portion in ½-pint containers in freezer.

Makes about two quarts hot sauce.

Sour Cream Enchiladas

These are fantastic and have mild flavor

1	12-ounce can unsalted tomato paste
2	cups water
3	tablespoons unsalted chili powder (use an unsalted blend)
1	teaspoon ground cumin
2	pints (4 cups) sour cream or yogurt
1	cup green onions, chopped
½	teaspoon ground cumin
4	cups unsalted cheddar cheese, grated
12	unsalted corn tortillas

Oil for frying tortillas

4	green onions, chopped (for garnish)

Sauce: In 3-quart saucepan, combine tomato paste, water, chili powder, and 1 teaspoon cumin. Simmer uncovered while preparing filling and frying tortillas.

Filling: In medium mixing bowl, combine 1 pint of the sour cream, 1 cup green onions, ½ teaspoon cumin, and 1 cup of the cheese. Mix thoroughly.

Tortillas: In an 8-inch skillet, heat 1 tablespoon oil and fry tortillas for 30 seconds on each side. Remove from skillet and drain on paper towels. Add oil to skillet as needed.

To assemble: One at a time, dip tortillas in heated sauce. Remove tortillas immediately from sauce and place in an ungreased 8x10-inch casserole. Overlap two tortillas at one end of the pan, allowing part of the tortilla to extend over the edge of the pan. Spread about 6 tablespoons of filling down center of the tortillas and fold extending sections down over the filling. Continue with remaining tortillas and place side by side in pan. Spoon remaining sauce over top of enchiladas. Sprinkle remaining 3 cups of cheese over top of rolled enchiladas.

Bake uncovered in 375° F. oven for 20 minutes.

To serve: Garnish with remaining sour cream and sprinkle with green onions.

Yields 6 large enchiladas; serves 6.

Pizza

Double this recipe for extra pizza crusts and sauce to freeze. Roll crusts out to fit pans, brush with prepared sauce, and freeze for later use.

Crust

1	tablespoon (1 package) yeast

1¼   cup very warm (110°-115°) water
3-3½ cups unbleached flour, sifted (may use half
          whole wheat flour, if desired)
1   tablespoon vegetable oil
⅛   teaspoon salt substitute

In a large bowl, dissolve yeast in water. Beat in 1½ cups of the flour; add oil and salt substitute. Gradually stir in remaining flour until dough is no longer sticky. Turn out onto a floured board and knead until smooth—about 10 minutes. Place in an oiled bowl; let rise in a warm place, covered, for 1½-2 hours. Punch down. Dough may be refrigerated at this point until about one hour before serving.

Prepare sauce.

Cut dough in half. On lightly floured surface, roll each half into the shape and size of greased pizza pan or cookie sheet on which the pizza will be cooked. Place on pan, shaping further with knuckles; turn edges up slightly. Brush each crust lightly with vegetable oil.

Sauce

1   6-ounce can unsalted tomato paste
1   6-ounce can unsalted tomato juice or
          low-sodium vegetable-tomato juice
1   cup water
3   tablespoons dried parsley flakes
4   teaspoons dehydrated minced onion
2   teaspoons Italian seasoning
1   clove garlic, minced

Combine ingredients in 2-quart saucepan and simmer, covered, for about one hour. About 30 minutes before serving, put simmered sauce on prepared crusts, dividing sauce equally for each crust. Place toppings on pizzas and garnish with grated cheeses. Bake in 425° F. oven for 20-25 minutes or until crust is browned and cheese is bubbly.

Makes two pizzas.

Suggested Toppings

Fresh mushrooms, sliced
Green peppers, sliced or chopped
Tomatoes, diced or sliced
Hamburger, browned and grease drained off
Onions, chopped or sliced
Pineapple chunks or slices
Unsalted cheddar cheese, grated
Unsalted Monterey Jack cheese, grated

Lasagne

Make ahead and refrigerate until ready to cook, if desired.

½   pound lean ground beef
¼   cup onion, chopped
1   12-ounce can unsalted tomato paste
1¾   cups water
1   cup fresh mushrooms, sliced
1   clove garlic, crushed
1   teaspoon crushed sweet basil
1   teaspoon dried parsley flakes
½   teaspoon salt substitute
½   teaspoon crushed oregano
¼   teaspoon black pepper
8   ounces lasagne noodles
2   cups unsalted dry curd cottage cheese
¼   cup sour cream, *or* 3 tablespoons milk
1   15-ounce can low-sodium spinach, *or*
         1 10-ounce package frozen spinach,
         thawed
1   egg
¼   teaspoon pepper
2   cups shredded unsalted Monterey Jack
         cheese, *or* 2 cups shredded unsalted
         cheddar cheese

In a large skillet, brown beef with onion. Drain grease well. Add tomato paste, water, mushrooms, garlic, sweet basil, parsley flakes, ¼ teaspoon of the salt substitute, oregano and pepper. Simmer uncovered one hour.

Cook lasagne noodles as directed on package, omitting salt.

In a large bowl, combine cottage cheese, sour cream or milk, drained and chopped spinach, egg, the remaining ¼ teaspoon salt substitute and pepper.

Layer ingredients in a 9x13-inch greased baking dish by alternating with a layer of noodles, cottage cheese mixture, meat mixture, then cheese, ending with the cheese. Sprinkle with ¼ cup grated Parmesan cheese before baking, *if diet allows.*

Bake in 350° F. oven for 30 minutes or until cheese bubbles. Remove from oven and let stand covered for 15 minutes before serving.

Vegetarian version: This is equally as tasty if the ground beef is omitted. Brown onions in a small amount of vegetable oil (about 2 tablespoons). Proceed with the recipe as directed.

Meatballs in Spaghetti Sauce

2   cups onion, chopped
2   cloves garlic, crushed
6   tablespoons oil
7   1-pound cans unsalted tomatoes
2   12-ounce cans unsalted tomato paste
2   teaspoons crushed oregano
2   teaspoons crushed sweet basil
2   teaspoons dried parsley flakes
1   teaspoon black pepper
24 ounces spaghetti noodles

In a 6-quart kettle, brown onion and garlic in oil. Add remaining ingredients except for spaghetti noodles and simmer covered, stirring occasionally, for at least 1-2 hours. Add meatballs and simmer covered for at least one hour longer. Serve over hot spaghetti noodles which have been cooked according to package directions, omitting salt. May be *lightly* sprinkled with Parmesan cheese, if desired.

Serves 12. Leftovers freeze well.

Meatballs
3   pounds extra lean ground beef
2   eggs
¾   cup grated Parmesan cheese
¾   cup Cream of Wheat
2   teaspoons dried parsley flakes
    tablespoons finely chopped onion
1   teaspoon crushed oregano
1   teaspoon crushed sweet basil
1   teaspoon black pepper

In large mixing bowl, combine ingredients. Form into balls and put on rack in broiler pan.

Bake in 350° F. oven for 20 minutes. Add to sauce and simmer at least one hour.

Guacamole Spread

1   ripe avacado
1   cup sour cream
1   teaspoon dehydrated minced onion
½   teaspoon ground cumin
¼   teaspoon unsalted chili powder
⅛   teaspoon dehydrated minced garlic or
        ½ minced garlic clove
1   tablespoon lemon juice

Put ingredients in blender and blend together well.

Italian Meat Sauce

This always gets raves.

½ cup onion, sliced
1½ pounds lean ground beef
2 cloves garlic, minced
¼ pound fresh mushrooms, sliced
2 1-pound cans unsalted tomatoes
2 6-ounce cans unsalted tomato paste
¼ cup fresh parsley, chopped
2½ teaspoons oregano or sage
½ teaspoon seasoned salt substitute
½ teaspoon thyme
1 bay leaf
1 cup burgundy or rosé wine* or ½ cup
    water or unsalted tomato juice
1 green pepper, chopped
1 teaspoon brown sugar
1½ pounds spaghetti noodles

In a large skillet, cook onion and ground beef together until beef is browned. Drain all grease. Add garlic, mushrooms, and cook 3 minutes longer. Add the remaining ingredients, except for noodles. Simmer uncovered at least 2 hours or as much as 6 hours. (The longer the sauce cooks, the thicker the sauce gets.)

Cook spaghetti noodles according to directions on package, omitting salt.

Serve sauce over noodles and accompany with French Bread (pg. 70) and a tossed salad.

Serves 6.

*The wine adds a full-bodied flavor if burgundy is used and a lighter flavor if a rosé wine is used.

Chop Suey

8 ounces Chinese or Japanese noodles*
2 tablespoons vegetable oil
1 small onion, sliced
1 clove garlic, minced
½ pound extra lean beef, slivered into
    bite-size pieces**
2 tablespoons lemon juice
1 teaspoon granulated sugar
1½ tablespoons cornstarch
¼ cup water
1 cup fresh peas or fresh or frozen pea pods
1 5-ounce can water chestnuts, drained and
    sliced*
5 fresh mushrooms, sliced
1 8-ounce can bamboo shoots, drained*
¼ teaspoon black pepper
¼ cup almonds, slivered

Cook noodles according to package directions, omitting salt. Drain, rinse; set aside.

In a large skillet, warm oil and add onion and garlic. Cook 3-5 minutes. Add slivers of beef. Sprinkle with lemon juice. Cover and simmer until beef loses its red color. In a small bowl, blend sugar, cornstarch, and water. Add to pan of meat. Add remaining ingredients, except for the noodles, and cook for 5 minutes. Turn off heat and cover. Let set for 5 minutes and then spoon over noodles. Serves 4.

*Be sure to read the labels on these products, and only purchase brands that are packaged without salt.

**4 chicken breasts, boned; or 4 cups diced, cooked lean pork may be substituted.

Hungarian Goulash

This can simmer hours, if needed, and is a fine meal for both company and everyday.

2   tablespoons oil
1½   pounds boneless lean beef or chopped
         stew meat, cut into ½-inch cubes
2   medium onions, sliced
4   tablespoons unbleached flour
1   teaspoon paprika
¼   teaspoon thyme
1   1-pound can unsalted tomatoes
1   6-ounce can unsalted tomato paste
1   tablespoon unsalted beef broth concentrate or 3 unsalted bouillon cubes
2   cloves garlic, minced
⅓   pound fresh mushrooms, sliced
1   bay leaf
1   stalk celery, with leaves, chopped
3   tablespoons fresh parsley, chopped
8   ounces spinach noodles
Sour cream, optional

In 6-quart kettle, brown beef in oil to develop flavor; add onions and cook until onions are tender. Blend in flour, paprika and thyme. Add tomatoes, including juice, and remaining ingredients except for noodles. Heat to boiling; reduce heat, cover and simmer about 1½ hours, stirring occasionally. Remove bay leaf.

About 20 minutes before serving, boil noodles according to package directions, omitting the salt. Ladle meat sauce over noodles. Top each serving with 1 tablespoon sour cream, if desired. Great with a lettuce salad.

4-6 servings.

Sauerbraten

Because this is a marinated meat, planning and part of the preparation must be done four days ahead. The extra time is certainly well spent!

1	6-pound rolled beef roast
2	cups vinegar
2	cups water
1	large onion, sliced
¼	cup granulated sugar
10	peppercorns
3	whole cloves
2	bay leaves
1	lemon
2	tablespoons unsalted margarine

Four days before serving, in a large saucepan, combine vinegar, water, onion, sugar, peppercorns, cloves and bay leaves. Heat but do not boil. Pour hot mixture over meat which has been placed in a glass or plastic (not metal) bowl and allow to cool. Add one lemon which has been thinly sliced. Cover with tight fitting lid or tightly sealed plastic wrap and set in refrigerator. Marinate 4 days, turning meat once each day.

On day of serving, remove meat from marinade. Strain large ingredients from marinade. Reserve liquid. Heat margarine in a 5-quart kettle over low heat. Brown meat slowly on all sides. Slowly add 3 cups of reserved liquid and bring to a boil. Reduce heat; cover and simmer, but do not allow to boil, for 3 hours, or until meat is tender. Remove meat to serving platter, cover and keep warm.

Gravy

¼	cup unsalted margarine
⅓	cup unbleached flour
3	cups reserved liquid
⅓	cup sour cream

In a large saucepan, melt margarine; blend in flour and heat until bubbly. Add liquid from kettle. Bring to boil, stirring frequently, and cook until thickened. Remove pan from heat. Add sour cream and beat. Stirring constantly, cook over low heat until heated thoroughly.

Serve with Sweet Sour Red Cabbage and German Potato Pancakes (see pp. 113, 115).

6-8 servings.

Chicken

Almost all scientists agree that there is an increasing amount of evidence linking poor diet and disease to justify changing eating habits. The Senate Select Committee on Nutrition and Human Needs listened to experts on nutrition. The results of these hearings are published in a report which lists dietary goals for the American public. They are:

1) Increase consumption of fruits and vegetables and whole grains.
2) Decrease consumption of refined and other processed sugars and foods high in such sugars.
3) Decrease consumption of foods high in total fat, and partially replace saturated fats, whether obtained from animal or vegetable sources, with polyunsaturated fats.
4) Decrease consumption of animal fat, and choose meats, poultry, and fish that will reduce saturated fat intake.
5) Except for young children, substitute low-fat and non-fat milk for whole milk, and use low-fat dairy products instead of high-fat dairy products.
6) Decrease consumption of butter fat, eggs and other high-cholesterol sources. Some consideration should be given to easing the cholesterol goal for premenopausal women, young children, and the elderly in order to obtain the nutritional benefits of eggs in the diet.
7) Decrease consumption of salt and avoid all foods that are high in salt content.

It would seem that eating poultry would be a positive, logical step in following these guidelines. Chicken has been used extensively in the following recipes because of its availability and ease in preparation.

Because of its low fat content and delicate flavor, chicken "sits well" in the stomach and easily takes on flavors with which it is cooked. It then becomes a very versatile meal—and one very good for you!

Stir-fry Chicken

This is surprisingly delicious because of the unique blend of ingredients.

6   cut chicken breasts, fat and skin removed,
       cut into bite-size pieces
2   tablespoons oil
1   clove garlic, minced
6   green onions, chopped into ½" pieces
1   unsalted chicken bouillon cube
2   tablespoons grated fresh ginger*
2   tablespoons cocktail sherry (optional)
½   lemon, juiced
1   medium head Romaine lettuce, cut in
       ½" strips
1   large stalk celery, sliced diagonally
½   cucumber, sliced, cut in half lengthwise
½   cup frozen peas, thawed
½   cup almonds or cashews, chopped
       (optional)

In a large skillet, sauté chicken breast pieces in oil over high heat. Add the garlic and onions, stirring constantly. Dissolve the bouillon cube in the cocktail sherry and lemon juice in a small cup. Continuing to stir the chicken, add the remaining ingredients, including the bouillon mixture. Stir only until all the ingredients are heated through.

The vegetables should remain crisp. Serve over hot rice cooked according to package directions, omitting salt.
4-6 servings.

*Labeled in the produce section of your supermarket as ginger root.

Oven-fried Herbed Chicken

Good to make ahead and take to a picnic. Serves equally well as a family or company meal.

1   cup dry unsalted bread crumbs
1   teaspoon basil
1   teaspoon tarragon
½   teaspoon onion powder
¼   teaspoon ground pepper
1   egg, beaten
1   tablespoon lemon juice
1   frying chicken
2   zucchini, cut in 2-inch long wedges

Mix crumbs, herbs and pepper in a medium-sized bowl. Combine egg and lemon juice in a separate bowl. Rinse and dry chicken and zucchini. Dip the chicken and zucchini in egg mixture and coat with seasoned bread crumbs. Grease broiler pan with 2 tablespoons unsalted margarine. Place chicken and zucchini in the pan in a single layer. Bake at 350° F. for about 1½ hours, or until chicken is fork tender and the crust is crisp.

Fun when served with mashed potatoes and a green vegetable.

3-4 servings.

Chicken Eleganté

This takes a little extra time to prepare, but it is so outstanding and unique, it is worth the effort.

4	whole chicken breasts, split
¼	teaspoon seasoned ground pepper
½	cup unbleached flour
2	tablespoons oil
2	tablespoons unsalted margarine
2	garlic cloves, minced
3	tablespoons sliced green onions
3	tablespoons lemon juice
¾	cup dry white wine *or* apple juice *or* chicken broth
1	teaspoon granulated sugar *or* honey
½	teaspoon tarragon leaves, crushed
¼	teaspoon seasoned salt substitute
¾	cup sour cream or yogurt

Remove bones and skin from chicken breasts. Pound each half between waxed paper to ¼″ thickness. Mix the seasoned pepper and flour. Dredge the chicken in the flour, shaking off the excess. Heat the oil and margarine in a large frying pan over medium high heat. Add four pieces of the chicken at a time, brown for 3 minutes on each side. Remove from pan. Keep warm.

To the pan drippings add the garlic, onions, lemon juice, wine, sugar, tarragon and seasoned salt substitute.

Cook, stirring up browned bits, until mixture boils. Remove from heat. Stir 2-4 teaspoons of the seasoned flour used to dredge the chicken into the sour cream. Stir the sour cream mixture into the garlic onion mixture. Add the chicken pieces. Cook over low heat, covered, just until the sauce comes to a gentle boil. This should take about 5 minutes. Do not let mixture boil! The sour cream will curdle and get thin. Serve with brown rice and a green vegetable. Makes a great company meal and is well worth the extra few minutes to de-bone and skin the chicken.

Serves six. For two people, cut the recipe in half.

Hot Chinese Chicken Salad

8	chicken thighs, skinned and boned; each cut into about 12 pieces
¼	cup corn starch
¼	cup vegetable oil
⅛	teaspoon garlic powder
1	large tomato, diced in large pieces
1	can sliced water chestnuts, drained
¼	pound fresh mushrooms, washed and sliced
1	stalk celery, sliced diagonally
1	cup green onion, chopped
2	low-sodium beef bouillon cubes dissolved in ¼ cup water and 1 tablespoon sherry or lemon juice
2	cups lettuce, shredded

Roll the chicken pieces in corn starch. Heat oil in a large frying pan; add chicken and brown quickly over medium high heat. Sprinkle with garlic powder. Add tomatoes, water chestnuts, mushrooms, celery and onions. Stir. Stir in bouillon mixture. Cover and reduce heat. Simmer 5 minutes. Remove from heat. Add lettuce and toss. Serve with unsalted brown rice and/or Angel Rolls (page 66).

Serves 6 to 8.

Chicken with Nut Sauce

1	3½-pound chicken, whole
4	tablespoons melted unsalted margarine or unsalted butter
1	tablespoon oil

Freshly ground black pepper
Nut Sauce (pg. 161)

Rinse chicken and pat chicken dry inside and out with paper towels. Mix the melted butter and oil together and thoroughly coat the chicken with a pastry brush.

Preheat oven to 475° F. (While baking chicken, prepare Nut Sauce.) In a shallow roasting pan, set chicken on its side on a rack. Roast in the center of the oven for about 10 minutes, then turn it on its other side. With a pastry brush, baste chicken with butter-oil mixture and again roast for 10 minutes. Turn the chicken on its back and lower the heat to 400° F. Baste again and sprinkle the bird with a few grindings of pepper. Roast uncovered 40 minutes longer, basting every 10 minutes with the remaining butter-oil mixture and then with the juices in the pan. Make Nut Sauce.

To test for doneness, pierce the thigh of the bird with the tip of a sharp knife. The juice that trickles out should be yellow; if it is pink, roast the bird for another 6 or 10 minutes.

Carve the chicken into quarters and arrange attractively on a deep serving platter. Pour the Nut Sauce over the bird and serve at once.

Makes 4 servings.

Nut Sauce

2   tablespoons unsalted margarine
2   tablespoons onion, finely chopped
2   teaspoons garlic, finely chopped
1   tablespoon unbleached flour
1½   cups unsalted chicken broth *or* unsalted
       bouillon
2   tablespoons red wine vinegar
⅛   teaspoon powdered cloves
⅛   teaspoon cinnamon
⅛   teaspoon cayenne pepper
1   small bay leaf
⅛   teaspoon powdered saffron (if available)
       or paprika may be substituted
1   tablespoon parsley, finely chopped
1   cup walnuts, pulverized in blender or very
       finely chopped

Prepare the sauce while the chicken is baking. In a heavy 10-inch skillet, melt the margarine; add the onion and garlic. Lower the heat and cook uncovered for 3 to 5 minutes, stirring occasionally.

When the onions are soft but not brown, stir in the flour and mix to a paste. Then pour in the chicken stock. Bring to a boil, stirring constantly, until the sauce thickens slightly. Stir in the remaining ingredients. Lower the heat and simmer uncovered for about 5 minutes. Taste for seasonings. Use to pour over one chicken.

Marinated Chicken

1   frying chicken, cut up
½   teaspoon rosemary or tarragon
¼   teaspoon pepper
2   tablespoons lemon juice
Rind of one lemon, grated
1   tablespoon parsley, chopped
2   tablespoons oil
Dash of paprika
¼   cup vinegar or sauterne wine

Rinse and dry chicken. Crush herbs, combine and blend with remaining ingredients. Put marinade and chicken pieces in a plastic bag or covered mixing bowl and store in refrigerator for 6 to 8 hours. Remove from refrigerator. Place chicken pieces in roasting pan and bake at 325° F., basting with marinade occasionally, for 1½ hours or until fork tender.

Serves 4.

Easy Chicken Bake

⅔   cup long grain brown rice
½   cup onion, chopped
2   tablespoons green pepper, chopped
½   cup chopped fresh mushrooms
4   chicken breasts, boned, skinned and split
       lengthwise
2   7¼-ounce cans low-sodium cream of
       mushroom soup
¼   cup water, lemon juice, or white wine
2   cubes unsalted chicken-flavored bouillon,
       crushed, or 2 teaspoons low-sodium
       chicken soup base
¼ to ½ teaspoon dried sage, crushed
¼   teaspoon dried thyme, crushed
Paprika

In a greased 3-quart casserole, combine rice, onion, green pepper and mushrooms. Place chicken on top of rice. In a separate mixing bowl combine soup, water, bouillon, sage and thyme; pour over chicken. Sprinkle with paprika. Cover and bake in 375° F. oven for 45 minutes. Uncover and bake 10 minutes more. Serve with a colorful vegetable. Fresh fruit is also a nice accompaniment to this meal.
       Serves 4

Camp Pack Chicken à la Felice

For camping, at home, or taking to a potluck. This is a good make-ahead dish.

1½   frying chickens, cut into pieces
¼   cup vegetable oil
2   1-pound cans unsalted tomatoes
Water
2   green peppers, chopped
3   onions, chopped
2   cloves garlic, minced
2   bay leaves
1   tablespoon celery seed
1   unsalted chicken bouillon cube or 1 tea-
        spoon low-sodium chicken soup base
        concentrate
2   7¼-ounce cans low-sodium cream of
        mushroom soup
1   6-ounce package egg noodles

In a 6-quart kettle, brown chicken pieces in small amount of oil. Add tomatoes and enough water to cover the chicken. Add the remaining ingredients, except for the noodles, and cook over medium heat until done. This takes about an hour, but can cook much longer, if needed. Remove chicken bones. This can be frozen for later use.* Twenty minutes before serving, turn heat up to medium high and add egg noodles and more water if necessary to chicken. Cook until the noodles are just done, about 10-20 minutes.

Good served with green salad and biscuits. Serves 6-8.

*Can be frozen in half-gallon milk cartons for easy packing and handling. Simply pull out of the freezer before leaving on camping trip and it's ready to go. Make this recipe in a big batch and save time!

Fines Herbes Chicken

This is a sure hit, even though there is a little "extra" in preparation.

1 stick (¼ pound) unsalted butter or unsalted margarine
½ teaspoon fines herbes
½ teaspoon dehydrated parsley flakes
½ teaspoon ground marjoram
½ teaspoon ground oregano
½ pound unsalted jack cheese
6 chicken breast halves
½ cup unbleached flour
1 egg, beaten
Water
¾ cup unsalted bread crumbs
½ cup white wine *or* unsalted chicken broth

In a small mixing bowl, whip margarine until smooth. Add fines herbes, parsley, marjoram and oregano. blend well.

Slice cheese to ½-inch thickness. Remove and discard skin and bones from chicken halves. Pound chicken breasts on board until ¼-inch uniform thickness. Place a slice of jack cheese in center of chicken and spread with one tablespoon of butter-herb mixture. Roll up chicken around cheese slice, trimming cheese if necessary.

In a small bowl, add water to beaten egg to make ½ cup. Dip chicken rolls in egg-water mixture, then in flour, again in the egg-water mixture, then in bread crumbs. Place seam side down in 9x13x2-inch pan.

Bake in preheated 350° F. oven for 20-25 minutes. Remove from oven and add wine or broth and remaining butter mixture (which has been melted). Return to oven and bake for another 20-25 minutes, or until chicken is done.

Remove from oven. To serve, put chicken roll on plate, and spread some pan drippings over top.

Very attractive when served with green salad and Rice with Nuts (pg. 114).

3-4 servings.

Chicken Paprika

2   frying chickens, cut into serving pieces
½   teaspoon pepper
½   cup unbleached flour
¼   cup unsalted margarine
2½   tablespoons paprika
1   onion, finely diced
1½   cups unsalted chicken broth (2 unsalted
         bouillon cubes dissolved in 1½ cups
         boiling water)
4   tablespoons unbleached flour
1   cup skim milk
½   tablespoon paprika
½   cup sour cream or plain skim milk yogurt
¼   cup fresh parlsey, chopped

Dredge the chicken pieces in a combination of pepper and ½ cup flour. Melt margarine in heavy large skillet and sauté chicken pieces until lightly browned. Sprinkle 2½ tablespoons of the paprika evenly over chicken. Add onion and chicken broth; cover and simmer for 1½ hours, or until chicken is tender. Remove chicken to serving platter. Stir the 4 tablespoons flour into the milk; add the ½ tablespoon paprika. Stir into remaining liquid in skillet and cook until thickened, stirring constantly. Add sour cream or yogurt and cook just until heated. Pour over chicken and serve.

Garnish with chopped fresh parsley. This also is nice served over cooked rice and looks colorful when accompanied by a green vegetable.
    4-6 servings.

Chicken Crepes

Crepes
1½   tablespoons oil
1½   cups unbleached flour
4   eggs
2   cups skim milk
Vegetable oil for cooking

Combine all ingredients in a deep bowl. Beat with a rotary beater until smooth. Heat an 8-inch skillet to 400° F. For each crepe, use about one teaspoon oil for frying. Fill ¼-cup measure with batter; pour into pan and quickly rotate pan in one motion to cover the entire pan bottom evenly. Cook until edges of crepe turn light brown. Turn; cook 20-30 seconds longer. These can be made ahead and stacked on top of each other. Can be kept in refrigerator for 2-3 days.

Filling and Topping
1   whole frying chicken, or 4 chicken breasts
         boiled, boned and cut into bite-size

pieces. Save broth from boiling chicken
¼   cup unsalted margarine
¼   cup unbleached flour
Broth from chicken plus enough water or wine to make 2 cups liquid, mixed with 2 teaspoons unsalted chicken broth concentrate or 2 unsalted chicken bouillon cubes
1   tablespoon unsalted margarine
10   large fresh mushrooms, washed and chopped
1   crushed clove garlic or ⅛ teaspoon garlic powder
2   tablespoons fresh parsley, chopped
1   tablespoon lemon juice
½   cup almonds, slivered or sliced
¼   teaspoon seasoned salt substitute
2-3   drops red pepper sauce*
Paprika
2   green onions, chopped
1   tablespoon Parmesan cheese

In a large kettle, boil chicken in enough water to cover. Remove from broth, reserving liquid for making following sauce; remove and discard bones and skin. Chop meat and set aside.

In large saucepan, melt ¼ cup margarine; add flour and stir. Add 2 cups liquid and stir until sauce thickens. Remove from heat. This is the sauce.

In large skillet, melt one tablespoon margarine. Sauté mushrooms and garlic in melted margarine until mushrooms are tender. Add chicken, parsley, lemon juice, almonds, seasoned salt substitute, red pepper sauce and ½ cup sauce. Mix thoroughly.

Put about 2 tablespoons filling on each crepe and roll up. Place each crepe in greased 9x13x2-inch pan. Pour remaining sauce over top of crepes. Bake 20 minutes at 350° F. Sprinkle liberally with paprika to add color. Sprinkle with green onions and Parmesan cheese. Good with tossed green salad and French cut green beans.

4 servings.

*One common brand is Tabasco Sauce.

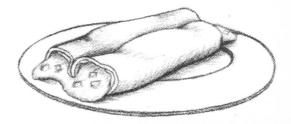

Oven-fried Chicken

Nice way to "dress up" a family meal. A good way to experiment with herbs and spices.

2½   pounds fryer chicken, cut into pieces
¼   cup soft margarine, unsalted
⅔   cup unsalted bread crumbs or low-sodium cracker crumbs, seasoned*
2   tablespoons unbleached flour

Rinse chicken pieces and dry between paper towels. Brush entire surface of each piece of chicken with margarine. Roll in seasoned crumbs. Place chicken pieces, skin side up, on a cookie sheet. Bake at 425° F. for 45 minutes or until chicken is fork tender. Do not turn.

*Seasonings may be added such as garlic powder, salt substitute, seasoned salt substitute, paprika, onion powder, pepper (black and cayenne), basil. Also, you may desire to add some cornmeal to bread or cracker crumbs for added taste.

Calico Chicken

1   whole fryer chicken, skinned and cut into serving-sized pieces
1   10-ounce package frozen corn
1   one-pound can unsalted tomatoes, chopped (undrained)
1   small onion, chopped
1   large green pepper, cut into pieces
2   tablespoons lemon juice
Paprika
1   tablespoon chopped fresh parsley
2   cups raw brown rice, cooking according to package directions, omitting salt

Place the chicken in a 3-quart casserole dish. Combine the corn, tomatoes, onion, green pepper and lemon juice in a bowl. Pour over the chicken. Sprinkle with paprika. Cook, covered at 350° F. for one hour. Remove lid. Sprinkle with parsley. Serve over brown rice. Complement with a tossed green salad.
Serves 4.

Meat and Fish Dishes

We have already suggested that low-cholesterol chicken and fish be considered when choosing "every-day" meals. Chicken and fish have the added benefit of being lower in natural sodium than beef. They also provide low calorie options for menus.

Beef, however, has been considered "traditional" eating in America. Included in this section are both meat and fish dishes.

When purchasing beef, look for brightly-colored meat. Watch for the lean cuts that have little or no fat marbling. When fat is on meat, trim as much as you can before cooking. When meat is cooked, always drain fat from meat or skim fat from juices.

As with many recipes in preceding sections, most of these meat dishes freeze well after cooking. These meat recipes are usually short in actual preparation time, although the cooking period may require an early start.

In using the recipes herein, those in other low-sodium cookbooks, and when adapting your own recipes to low sodium, try to use as many fresh foods as possible. Using fresh foods will also make your meal appear more attractive. The flavor and nutritional qualities of fresh foods are also greater, and hence the desire to use salt to enhance flavor will decrease.

Meat Loaf

Great served with mashed or baked potatoes and a vegetable.

1½   pounds lean ground beef
3   tablespoons minced dehydrated onion
½   cup green pepper, chopped
2   slices unsalted whole wheat bread,
           crumbled
¼   cup quick-cooking oatmeal
¼   cup unsalted catsup or unsalted chili sauce
1   unsalted beef bouillon cube, crushed and
           dissolved in small amount of boiling
           water
1   egg
⅛   cup dehydrated parsley or ¼ cup fresh
           parsley, chopped
¼   teaspoon pepper

In a large mixing bowl, mix above ingredients. Pack into a greased 9x5x3-inch bread loaf pan. Baste top of loaf with Catsup Coating. Bake at 350° F. for 1 to 1½ hours.

Catsup Coating

½   cup unsalted catsup
1   tablespoon firmly packed brown sugar
¼   teaspoon onion powder

Mix together in a small bowl and use as a glaze over the meatloaf.
8 servings.

Beef Simmer

2   pounds lean beef cubes
8   medium carrots, cut in thick slices
1   1-pound can unsalted tomatoes, or 6 whole
           fresh tomatoes
½   cup cocktail sherry or beef broth
1   tablespoon celery seed, mashed
1   large onion, diced
4   tablespoons tapioca
1   tablespoon granulated sugar
½   teaspoon thyme
½   teaspoon marjoram
½   teaspoon ground rosemary
1   15-ounce can unsalted peas

Brown beef in medium-sized skillet. In a 3-quart casserole or slow cooker, combine all of the ingredients, except for the peas. Cook, covered, in a 250° F. oven for 6-8 hours. The last 20 minutes of baking, add peas and continue cooking for 20 minutes.
Serves 6 to 8.

Pepper Pot

A dish with an oriental flair.

1   cup brown rice, uncooked
2   cups pork, diced (about 4 lean loin chops)
2   tablespoons vegetable oil
1   large onion, sliced
4   green peppers, seeded and diced
1   stalk celery, sliced
1   1-pound can unsalted tomatoes
½   teaspoon ground black pepper
4   carrots, peeled and diced
1   tablespoon lemon juice

Cook rice according to package directions, omitting salt. Trim all fat from pork. In a 6-quart kettle, fry the pork in the oil until browned. Add the onion, green peppers, and celery. Sauté for 2-3 minutes. Add the tomatoes, pepper, carrots and lemon juice. Cook the bones with the vegetables as they add flavor. Simmer for 20 minutes but it is best to cook vegetables so they remain crisp. Remove bones before serving.

Serve Pepper Pot in bowls and add ½ cup of cooked rice in the center of each bowl on top of the vegetable-meat mixture.

4 servings.

Pot Roast

Good served with mashed, oven baked, or baked potatoes.

1   4-6 pound beef blade, chuck, or rolled
         roast
1½   cups boiling water mixed with 2 unsalted
         beef bouillon cubes
1   onion, thinly sliced
½   teaspoon paprika
¼   teaspoon seasoned salt substitute
3   tablespoons dried soup greens
½   teaspoon garlic powder
¼   pound fresh mushrooms, sliced (optional)

Place the roast in a 9x13-inch pan that is lined with heavy duty aluminum foil. Pour the beef bouillon over the roast and top with sliced onion. Sprinkle the top of the roast with paprika, seasoned salt substitute, dried soup greens, garlic powder and mushrooms. Cover with foil and bake at 350° F. for 3-4 hours or 300°-325° F. for about 6 hours until roast is tender and falls away from bone.

8 to 12 servings.

Beef Stroganoff

Excellent served with a tossed salad and a green vegetable. This is a great company dish.

1   cup brown rice or 8 ounces wide egg noodles, cooked according to package directions, omitting salt
1   tablespoon unsalted margarine
1   medium onion, sliced
1   clove garlic, minced
15   fresh mushrooms, sliced
1   pound lean round steak or left-over roast beef or steak, cut into bite-size pieces, all fat removed.
2   tablespoons unsalted ketchup
2   tablespoons cocktail sherry or water
10   drops tabasco sauce
¼   teaspoon ground pepper
2   unsalted beef bouillon cubes or 2 teaspoons unsalted beef soup base
1   7-ounce can low-sodium cream of mushroom soup
½   cup sour cream or yogurt

Prepare rice or noodles, according to package directions, omitting salt.

In a large skillet, melt margarine and saute onion, garlic and mushrooms until onion is tender. Add the steak (if raw, cook until the meat is just pink). Add remaining ingredients, except for the sour cream and rice or noodles. Simmer 10 to 15 minutes to let flavors mingle. Just before serving, add the sour cream and heat on low until stroganoff is serving temperature, but do not allow to boil. The sour cream curdles if heated to a high temperature. If boiling should occur only the texture will be affected—not the taste.

4 servings.

Sweet Sour Meatballs

Sauce
2   1-pound cans unsalted tomato pureé
2   cups water
¼   cup cider vinegar
¼   teaspoon celery seed
1   teaspoon paprika
2   tablespoons brown sugar
1   teaspoon ground cinnamon
¼   teaspoon unsalted chili powder
¼   teaspoon ground cloves
2   tablespoons cornstarch

Meatballs
1   pound lean ground beef or pork
1   egg
½   cup unsalted Matzo Meal

½   teaspoon garlic powder
1   tablespoon minced dehydrated onion
½   teaspoon sage
½   teaspoon ground ginger
½   teaspoon mace
1   teaspoon dried mustard
2   green peppers, washed, seeded and cut
        into 1-inch pieces
12   whole mushrooms, washed and sliced

To make sauce, empty tomato purée and water into a 5-quart kettle. Add the remaining sauce ingredients, except cornstarch. Mix cornstarch with enough water to moisten; add to sauce. Stir to mix thoroughly. Sauce will thicken as it simmers; stir occasionally. Simmer over low heat while preparing meatballs.

To make meatballs, in a medium-sized bowl mix meat, egg, and Matzo Meal along with spices and herbs. Form into balls approximately one-inch in diameter.

Place the meatballs in a 9x13-inch pan in rows. Add the green peppers and mushrooms alternately in between the rows of meatballs. Pour sauce over meatballs.

Cook in a 350° F. oven, uncovered, for one hour. Serve over cooked rice or use as a hot hors d'oeuvres.

Makes about 24 meatballs.

Jackpot

The name Jackpot came about when one eager diner told us, "You have hit the jackpot with this recipe!"

1½   pounds lean ground beef
1   cup onion, chopped
4⅓   cups (9-ounces) curly egg noodles
1   7¼-ounce can low-sodium tomato soup
1   16-ounce can unsalted tomato purée
1   6-ounce can unsalted tomato paste
1   cup unsalted cheddar cheese, grated
2   7¼-ounce cans unsalted creamed corn
¾   teaspoon garlic powder
5   drops tabasco sauce
1   teaspoon rosemary, crushed
½   teaspoon black pepper
¼   pound fresh mushrooms, sliced and
        sautéed (optional)

In a large skillet, brown the beef and onion until tender. Drain off all fat. Cook egg noodles in unsalted boiling water according to package directions. Drain water from noodles. Mix ingredients together and put in a 3-quart deep, greased casserole dish.

Cook, covered, at 350° F. for 45 minutes or until bubbly.

6 servings.

Sautéed Beef Strips

1   cup brown rice
1½   pounds steak (sirloin, sirloin tip, or top
       round)
1   tablespoon vegetable oil
1   medium red onion, sliced
8   large fresh mushrooms, sliced
3   fresh tomatoes, chopped
1½   teaspoons paprika
3   tablespoons unbleached flour
½   cup low-sodium beef broth*
1   cup red wine or low-sodium beef broth
¾   teaspoon ground thyme
¼   teaspoon crushed rosemary
½   green pepper, chopped
½   teaspoon black pepper
½   cup fresh parsley, chopped

Cook rice in saucepan, according to package directions, omitting salt.

Cut beef in thin strips. In a large skillet, sauté beef strips in oil over medium-high heat. Add onion and mushrooms. Cook until meat is lightly browned. Stir in tomatoes and paprika. Stir in flour; add broth and wine (if used) and stir to form a medium-thick sauce. Add thyme, rosemary, green pepper and pepper; simmer 3-4 minutes or until beef is tender. Serve over brown rice. Garnish with chopped fresh parsley.
4-6 servings.

*Make the beef broth by adding one unsalted bouillon cube to ½ cup boiling water.

Curried Beef Ring

This dish is very attractive!

¾   cup brown rice, cooked according to
       package directions, omitting salt;
       set aside

Mix in large bowl:
2   pounds lean ground beef
2   eggs
1   large, tart diced apple
1   tablespoon lemon juice

Sauté in skillet and pour into bowl:
1   large onion, chopped
1   clove garlic, chopped
4   tablespoons unsalted margarine or un-
       salted butter

Heat (in same skillet as above):
1   tablespoon curry powder

1   tablespoon unsalted margarine or unsalted
        butter
¼   teaspoon ground ginger

Add to above:
1   unsalted chicken bouillon cube
1   cup skim milk

Pour all ingredients into bowl and add rice. When mixed, put into large casserole or bundt pan. Bake at 350° F. for one hour. Remove from oven. Turn out onto large serving platter. Put Vegetable Chutney in center of beef ring.

Vegetable Chutney
1   large onion, diced
2   large tomatoes, diced
2   green peppers, diced
1   teaspoon celery seed
½   stick unsalted butter

Heat in large skillet for 2 to 3 minutes, tossing lightly. Drizzle over vegetables a combination of:
1   teaspoon granulated sugar
2   tablespoons lemon juice
¼   teaspoon cayenne pepper

4 to 6 servings.

Quick Chili

This is quick if you have already soaked, cooked and frozen the beans. Otherwise, soak the beans the night before and the following morning begin the cooking process.

1   cup dried kidney or red beans, cooked
        (see introduction to Ethnic Dishes
        section for cooking directions)
1½-2 pounds lean ground beef
1   large onion, chopped
2   7¼-ounce cans low-sodium tomato soup
¼   teaspoon seasoned salt substitute
1   clove garlic, minced
2-3 teaspoons unsalted chili powder
1   1-pound can unsalted tomatoes, undrained

In a 6-quart kettle, brown the meat and onion; drain off fat. Add remaining ingredients and simmer for at least 30 minutes. The more this cooks, the richer the taste becomes.

If desired, serve with grated unsalted cheddar cheese on top. Good with a lettuce salad and French Bread (pg. 70).

4-6 servings.

Western Spuds

If the potatoes are cooked in a microwave oven, this is a quick dish to prepare.

4   large potatoes, baked
½   pound lean ground beef*
1   large onion, chopped
1   green pepper, seeded and chopped
10-15 fresh mushrooms
2   7¼-ounce cans low-sodium cream of
        mushroom soup
1   teaspoon unsalted beef bouillon concen-
        trate *or* 1 unsalted beef bouillon cube
½   teaspoon garlic powder
½   teaspoon paprika
¼   teaspoon ground black pepper
Unsalted cheddar cheese, grated
Sour cream or plain yogurt

Wash potatoes and bake in a 400° F. oven for about one hour or until done. Prepare the filling.

Filling: Brown beef in a large skillet with onion, green pepper, and mushrooms. Drain grease and add soup, bouillon, garlic powder, paprika, and pepper. Simmer, uncovered, for 10 to 30 minutes until flavors are blended.

To serve, spoon the hamburger mixture over baked potatoes which have been slit and fluffed. Top with unsalted cheese and/or sour cream.

These potatoes are good served with a green vegetable and tossed salad.

4 servings.

*To make this a complete-protein vegetarian meal, omit beef, increase mushrooms to 20 to 25, add another green pepper, and use vegetable bouillon instead of beef bouillon.

Shish Kebabs

Serve with Rice with Nuts (pg. 114) and a fruit salad for a special bar-b-que.

3-4   pounds lamb, fat removed, cut into
        1½-inch cubes, marinated
Herbed Marinade (pg. 102)
2   green peppers, washed, seeds removed,
        cut into sections
1   pound cherry tomatoes, washed (or 2
        sweet red peppers, seeds removed,
        cut into sections)
2   medium onions, cut into sections
¼   pound fresh mushrooms, whole
Skewers

Prepare lamb and marinate in Herbed Marinade for several hours before serving time.

Fill skewers, alternating meat cubes with vegetables.

Broil over *hot* coals or broil in oven, turning often, to medium-rare doneness, brushing frequently with marinade.

6 to 8 servings.

Quick Sloppy Jims

1	pound lean ground beef
1	large onion, finely chopped
1	stalk celery, finely chopped
1	6-ounce can unsalted tomato paste
¾	cup water
6	drops tobasco sauce
2	tablespoons vinegar
½	teaspoon unsalted chili powder
2	tablespoons brown sugar
¼	teaspoon pepper
¼	teaspoon seasoned salt substitute
¼	teaspoon garlic powder
4	hamburger buns

In a large skillet, brown the ground beef, onion and celery. Drain off all fat. Add remaining ingredients, except for hamburger buns, and simmer uncovered for 30 minutes.

To serve, spoon over hamburger buns (see recipe in Breads section or use commercially prepared hamburger buns if diet allows).

4 servings.

Baked Fish

Serve with tartar sauce (pg. 104), salad, bread (Dilly Bread, page 71, is excellent with fish) and enjoy yourself!

Fish, whole or fillets, cleaned and rinsed
Aluminum foil
Onion, sliced thinly
Lemon, sliced thinly (do not peel)
⅓ cup white wine or unsalted chicken broth

Lay fish on aluminum foil. Lay onion slices and lemon slices inside cavity of fish or on top of fillets. Pour white wine or broth on top of fillets and on inside of whole fish. Wrap tightly with foil, making sure that there are no holes for the moisture to escape.

Bake at 400° F. for approximately 10 minutes per inch of thickness. Test for doneness. Fish should be moist and should lightly flake away from bones. Use ½ pound of fish per serving.

Fish Fillets Italiano

Sauce Italiano

¼   cup chopped onion
1   clove garlic, minced
1   tablespoon vegetable oil
2   cups chopped fresh tomatoes
1   6-ounce can unsalted tomato paste
½   green pepper, finely chopped
¼   cup chopped green onion
½   teaspoon oregano
½   teaspoon basil
⅛   teaspoon black pepper

In a 3-quart saucepan, cook the onion and garlic in the oil until the onion is limp. Add the remaining ingredients and simmer, covered, for 20 minutes.

Fish fillets

4-6   mild fish fillets
1   egg
½   cup cornmeal
2   tablespoons unsalted butter or margarine

Wash the fish fillets and pat dry. In a small, shallow bowl, beat the egg. Dip the fillets in the egg and roll in the cornmeal. In a 12-inch skillet heat the butter. Fry the fillets until they are browned and flake with a fork. Serve on in-dividual plates and pour sauce over each serving. 4 servings.

Crab or Fish Quiche

1   9-inch unsalted Pastry Shell, baked
1½   cups unsalted crab meat or fish fillet
         cut into bite-size pieces
1   tablespoon chopped fresh parsley
1   tablespoon chopped celery
4   eggs, lightly beaten
2   cups skim milk
¼   teaspoon white pepper
¼   teaspoon nutmeg

Prepare pastry shell following directions in the Desserts section (pg, 197). Bake.

Brush baked pastry shell lightly with beaten egg. Refrigerate for 15 minutes.

Arrange crab or fish in pastry shell. Add parsley and celery evenly over top of fish. In medium-sized mixing bowl, beat eggs. Add milk and spices. Mix thoroughly and pour over top of ingredients in pie shell.

Bake at 425° F. for approximately 35 minutes, or until pie is just set. Remove from oven and allow to stand until lukewarm before cutting.

4-6 servings.

Fish Cassolet

2   pounds fish fillets
3   tablespoons vegetable oil
1   one-pound can unsalted tomatoes *or*
       2 cups chopped fresh tomatoes
3   medium sized potatoes, boiled, peeled and
       chopped
1   tablespoon minced onion
1   teaspoon vinegar
1   teaspoon granulated sugar
¼   teaspoon black pepper
Juice of one lemon
1   teaspoon minced fresh parsley
2   heaping tablespoons slivered almonds

In a 3-quart saucepan, cook the tomatoes, potatoes, onion, vinegar, sugar and pepper until the mixture is quite dry. Brush the fillets with the oil and place one half of the fish in the bottom of a 3-quart casserole dish. Cover the fish in the casserole with the tomato mixture. Top with the remaining fillets. Pour the lemon juice, parsley and almonds over the top of the layered fish. Cover. Bake at 350° F. for 35-45 minutes or until the fish is moist and flaky when tested with a fork.

4 servings.

Taco Casserole

1   one-pound package unsalted corn chips,
       crushed
1   pound lean ground beef, browned, fat
       drained
2   7¼-ounce cans unsalted Chili Con Carne *or*
       half of 11-ounce bottle unsalted chili
       sauce
½   cup dry kidney or pinto beans, cooked
       (see introduction to Ethnic Dishes
       section for directions on basic cooking
       of the dry beans)
2   onions, chopped or sliced
5   leaves Iceberg lettuce
2-3 tomatoes, sliced
1   pound unsalted Monterey Jack cheese,
       sliced

Layer ingredients, in order given, in 2½-quart casserole. Bake uncovered in 350° F. oven for 40 minutes or until the cheese is melted and slightly browned on top. To serve, be sure each portion has a part of each layer. May be topped with Basic Hot Sauce (pg. 149).

4 servings.

Tamale Pie

1	onion, chopped
1	pound lean ground beef
2	tablespoons unsalted chili powder
½	teaspoon ground cumin
½	cup chopped green pepper
1	1-pound can unsalted whole kernel corn, undrained
1	12-ounce can unsalted tomato paste
1	cup dried red kidney beans, cooked (see introduction to Ethnic Dishes section for cooking directions)
2½	cups cold water
¼	teaspoon seasoned salt substitute
½	teaspoon unsalted chili powder
1¼	cups cornmeal
½	cup unsalted cheddar cheese, shredded

Cook kidney beans according to directions in introduction to Ethnic Dishes section.

Brown onion and ground beef in very large frying pan. Drain off all fat. Add 2 tablespoons chili powder and cumin. Mix thoroughly. Add green pepper, corn, tomato paste and beans; mix well. Gently simmer over low heat while preparing cornmeal mixture.

Combine water, seasoned salt substitute, ½ teaspoon chili powder and cornmeal in a 2-quart saucepan over medium heat. Cook until quite thick and stiff (about 10 minutes), stirring frequently. Set aside ¾ cup of the mixture, then line sides and bottom of a greased 3-quart casserole dish with the rest.

Put beef mixture in the casserole dish which has been lined with the cornmeal crust. Top with the ¾ cup crust mixture which was set aside. Top crust mixture with shredded cheese.

Bake in 350° F. oven for 25 minutes or until the cheese is bubbly throughout.

6 to 8 servings.

Skillet Tuna Scramble

Easy to fix and quick once the rice is cooked.

1½	cups raw brown rice*, cooked according to package directions, omitting salt
2	tablespoons chopped green pepper
2	tablespoons chopped onion
¼	cup sliced mushrooms
4	tablespoons unsalted margarine
¼	cup unbleached flour
2	cups skim milk
¼	teaspoon curry powder
1	6½-ounce can unsalted tuna, drained**

Prepare rice in a 3-quart saucepan, according

to package directions, omitting salt.

In a large skillet, sauté the green pepper, onion and mushrooms in 2 tablespoons of the margarine until the vegetables are just tender. Remove vegetables from the skillet and keep warm. In the same pan, melt the remaining 2 tablespoons of margarine. With a wire whisk stir the flour into the margarine. Add the milk gradually to the flour mixture until a medium thick sauce is obtained. Stir in the curry powder. Add the tuna and the reserved vegetables to the skillet. Stir until all ingredients are hot. Serve over the rice.

4 servings.

*Unsalted biscuits or mashed potatoes may be substituted for the rice.
**Any left over fish may be used here, as well as canned unsalted salmon.

Salmon Loaf

Especially easy with left-over or canned fish

2   cups cooked, unsalted salmon*
½   cup onion, chopped
1   tablespoon unsalted margarine
⅓   cup unsalted bread crumbs
2   eggs
¼   cup fresh parsley, chopped
1   teaspoon dry mustard

In a small skillet, sauté onion in margarine. Mix all ingredients together in a large mixing bowl. With a fork, gently put ingredients into a greased 9x5x3-inch loaf pan taking care not to press into pan. (This keeps the loaf nice and flaky.) Bake for approximately 30 minutes in a 350° F. oven.

*Any mild, white fish may be substituted.

Lemon Cheese Sauce

2   tablespoons unsalted margarine or unsalted butter
2   tablespoons unbleached flour
1   cup skim milk
1   egg yolk, beaten
½   cup unsalted cheddar cheese
4   tablespoons lemon juice

Melt margarine in a one-quart saucepan. Add flour and stir until blended. Gradually add milk, stirring constantly. Continuing to stir, add egg yolk, cheese, and lemon juice. Cook until thick. Serve over Salmon Loaf.

4 to 6 servings.

Entrée Salad

This is low in calories and makes a good summertime main dish!

Dressing
1   clove garlic, crushed
½   lemon, juiced
1½ tablespoon unsalted prepared mustard
1   egg
1   teaspoon tarragon
1½ tablespoon wine vinegar
¾   cup frozen, plain yogurt, thawed
¼   teaspoon pepper

In a quart jar, mix the garlic, lemon juice, egg and other ingredients (except yogurt) with a wire whisk. Set aside.

Salad
2   heads Romaine lettuce, washed and torn into bite-size pieces
2   green onions, chopped
1   can unsalted tuna, drained, or other left-over unsalted cold meat
1   turnip, rutabaga, or jícama, peeled and chopped
4   slices unsalted bread, cubed, sautéed in unsalted butter and ¼ teaspoon garlic powder
½   medium bunch broccoli, cut into bite-size pieces
½   pint cherry tomatoes
½   cup alfalfa sprouts
6   large mushroom caps, washed and sliced

Put prepared salad ingredients in a large salad bowl. Mix the yogurt with the dressing. Pour the dressing over the top of the salad and toss.
Serve immediately.
4 servings.

Cookies, Desserts and Bars

Sweets. A Treat. Something Special. Something salty? Something bought at a bakery??

Relax. A non-salty does not have to forego that "something special" at the end of a meal. Once tried, homemade baked goods can become relatively quick, easy, and *much* more flavorful.

A Few Things to Remember

1) Throw out the *baking powder* and *baking soda* that you have usually used. One teaspoon of regular baking powder has 250 to 405 milligrams of sodium and baking soda has 1,000 mg of sodium per teaspoon.

2) Go to the health food store and purchase low-sodium baking powder, (referred to as "baking soda substitute" in these recipes). Low-sodium baking soda can be purchased in the prescription department of a drug store or a grocery store. It is called Potassium Bicarbonate, N.F.-F.C.C., Food Grade. It is more expensive than the soda on the market shelf, but one pound goes a *long* way!!

3) There is a reason the amounts in the recipes calling for baking powder seem excessive. Low-sodium baking powder requires 1½ times the amount needed of regular, salty baking powder.

4) Always preheat the oven. The texture and shape of your baked goods will be much improved and the cooking times given will be more accurate.

5) Be careful to use the size and shape pans specified. Changing these items may produce inferior results or, at worst, a failure.

6) Enjoy your baking! Perhaps you will want to consider making double batches and freezing a portion of your efforts. Thus, you will be cooking half as often. This also reduces the temptation to buy bakery products, because there will be "a little something" on hand.

7) Talk to personnel in a local bakery. Perhaps the baker will cook special non-salted foods for you, if ordered in advance or in large quantities.

Another Alternative: Call a person you know who loves to bake. Ask if he or she would be willing to bake for *you.* Supply the recipes and low-sodium products and have your friend bake what you would like. The fee may be lower than buying in the store, the flavor will be greater, and the health of your family will be more protected.

As you prepare to bake, remember the saying: "Sweets to the Sweet"!

Chocolate Bit Cookies

This makes the "old favorite" taste even more special.

2¼   cups whole wheat flour
¼   cup wheat germ
1   teaspoon baking soda substitute
1   cup (2 sticks) unsalted margarine
1   cup granulated sugar (¾ cup in altitudes above 4,000 ft.)
¾   cup plus 1 tablespoon brown sugar (½ cup plus 2 tablespoons in altitudes above 4,000 ft.)
1   teaspoon vanilla
½   teaspoon water
2   eggs
2   cups or 1 12-ounce bag chocolate chips
1   cup walnuts, chopped

In a small bowl, mix flour and wheat germ with soda substitute. In a separate large mixing bowl, cream margarine and gradually add granulated sugar; add brown sugar and cream thoroughly. Add vanilla, water and eggs to the creamed mixture; blend thoroughly. Add flour and wheat germ; mix. Stir in chocolate chips and nuts. Drop by teaspoonfuls onto greased cookie sheets. Bake at 350° F. for 10-12 minutes or until lightly browned. Remove from oven. Store cooled cookies in air-tight container.

Makes approximately 3 dozen cookies.

Banana Oatmeal Cookies

1   cup shortening or unsalted margarine
1   cup granulated sugar
2   eggs
1   cup ripe bananas (about 2), mashed
1   cup whole wheat flour
1   cup unbleached flour
¼   teaspoon nutmeg
Dash of salt substitute
2   teaspoons baking powder substitute (1½
          teaspoons in altitudes above 4,000 ft.)
¼   teaspoon baking soda substitute
2   cups quick cooking rolled oats
Powdered Sugar Icing (pg. 201)

In a large mixing bowl, cream together shortening and sugar. Add eggs, mixing until well blended. Mix in bananas. Sift together flour, nutmeg, salt substitute, baking powder substitute, and baking soda substitute.

Gradually add flour mixture to banana mixture, blending thoroughly. Stir in oats. Drop dough from teaspoon onto greased cookie sheets. Bake in preheated 375° oven for 10-15 minutes, or until lightly browned. Cool and top with Powdered Sugar Icing. Freezes well. Keep in tightly covered container.

Makes about 4 dozen 2-inch cookies.

Peanut Butter Cookies

½   cup (1 stick) unsalted margarine
½   cup shortening
1   cup granulated sugar
1   cup brown sugar, packed
1½   teaspoons vanilla
2   eggs, beaten
1   cup low-sodium peanut butter*
½   cup raw or roasted unsalted peanuts,
          chopped (optional)
2   cups unbleached flour
1   cup whole wheat flour
1½   teaspoons baking soda substitute

In a large mixing bowl, cream margarine, shortening, sugars and vanilla. Add eggs. Beat thoroughly. Mix in peanut butter and nuts. Stir dry ingredients into creamed mixture. Form into one-inch balls and, if desired, roll in granulated sugar. Place on ungreased cookie sheets. Press lightly with the back of a fork to make a crisscross pattern and to slightly flatten. Bake in 350° oven for 12-15 minutes. Remove from oven and cool on wire racks.

Makes about 5 dozen cookies.

*If unhydrogenated peanut butter is used, add ¼ cup more whole wheat flour.

Blondies

A grand alternative to chocolate brownies. Easy preparation.

¼   cup (½ stick) unsalted butter or unsalted margarine
1   cup light brown sugar, packed
1   egg
1   teaspoon vanilla
½   cup whole wheat flour
1¾   teaspoons baking powder substitute (1¼ teaspoons in altitudes above 4,000 ft.)
Dash of salt substitute
1   teaspoon lemon juice
¾   cup pecans, coarsely chopped

In a 3-quart saucepan melt the butter over low heat. Stir in the sugar. Remove from heat and, when cool, beat in the egg and vanilla. Mix together the flour, baking powder substitute and salt substitute, and lemon juice. Stir into the butter mixture (which is still in the saucepan); add pecans.

Spread evenly in a greased 8-inch square cake pan and bake in a preheated 325° F. oven for about 30-35 minutes, or until just set. Do not over bake. These are best when lightly moist and chewy. Remove from oven. Cool. Cut into 16 squares. This recipe doubles easily and can be cooked in a 9x13-inch pan. Store in an airtight container.

Makes 16 squares.

Chocolate Drop Cookies

1   cup (2 sticks) unsalted margarine
1¼   cups granulated sugar
2   eggs
1½   teaspoons vanilla
1½   cups whole wheat flour
2   cups unbleached flour (plus 2 tablespoons in altitudes above 4,000 ft.)
2   tablespoons baking powder substitute (1½ tablespoons in altitudes above 4,000 ft.)
4   tablespoons unsweetened cocoa
⅔   cup skim milk

In a large mixing bowl, beat margarine and sugar until fluffy. Add eggs and beat again. Add vanilla. Mix dry ingredients together and add to creamed mixture alternately with milk. Bake at 350° F. (375° F. in altitudes above 4,000 ft.), for 12-14 minutes on ungreased cookie sheets. Remove from oven. Cool and frost. Store in airtight container.

Makes 4 to 5 dozen cookies.

Favorite Devil's Food Cake

1½ full cups soured skim milk* (1⅔ cups
        in altitudes above 4,000 ft.)
½   cup (1 stick) unsalted margarine or ½ cup
        vegetable shortening
1⅔ cups unbleached flour
1   cup granulated sugar
⅓   cup brown sugar, firmly packed
⅔   cup unsweetened cocoa
1½ teaspoons baking soda substitute
        (same for high altitudes)
¼   teaspoon salt substitute
2   eggs
2   teaspoons vanilla

Preheat oven to 350° F. (375° F. in altitudes above 4,000 ft.). Grease and flour a 9x13-inch pan or two 8- or 9-inch round pans. Sour the skim milk.

In a large mixing bowl, beat the margarine, flour, sugars, cocoa, baking soda substitute and salt substitute; mix until well blended and margarine is thoroughly blended with other ingredients and resembles fine particles. This equals 3¾ cups cake mix and, at this point, may be frozen in an airtight container for later use as a cake mix.

Add the soured milk, eggs and vanilla to the mixed dry ingredients. Beat on low speed for 30 seconds, then on high speed for three minutes, scraping the bowl several times. Do not over beat as cake will have a tendency to become more dry.

Pour into prepared pan(s). Bake approximately 30 minutes for a 9x13-inch pan, 25 minutes for layer pans, or until toothpick inserted in the center comes out clean.

Remove from oven and allow to cool for 5 minutes before removing from pan to cool on wire rack. After cake has completely cooled, frost as desired. A favorite frosting is the Cocoa Frosting (below).

*To sour milk: place 1½ tablespoons lemon juice in the bottom of a 2-cup container. Add milk to equal 1½ cups. Let sit for 10 minutes or until milk begins to curdle.

Cocoa Frosting

1   cup powdered sugar
2   tablespoons unsalted margarine
2   tablespoons unsweetened cocoa
4   tablespoons skim milk

Mix together until of spreading consistency.

White Create-A-Cake

Short preparation and very versatile. You can even make your own mix ahead of time!

2   cups all-purpose or unbleached flour
1¼   cups granulated sugar (one cup in altitudes above 4,000 ft.)
4½   teaspoons baking powder substitute (3¾ in altitudes above 4,000 ft.)
¼   teaspoon salt substitute
½   cup white vegetable shortening
1   cup skim milk
2   teaspoons vanilla
4   egg whites

Preheat oven to 350° F. (375° F. in altitudes above 4,000 ft.). Generously grease (do not use oil) a 9x13x3-inch pan or two 8″ square or round pans. Line the square or round pans with waxed paper; grease the top of the waxed paper also.

Sift the flour; remeasure to make 2 cups when spooned lightly into the cup measure and leveled with a knife blade.

In a large mixing bowl, combine the flour, sugar, baking powder substitute, salt substitute and shortening. Mix at medium speed until the shortening is cut into the flour in fine particles. At this point, these ingredients may be packaged in a freezer bag and labeled for later use. This way, you have your own cake mix waiting. Proceed with frozen mix as for unfrozen preparation.

Add the milk or liquid used (see variations below) and mix for two minutes at medium speed. Add the unbeaten egg whites and flavoring. Beat for two more minutes at medium speed.

Pour batter into prepared pans. Bake in preheated oven for 30-35 minutes for 8″ round or square layer pans or for 35-40 minutes for the 9x13-inch pan. A toothpick inserted in the center of the cake should come out clean if the cake is done. If using the frozen mix, cooking time may require an additional 5 to 8 minutes.

Remove cakes from oven and cool on wire racks—leave the 9x13-inch cake in pan, allow 8″ round or square layers to cool for ten minutes in pans resting on wire racks before inverting cakes onto wire racks for remainder of cooling process.

To frost cakes, allow to cool completely. Use any frosting in this cookbook for a tasty and attractive finish to these cakes!

Variations to White Create-A-Cake

Lemon: Add one teaspoon vanilla instead of two teaspoons of vanilla. Add ½ teaspoon lemon extract. Use two whole eggs instead of four egg whites. Use one stick (½ cup) unsalted margarine instead of shortening to give a nice, yellow color to the cake.

For either Powdered Sugar Icing, Fluffy White Frosting or Cream Cheese Icing (pp. 192, 200, 201), use fresh lemon juice instead of the liquid called for in the instructions.

Cherry: Stir one drained cup of chopped, pitted sour or bing cherries into batter before pouring into pan. Save juice for frosting—see Fluffy Frosting (pg. 200).

Yellow: Use 2 whole eggs instead of the 4 egg whites. Use unsalted margarine instead of shortening, if desired, to add more yellow color to the cake.

Almond: Use two whole eggs instead of the 4 egg whites. Use ¾ teaspoon almond extract instead of the vanilla. Sprinkle the top of the unbaked cake with one cup slivered or sliced almonds and bake as directed for white cake.

Orange: Use two whole eggs instead of the 4 egg whites. Substitute ½ cup orange juice and ½ cup skim milk for the one cup milk. Use one teaspoon vanilla and ½ teaspoon orange extract instead of 2 teaspoons vanilla. Unsalted margarine may be substituted for the shortening in the same proportions. Use orange juice for liquid in the frosting desired.

Coconut: Stir one cup flaked coconut into the batter just before pouring into baking pan(s). Sprinkle additional coconut over the frosting desired.

Banana Cake

This stays moist and flavors improve with time.

2   cups whole wheat flour, sifted
2½ teaspoons baking powder substitute (2 teaspoons in altitudes above 4,000 ft.)
1   teaspoon baking soda substitute
½   teaspoon salt substitute
1   teaspoon ground cinnamon
½   cup unsalted margarine
1   cup brown sugar, packed
2   eggs, well beaten
2   cups ripe bananas, mashed
1   cup walnuts, chopped
⅔   cup skim milk

In a large mixing bowl, sift the flour, baking powder substitute, baking soda substitute, salt substitute and cinnamon. Sift again. In a separate bowl, cream margarine, sugar and eggs. Beat well. Add bananas and milk alternately with dry ingredients to the creamed mixture. Stir in nuts. Bake in a greased 9x13-inch pan for 30 minutes at 350° F., or until a toothpick inserted in the center comes out almost clean.

Makes 12 servings.

Kärin's Double Fudge Brownies

Something to try when the chocolate desire becomes too strong.

2   sticks (½ pound) unsalted margarine
4   ounces (4 squares) unsweetened chocolate
1   cup unbleached flour
½   cup (plus 2 tablespoons in altitudes above
          4,000 ft.) whole wheat flour
1   teaspoon baking powder substitute (¾ tea-
          spoon in altitudes above 4,000 ft.)
4   eggs
2   cups granulated sugar
1   teaspoon vanilla
¾   cup chopped nuts (optional)

In a medium-sized saucepan melt the margarine and chocolate. Stir constantly. Cool. In a small bowl mix the flours and baking powder. In a large mixer bowl beat the eggs until frothy and lemon-colored. *Gradually* add the sugar to the eggs. Add the vanilla and cooled chocolate. Beat until well blended on medium speed of mixer. Lower speed and blend in the flour mixture to the sugar-egg mixture. Stir in the chopped nuts. Pour into a greased 9x13x2¾-inch pan. Bake at 350° F. for 30-35 minutes or until a toothpick inserted in the center comes out almost clean. Cool on a wire rack. While brownies are cooling make Fudge Frosting.

Fudge Frosting

2   ounces (2 squares) unsweetened chocolate
3   tablespoons unsalted margarine
5   tablespoons skim milk
½   teaspoon vanilla
Dash of salt substitute
2½   cups sifted powdered sugar

In a medium saucepan melt the chocolate and margarine over low heat. Add the milk, vanilla and salt substitute. Remove from heat. Add the sugar. Stir until well blended. Spread on brownies while the brownies and frosting are still warm. This makes a moist, cake-like brownie. Store tightly covered in the pan or a container. These also freeze well and make good gifts!

Eat sparingly!! With this much chocolate, each brownie tends to contain more caffein than might be recommended for hypertensives.

Makes at least 24 brownies.

Dark Pound Cake

This is really like a fruit cake baked in a loaf pan.

½   cup (1 stick) unsalted margarine
1   cup granulated sugar
3   eggs, beaten
1   cup whole wheat flour
1¼   teaspoons baking powder substitute
        (¾ teaspoon in altitudes above 4,000 ft.)
¾   teaspoon nutmeg
¼   cup water
¼   cup light molasses
¼   teaspoon baking soda substitute
3   cups raisins
2   cups pecans or walnuts, chopped
¼   cup orange juice

In a large mixing bowl, cream margarine with sugar and then add eggs. Separately, mix together the flour, baking powder substitute and nutmeg. While beating creamed mixture, gradually add the flour mixture to the sugar mixture. While continuing to beat, slowly add the water. Mix soda substitute with the molasses and add to previously mixed ingredients; mix. Add raisins, nuts and orange juice.

Grease a 9 x 5 x 3-inch loaf pan; line bottom of pan with waxed paper. Pour ingredients into pan and bake at 300° F. for 2 hours. Remove from oven. Invert onto rack to cool; remove wax paper. Cool thoroughly. Wrap well to store.

This will keep for a long time in the refrigerator if wrapped in a plastic bag. If cake gets dry, poke with a toothpick in a few places and drizzle with a very small amount of orange juice.

This doubles easily to make two loaves—one to eat and one to freeze.

Makes one loaf cake.

Caramel Frosting

¼   cup (½ stick) unsalted butter or unsalted margarine
¾   cup brown sugar, packed
3   tablespoons skim milk
2   cups (approximately) powdered sugar

Melt the butter or margarine in a 3-quart saucepan. Add the sugar. Cook over high heat for about two minutes, stirring constantly. Gradually add the milk and bring to boiling point. Cool to lukewarm. Add powdered sugar (enough for spreading consistency). Beat until smooth. Spread frosting immediately as it tends to harden quickly.

Whole Wheat Almond Pound Cake

This also can be used as a breakfast coffee cake.

1   cup plus 2 tablespoons unsalted margarine, softened
1   cup natural almonds, slivered
1½ cups brown sugar, packed
4   eggs
1   teaspoon almond extract
2   cups whole wheat flour, sifted
1   cup unbleached flour
⅓   cup almonds, natural or blanched, ground
5   teaspoons baking powder substitute (4 teaspoons in altitudes above 4,000 ft.)
1½ cups skim milk or water

Preheat oven to 350° F. Spread 2 tablespoons margarine on the bottom and sides of a 10-inch tube cake pan; press slivered almonds into margarine so that they are distributed evenly around the pan.

In large bowl, with electric mixer at high speed, beat one cup margarine until creamy. Gradually add sugar, beating until fluffy. Add eggs, one at a time, and almond extract; beat. Mix flours with ground almonds and baking powder substitute, beat into creamed mixture alternately with milk or water.

Pour batter into prepared pan. Bake for about one hour and 10 minutes, or until the top is golden brown and a pick inserted into center comes out clean. Cool 20 minutes in pan; invert and remove. Frost with Glaze.

Glaze

1   cup powdered sugar
1   tablespoon unsalted margarine, softened
½   teaspoon almond extract
2-4 tablespoons skim milk (to desired consistency)

Mix sugar and margarine together in a small bowl. Add almond extract and milk to desired consistency.

Makes 16 servings and keeps well.

Honey Graham Crackers

A better flavor than any you have ever purchased in a store!

2   cups whole wheat flour
2½   teaspoons baking powder substitute (2 teaspoons in altitudes above 4,000 ft.)
3   tablespoons brown sugar
½   cup (1 stick) unsalted margarine
2   tablespoons honey
2   tablespoons water

In a large mixing bowl, mix the dry ingredients. Cut in margarine with a pastry blender; mix in honey and water with a fork.

On a greased cookie sheet, roll out dough to ¼-inch thickness. With a knife, make slashes for desired cracker shape, being careful to not cut all the way through the dough. Prick each shape with a fork several times.

Bake in a preheated 400° F. oven for 4 to 6 minutes or until lightly browned. Remove from oven.

May be sprinkled with a cinnamon-sugar mixture, if desired, immediately after removing from oven. Use ¼ cup granulated sugar mixed with one teaspoon ground cinnamon.

Baked Apples

½   cup dry roasted, unsalted peanuts, chopped
⅓   cup unsalted bread crumbs
⅓   cup brown sugar, packed
1   teaspoon ground cinnamon
6   tart baking apples
1   tablespoon unsalted margarine
¾   cup water
1   cup granulated sugar or ½ cup honey

In a small bowl combine peanuts, bread crumbs, brown sugar and cinnamon.

Core apples and peel skins from top of each apple. Arrange in a shallow 9x13-inch baking dish. Fill apple centers with peanut mixture. Dot apple tops with unsalted margarine. Pour ¼ cup water into dish.

Bake at 350° F. for one hour, or until tender. During cooking, spoon water from pan over apples occasionally.

Meanwhile, combine remaining ½ cup water and one cup sugar or honey in a saucepan. Bring mixture to a boil and simmer for 5 minutes. When ready to serve, spoon syrup over apples. Garnish with additional chopped peanuts, if desired. Can be served hot or cold.

Serves 6.

Carrot Cake

The carrots add texture and moistness, but do not have a strong flavor.

2   cups granulated sugar
1¼   cups vegetable oil
3   eggs, beaten
2   cups unbleached flour
2   teaspoons ground cinnamon
2   teaspoons baking soda substitute
½   teaspoon salt substitute
3   cups carrots, grated or chopped
1   cup walnuts, chopped
1   cup currants

In a large mixing bowl, cream sugar and oil. Beat in eggs. In another bowl, sift flour, cinnamon, baking soda substitute and salt substitute. Add to the creamed mixture. Add carrots, nuts and currants. Pour into greased bundt pan or greased 9x13-inch pan and bake for 1¼ hours at 350° F., or until toothpick inserted comes out clean.

Good frosted with Cream Cheese Icing.

Cream Cheese Icing

¼   cup (½ stick) unsalted margarine, softened
4   ounces Neufchâtel cream cheese, softened
2   cups powdered sugar
1   teaspoon vanilla extract or ½ teaspoon lemon extract
1   tablespoon skim milk

Cream the margarine and cream cheese in a medium-sized bowl. Add the powdered sugar, extract and milk. Blend well and spread on cooled cake. (This will tend to be a thick frosting.)

Chocolate Frosting

2   squares (2 ounces) unsweetened chocolate
3   tablespoons unsalted margarine
5-6 tablespoons skim milk
½   teaspoon vanilla extract
2   cups sifted powdered sugar

Melt the chocolate and margarine in a 3-quart saucepan. Add the milk. Remove from heat. Add the vanilla. Cool to room temperature. Add the powdered sugar until frosting is smooth. Spread immediately.

Soft Gingerbread

This makes a dark, moist cake with a pleasant spicy flavor.

1   cup unbleached flour
2   cups whole wheat flour, sifted
1   teaspoon baking soda substitute
1   teaspoon ground ginger
1   tablespoon ground cinnamon
1   teaspoon ground cloves
1   cup brown sugar, lightly packed
1   cup vegetable oil
3   eggs, well beaten
1   cup sour skim milk*
1   cup light molasses
Whipped cream or Lemon Sauce (pg. 100)

Sour the milk. Sift dry ingredients together twice onto a paper towel. Beat in large mixing bowl the sugar, oil, eggs, sour milk and molasses. Beat in dry ingredients and bake in greased and floured 9 x 13-inch pan for 35-45 minutes at 350° F. or until firm when touched with fingertip. Top with whipped cream or Lemon Sauce, if desired. Store tightly covered.

*To sour the milk—put one tablespoon lemon juice or white vinegar in the bottom of a one-cup measure. Fill the cup with milk. Stir. Let it sit at room temperature for 5-10 minutes.
Makes 12 servings.

Chocolate Glazed Bar Cookies

Always a hit, and healthy, too!

½   cup (1 stick) unsalted margarine
½   cup brown sugar, firmly packed
1   teaspoon vanilla
2   eggs
1½ cups whole wheat flour
1   cup wheat germ
½   cup semi-sweet chocolate pieces

Cream margarine and sugar in a large bowl. Beat in vanilla and eggs. Stir in flour and wheat germ. Press evenly into ungreased 8-inch square pan. Bake in 325° oven for 20-25 minutes. Remove from oven.

Immediately, sprinkle top with chocolate pieces. When chocolate has softened, spread carefully over surface with metal spatula or knife.

Cool and cut into 16 bars. Store in an air-tight container.

Layer Raisin Bars

This recipe was created because a guest had a craving for a bar cookie rich in raisins and nuts.

Bottom Layer
1	cup whole wheat flour
¼	cup brown sugar
½	cup unsalted margarine
½	teaspoon vanilla

In a small mixing bowl mix flour and sugar. Cut in margarine until mixture looks like cornmeal. Add vanilla. Press into an ungreased 9x13-inch pan and bake for 10 minutes at 350° F.

Raisin Filling
2	cups raisins
5	tablespoons sugar
6	tablespoons water
2	tablespoons lemon juice
1	teaspoon grated lemon rind
1	teaspoon flour
1½	tablespoons unsalted butter or margarine
¼	teaspoon nutmeg
2	eggs

Mix all ingredients in a 2-quart saucepan, except eggs. Boil covered until mixture is thick, about 10 minutes. Add eggs. Spread on bottom layer.

Top Layer
½	cup PLUS 2 tablespoons unbleached flour
½	teaspoon cinnamon
½	cup quick rolled oats
⅓	cup unsalted margarine
½	cup chopped nuts

Mix dry ingredients in a medium-sized bowl. Cut in margarine until pieces resemble coarse cornmeal. Sprinkle over raisin layer. Bake at 350° F. for about 25 minutes or until topping is browned. Cut into squares.

Makes approximately 36 bar cookies.

Sugar Cakes

This is an adaption of an old favorite. Try it. You'll like it! Each cookie is like eating a small "cake."

2	eggs
2	cups granulated sugar
1	cup (2 sticks) unsalted margarine
1	cup shortening
1	cup skim milk, soured*
1	cup sour cream**

2   teaspoons baking soda substitute
1¼   cups whole wheat flour
5½   cups unbleached flour (6 cups in altitudes
         above 4,000 ft.)
3   teaspoons vanilla
½   teaspoon nutmeg
Raisins or walnuts
Granulated sugar

In a large mixing bowl, cream eggs and sugar with shortening and margarine. In a separate bowl, mix soured milk and sour cream together. Combine dry ingredients. Alternately add the dry ingredients and the milk mixture to the cream mixture. Add vanilla and nutmeg. Drop by tablespoonfuls on greased cookie sheets. Raisins or a walnut may be placed on each cookie center. Sprinkle each cookie top with sugar. Bake for 10-15 minutes in 350° F. oven until just barely browned. Remove from oven. Cool on wire racks. Store in an air-tight container.

Makes 6 dozen cookies.

*To sour the milk, put one tablespoon lemon juice or white vinegar in bottom of a one-cup measure. Fill the cup with skim milk. Stir and let it sit at room temperature for 5 to 10 minutes.

**Any sour cream can be used, but whipping cream "gone bad" is especially good.

Chocolate Chip Cookies

Another use for Basic Biscuit Mix. A quick version of a "standard cookie."

2   cups brown sugar, packed
1   cup shortening or ½ cup shortening and
         ½ cup (1 stick) unsalted margarine
2   eggs
2   teaspoons vanilla
4   cups Basic Biscuit Mix (pg. 61)
1   12-ounce package (2 cups) semi-sweet
         chocolate pieces or carob pieces
1½   cups walnuts or pecans, chopped
         (optional)

In mixing bowl, cream sugar, shortening, eggs and vanilla until fluffy. Stir in mix, chocolate or carob pieces, and nuts. Drop by teaspoonfuls two inches apart on ungreased cookie sheets. Bake in 375° F. oven for 10-12 minutes. Remove from oven. Cool on cookie sheets for one minute. Remove cookies from cookie sheets and cool on a rack.

Makes about 4 dozen cookies.

Glazed Strawberry Pie

This is truly an elegant looking and tasting pie.

1	10-inch pastry shell (pg. 197), baked
2	pints fresh strawberries, washed and hulled
¾	cup water
¾	cup granulated sugar
3	tablespoons cornstarch

About ¼ cup orange juice

½	pint whipping cream
½	teaspoon vanilla

Place one cup of strawberries in small saucepan; crush. Add water and boil for 3 minutes. Strain juice from berries into a measuring cup. Throw away boiled berries. Add orange juice to berry juice to make one cup liquid.

In saucepan, mix sugar and cornstarch. Add juices, and stirring constantly, simmer until thick and clear. Cool to room temperature.

Arrange remaining berries in shell with bottom of berry facing upward. Spoon cooled glaze over each berry. Refrigerate pie until just before ready to serve.

Whip whipping cream. Toward end of whipping, whip in vanilla. Top pie with whipping cream. Cut into 8 wedges and serve.

8 servings.

Pumpkin Pie

What would Thanksgiving or Christmas be without the traditional pumpkin pie?

1	10-inch unsalted pastry shell (pg. 197), unbaked
2	eggs, beaten
1½	cups canned pumpkin (no salt added)
¾	cup granulated sugar
1	teaspoon ground cinnamon
½	teaspoon ground ginger
¼	teaspoon ground cloves
½	teaspoon vanilla or rum extract
½	cup skim milk
1	cup whipping cream, unwhipped
1	cup whipping cream or non-dairy topping, whipped

In a large mixing bowl beat the eggs, and then add the remaining ingredients (except one cup whipping cream or topping). Pour into unbaked pastry shell and bake in a preheated 425° F. oven for 15 minutes. Reduce oven temperature to 350° F. and continue baking for 45 minutes or until knife inserted into center comes out clean. Cool. Garnish with whipping cream or topping, if desired.

Serves 8.

Poor Man's Cake

This is so named because it requires no eggs or milk. It also can be made with items generally stored on the shelf.

1½   cups brown sugar, packed lightly
¾   cup shortening
1   cup raisins
1½   teaspoon ground cinnamon
¾   teaspoon ground cloves
¾   teaspoon nutmeg
2¼   cups hot water

Combine above ingredients in a 3-quart saucepan and boil one minute, COOL (at room temperature—do not put in refrigerator)—this allows the raisins to plump and it's very important not to rush this step. In a large mixing bowl, place cooled mixture and add the following ingredients:

2¼   cups unbleached flour
1¼   cups rolled oats
1½   teaspoons baking soda substitute
2   tablespoons unsweetened cocoa
½   cup nuts, chopped

Mix together with wooden spoon. Pour into greased and floured 9 x 13-inch pan. Bake in 350° F. oven for 40 minutes.
Serves 12.

Pastry Shells

This is the basic pastry shell referred to in other recipes. Good for quiches and pies.

1   cup unbleached flour
1   cup whole wheat flour
⅔   cup shortening
¼   cup ice water (maybe less)
1½   tablespoons lemon juice

Mix the flours in a large mixing bowl. Cut in the shortening with two knives or a pastry blender until the mixture is the size of small peas. Add the ice water and lemon juice. Mix with a fork until moistened. Divide dough into two parts. Roll out between plastic sheets or wax paper with short, light strokes with a rolling pin. Place one circle of dough in a pie plate. Fill and bake as directed in recipe.

When recipe calls for a baked pastry shell, prick the bottom and sides of the shell with a fork. Bake in preheated oven at 400° F. for 10-15 minutes, or until lightly browned.

Makes two 10-inch crusts.

Lucious Apricot Squares

A more mild flavor is obtained if canned apricots are used, and a more tart, pronounced apricot flavor is noticeable if the dried are used.

⅔   cup dried apricots or canned apricots
½   cup (1 stick) unsalted margarine or
        unsalted butter, softened
¼   cup granulated sugar
⅔   cup unbleached flour
⅔   cup whole wheat flour
¾   teaspoon baking powder substitute (½ tea-
        spoon in altitudes above 4,000 ft.)
1   cup brown sugar, packed
2   eggs
½   cup walnuts, chopped
½   teaspoon vanilla extract
Powdered sugar

Cook the dried apricots according to the directions on the label, omitting salt if called for. Drain apricots and chop finely. Set aside.

In a large mixing bowl, cream the butter and granulated sugar. In a separate medium-sized bowl, mix the flours thoroughly; stir one cup of the flour mixture into the creamed mixture until crumbly, or until completely blended. Pack this crumb mixture into a greased 8-inch square pan.

Bake for 25 minutes in a 325° F. oven.

Meanwhile, mix together the remaining ⅓ cup flour, and the baking powder substitute. (Use the bowl you just dirtied up for the crumb mixture.) In a large bowl, with an electric mixer at medium speed, beat the brown sugar and eggs until well blended. Beat in the flour mixture, walnuts, vanilla and apricots. Spread over the baked crumb layer and cook 25-30 minutes more or until the top is golden and a toothpick inserted in the center comes out clean.

Remove from oven. Cool in the pan on a wire rack. If desired, sprinkle lightly with powdered sugar. Store tightly covered. This doubles easily and fits into a 9x13-inch pan.

12 servings.

Kringles

These are really quite easy and fast to prepare, despite the three-part directions.

Dough

1   cup unbleached flour
½   cup (1 stick) unsalted margarine
1   tablespoon water

In a small mixing bowl cut margarine into flour. Add water and mix lightly with a fork.

Divide dough in half. Form into 2 strips almost as long as the cookie sheet and 3 inches wide, on ungreased cookie sheet.

Filling

1   cup water
½   cup unsalted margarine
1   cup unbleached flour
3   eggs
½   teaspoon almond extract

In a 3-quart saucepan, combine water and margarine; heat to boiling. Remove from heat. Add flour. Stir until smooth. Stirring constantly, add eggs, one at a time. Add almond extract. Smooth cooked mixture on top of dough strips, covering dough strips completely. Bake 45 minutes at 375° F. Cool and frost.

Frosting

1   cup powdered sugar
1   tablespoon unsalted margarine
½   teaspoon almond extract
2   scant tablespoons skim milk

Mix the above ingredients in a bowl, stirring to blend well. When frosted, cut crosswise into about 20 strips. Store by covering lightly. If these are kept air-tight, they get soggy. Best when served soon after cooled.

Cinnamon Stixs

Companions for ice milk. These are also a festive cookie special enough for holidays.

½   cup (1 stick) unsalted butter, softened
½   cup (1 stick) unsalted margarine, softened
5   tablespoons granulated sugar
1   teaspoon vanilla
2   cups unbleached flour
Cinnamon-sugar*

In a medium-sized bowl cream together butter, margarine, sugar and vanilla. Blend in flour, using a pastry blender. Pinch off pieces of dough and roll into two-inch lengths about the thickness of a finger. Bake on ungreased cookie sheets at 375° F. for about 12-15 minutes or until lightly browned. While cookies are still warm, roll them in cinnamon mixed with sugar.

Makes approximately 2 dozen cookies.

*Use proportions of one teaspoon cinnamon to ¼ cup sugar.

Fluffy White Frosting

¾   cup granulated sugar
¼   cup honey
¼   teaspoon cream of tartar
2   tablespoons water
2   egg whites
1   teaspoon vanilla extract

In the top of a double boiler (this recipe will not work in a regular saucepan—a double boiler is necessary!) combine sugar, honey, water, egg whites and cream of tartar. Cook over rapidly boiling water, beating constantly with a hand, rotary, or electric beater until mixture stands in peaks—about 6-8 minutes. Remove top of double boiler from heat; add vanilla. Continue beating until frosting is shiny and holds swirls. Be careful to not overbeat.

This frosts a 9x13-inch cake or two layer cakes.

Variations

Lemon: Add 2 tablespoons lemon juice instead of water. Reduce vanilla to only ½ teaspoon instead of one teaspoon.

Cherry: Add 2 tablespoons reserved cherry juice from cherry cake in place of water. Fold in ¼ cup chopped, drained cherries into frosting after it has been completely cooked.

Orange: Add 2 tablespoons orange juice in place of water. Add one teaspoon grated orange peel to finished frosting and fold in carefully.

Pecan Pie

This pie has a special "tang" that sets it apart from all other pecan pies.

1   9-inch unsalted pastry shell (pg. 197), unbaked
3   eggs
¾   cup granulated sugar
¾   cup brown sugar, packed
1   tablespoon unsalted butter or unsalted margarine
1   tablespoon white vinegar
1⅓   cups pecans, chopped

In a large mixing bowl, beat eggs until thick. Add remaining ingredients, making sure that the sugars are added to the eggs gradually so the filling does not have a grainy texture. Beat thoroughly. Pour into unbaked 9-inch pastry shell. Bake in 375° F. oven for about 45 minutes or until center of filling is just set. Remove from oven. Cool on wire rack. Cut into 6 pieces.

Serves 6.

Puddings

Packaged puddings can be very high in sodium. Try these.

1½   tablespoons cornstarch
2   tablespoons granulated sugar
1   cup skim milk
1   teaspoon vanilla

Mix cornstarch and sugar in a 2-quart sauce-pan. Heat milk in a separate small saucepan. Pour a little milk on the cornstarch mixture and blend well. Add remaining milk. Heat in a double boiler, stirring very frequently, until thick.* Cover and cook for approximately 2-5 minutes. Remove from heat. Mix in vanilla. Pour into individual serving dishes. Sprinkle with nutmeg on top, if desired. Refrigerate, covered, until ready to serve.

* Varieties

Chocolate: Add 1 square unsweetened choco-late, melted, to the pudding mixture after it has just thickened. Increase sugar to 4 tablespoons. Omit nutmeg on top.

Butterscotch: Substitute 2 tablespoons liquid brown sugar for the granulated sugar. Omit nutmeg.

Strawberry: Fold washed, hulled, chopped fresh strawberries into pudding mixture just before pouring into individual dishes. Omit nutmeg.

Banana: Slice ½ of a small banana into each serving dish. Pour the pudding mixture over the bananas. Omit nutmeg.

Powdered Sugar Icing

¼   .cup (½ stick) unsalted margarine or un-salted butter, softened
2   cups powdered sugar
1   teaspoon vanilla
2-4 tablespoons skim milk or orange juice

In a small mixing bowl, cream margarine or butter. Gradually add sugar; mixing after each ad-dition. Add vanilla and mix. Add milk, one table-spoon at a time, mixing thoroughly after each ad-dition, until icing is of desired spreading consis-tency. Using an electric mixer makes a creamier, fluffier frosting.

Cocoa Frosting: add one tablespoon un-sweetened cocoa to powdered sugar icing. This frosting is delicious on Favorite Devil's Food Cake (pg. 185).

Lemonade Cookies

Delicious, fresh taste. You'll be asked to share this recipe!

1   cup (1 stick) unsalted margarine
1   cup granulated sugar
2   eggs
3   cups unbleached flour
1   teaspoon baking soda substitute
1   6-ounce can frozen lemonade*
Granulated sugar

Preheat oven to 400° F. In a mixing bowl, cream together margarine and sugar. Add eggs, one at a time, beating well after each addition. In a separate bowl combine flour and baking soda substitute. Stir dry ingredients into egg mixture alternately with ½ cup of the lemonade concentrate. Drop by teaspoonfuls two inches apart onto ungreased cookie sheets. Bake about 8 minutes or until edges of cookies are lightly browned. Remove from oven, brush each cookie lightly with some of the remaining concentrate and sprinkle with sugar. Return to oven for a few minutes. Remove from oven. Cool.

This makes about 3 dozen cookies. They will remain soft and cakey if kept in an air-tight container. These freeze very well.

*See Helpful Hints.

Prune Whip Pie with Coconut

Unusual, yet subtle taste. Always a success with company.

5   egg whites
½   cup granulated sugar
1½   teaspoons lemon juice
1   cup dried pitted prunes (boil until plump; cool, and put into blender)*
Baked 10-inch unsalted pastry shell (pg. 197)
1   cup heavy cream, whipped
½   teaspoon vanilla
Cinnamon
Freshly grated coconut, or packaged flake or grated coconut

In a saucepan, boil prunes in water to cover until plump; cool. Drain. Put in blender and purée with the lemon juice.

In a deep bowl, whip egg whites until stiff. Gradually beat in sugar. Fold in the prunes. Spoon into baked 10-inch pie shell. Bake in 325° oven for 15 minutes. Cool. Top with whipped cream mixed with the vanilla. Sprinkle with cinnamon and coconut.

*If desired, substitute equivalent amount of strained unsalted baby food.

Little Gems

½   cup (1 stick) unsalted margarine
¼   cup shortening
½   cup unsalted peanut butter, crunchy style
½   cup brown sugar, firmly packed
1   egg
1   teaspoon vanilla
1   cup unbleached flour
¾   cup whole wheat flour
½   teaspoon baking powder substitute (scant
       half teaspoonful in altitudes above
       4,000 ft.)
Granulated sugar
Berry jelly or chocolate kisses

Blend margarine, shortening and peanut butter in a medium-sized bowl. Cream in brown sugar gradually. Add egg and vanilla. Beat well. Mix dry ingredients and stir in. Form dough into one-inch balls. Roll each ball in a small dish of granulated sugar. Place on ungreased cookie sheet. With teaspoon or fingertip depress center of unbaked ball of dough. Bake 12-15 minutes at 350° F. Immediately place one unwrapped chocolate kiss or ½ spoonful of jelly in the center depression of each cookie. When the chocolate has melted slightly, flatten with a knife. The heat of the cookie will be enough to soften the chocolate.

Makes about 3 dozen "tea" sized cookies.

Oatmeal Cookies

This makes a giant batch. Good for crowds or freezing.

1½   cups vegetable oil
3   cups honey
2   eggs
½   cup water
2   teaspoons vanilla
2   cups whole wheat flour
1   teaspoon baking soda substitute
½   cup soy flour
3   teaspoons ground cinnamon
1   cup raisins
1   cup coconut
1   cup nuts, chopped
6   cups rolled oats

In large mixing bowl, cream oil, honey and eggs until fluffy. Add water and vanilla; blend. Mix flour, baking soda substitute, soy flour and cinnamon together; add to liquid; mix until moist. Add remaining ingredients, mixing after each addition. (This dough may be wrapped in wax paper and frozen for use at a later time.) Drop by rounded tablespoonfuls onto greased cookie sheets. Bake for 12 minutes in 350° F. oven. Cooked cookies may be frozen also.

Makes 10 dozen.

Fruity Fill-ups

1½   cups whole wheat flour
¾   cup unbleached flour
1   teaspoon baking soda substitute
¾   teaspoon cinnamon
½   cup (1 stick) unsalted margarine
½   cup shortening
¾   cup packed brown sugar
½   cup granulated sugar
2   eggs
½   cup water
1   teaspoon almond extract
2   cups rolled oats
About ¾ cup fruit preserves (apricot, raspberry, etc.)

In a large bowl, mix the flours, baking soda and cinnamon. Set aside. In a large mixing bowl cream margarine, shortening and sugars until light and fluffy. Beat in eggs, water and extract. Add the oats. (Mixture will look curdled.) Add the flour mixture. Stir until blended. Drop by rounded tea-spoonfuls 3-inches apart on ungreased cookie sheets. With the back of a spoon or finger make a dent in the center of the dough. Fill each with ½ teaspoon preserves and top with additional level teaspoonful of dough. Bake in preheated 400° F.

oven for 10-12 minutes. Remove cookies to racks to cool.

Makes about 48.

Rhubarb Pie

5   cups peeled and diced rhubarb
1   cup sliced strawberries
1¼   cups granulated sugar
¼   cup brown sugar
4   heaping tablespoons unbleached flour
Dash salt substitute
3   eggs
1   10-inch unsalted pastry shell

Put the rhubarb and strawberries in a large bowl. In another medium-size bowl mix the sugars, flour, salt substitute and eggs. Mix well. Fold into the rhubarb and strawberries. Pour into the pastry shell. Bake at 400° F. for 20 minutes. Reduce the oven temperature to 350° F. and cook for 60 minutes longer, or until a brown crust forms over the top. Cool slightly before serving. May be cooled completely and then refrigerated until ready to serve.

Makes 8 servings.

Holiday Cooking

Holidays remind us of warm, shared moments with family and friends. Holidays remind us of celebrating. Often those moments of celebration include memorable meals with special dishes that are associated with that holiday.

Because of the special nature of holidays, we have included special menus with extra fancy dishes. Most of these dishes are just as easy to prepare as any other traditional ones you may have made in the past. Perhaps you would like to try some of these new recipes. This will give you the opportunity to create some new traditions and new memories of shared meals. Or you may wish to adapt some of your favorite recipes.

Many people, no matter what their dietary needs, associate holidays with "going off" the diet. No need to worry—that is not necessary. Many of these recipes are able to fit into the dietary guidelines of the guests at your table, and you will feel doubly satisfied with the elegant offerings you present.

For your shopping, meal planning, and cooking convenience, complete menus are provided for some of the major holidays. Of course, these can be interchanged or switched according to your desires.

Whatever the special day, we wish you a happy, carefree, delicious meal. Enjoy, and bon appétit.

Traditional Christmas Menu

Turkey
Poultry Dressing
Gravy
Aunt Jenny's Potato Refrigerator Rolls
   (see Breads)
Cranberry-Orange Relish
Gary's Festive Broccoli
Linda's Christmas Carrot Pudding

Serves 8.

Turkey

To Buy Turkey: Purchase either a fresh turkey that has not been injected with additives or a frozen turkey that is not self-basting. Some turkeys have a pop-up timer inserted in the meat to tell you when the turkey is fully cooked. The timer may be used, as long as the turkey is free of *all* additives, including the undesirable self-basting feature. Buy a 12-14 pound bird.

To Prepare: Thaw according to directions. Wash turkey, inside and out, with cold water. Dry cavity with paper toweling. Stuff with Poultry Dressing (pg. 208), if desired. Place in a large roasting pan. Use the Easy, No-baste Turkey method (pg. 207) or bake in a roasting pan, basting with the following stock. Turkey may be covered with a tent made of aluminum foil.

Stock

1	quart water
1	unsalted chicken bouillon cube
½	stalk celery
1	sprig parsley
½	teaspoon black pepper
½	teaspoon seasoned salt substitute
¼	teaspoon garlic powder
½	onion, chopped or 2 green onions, chopped
1	bay leaf

Wash giblets and neck. Combine all stock ingredients in a 5-quart saucepan. Simmer uncovered, while turkey is baking; add more water if necessary. Baste turkey every 1-1½ hours until done. Use stock in the poultry stuffing and also as an added liquid for the gravy.

Easy, No-Baste Turkey

½   cup (1 stick) unsalted margarine
2   teaspoons paprika
1   teaspoon garlic powder
½   teaspoon onion powder
¼   teaspoon salt substitute
¼   teaspoon black pepper

In a small bowl, cream margarine; add remaining ingredients and mix thoroughly. Slip some of mixture under breast skin as far back as you can. Spread the remaining mixture over skin. Put turkey into brown paper bag(s); seal. Bake according to the package directions, checking the turkey one hour before stated time. It is not necessary to baste turkey when baked with this method. Make Stock (pg. 206) and use for gravy, adding any cooked pan juices.

To test for doneness: Pierce the thigh between the breast and leg portions with a fork. Liquid that runs out should be almost clear, not pink. The legs should also wiggle when gently pushed. When cooking in a brown bag, birds have a tendency to get done more quickly than normally stated. As a rule of thumb, a bird should take 20 minutes per pound to cook if it is unstuffed, and 30 minutes per pound if it is stuffed.

Cranberry-Orange Relish

The extra special side dish.

1   16-ounce package fresh cranberries, washed, sorted and stems removed
1½-2 scant cups granulated sugar, according to desired sweetness
1   teaspoon grated orange peel
1¼ cups orange juice

In a 3-quart saucepan, mix ingredients and boil over medium high heat, uncovered, for 8-10 minutes or until cranberry skins pop. Store in an airtight container in the refrigerator until ready to serve. Relish thickens as it cools.

Makes approximately 3 cups.

Poultry Dressing

1   loaf unsalted white bread, cut into about
        ½-inch squares
½   cup (1 stick) unsalted margarine, melted
2   onions, chopped
2   stalks celery, chopped, including leaves
1   tablespoon paprika
1   tablespoon sweet basil
1   tablespoon celery seed
1   tablespoon poultry seasoning or sage
¼   cup chopped fresh parsley
1   egg
¾   teaspoon seasoned salt substitute
1   tablespoon honey dissolved in 1½ cups
        water (giblet water)
1   tablespoon unsalted chicken broth
        concentrate

In a large skillet, sauté onions and celery in margarine just until soft. Put bread squares in a large bowl. Add spices and sautéed ingredients. Add remaining ingredients and liquid. Add more liquid if a more moist stuffing is desired. Add egg and mix all together. Stuff poultry. This makes enough stuffing for a 12-pound bird.

The stuffing moistness may vary according to individual taste. Some like a dry dressing. The dressing tends to get a bit more moist as it cooks in the bird, and a bit more dry if placed in a greased 3-quart casserole dish and cooked one hour before serving.

If cooked separately in the casserole, refrigerate until ready to bake. Cook at 350° F. for 45 minutes.

Gravy

Terrific ladled over turkey and mashed potatoes.

3-4   cups Stock (See recipe, pg. 206)
¼-½ cup unbleached flour
½   cup cold water
2   teaspoons paprika
½   teaspoon seasoned salt substitute
¼   cup skim milk *or* white wine
¼   teaspoon garlic or onion powder
½   teaspoon pepper
Giblets, chopped with gristle removed (omit liver)

Skim the fat off the drippings in the roasting pan in which the turkey has been cooked. Discard the fat. Heat the drippings over medium heat and scrape the bottom of the pan using a wire whisk. Add approximately 3 cups of the giblet stock. Cook until boiling. Mix the flour into the ½ cup cold water until a smooth paste is formed. Slowly add the flour mixture to the liquid in the pan, stirring constantly so as to avoid lumps. Add the paprika, seasoned salt substitute, milk or wine, garlic or onion powder and pepper. Stir until flavors are well blended and gravy is of the desired consistency. The longer it cooks the thicker the gravy should become. If a thicker gravy is desired, more flour and water mixture could be added. If a thinner gravy is desired, add more stock or some skim milk. Adjust seasonings to taste.

Serve very hot.

Enough gravy to serve 8.

Gary's Festive Broccoli

Gorgeous to look at and delicious to eat. Cook ahead, if desired.

16-20 small white onions
1   large head broccoli
3   tablespoons unsalted margarine
3   tablespoons unbleached flour
2   cups skim milk
1   pint cherry tomatoes, washed with stems
        removed

In a 3-quart saucepan, boil onions with skins until just barely fork tender; drain. Remove skins, set aside. Wash broccoli and cut into spears. Boil, covered, for 5 minutes. Rinse in cold water. Set aside. Use same saucepan to make white sauce.

Preheat oven to 350° F. In a greased 3-quart casserole, layer half of the broccoli, then 8-10 onions, then the remaining broccoli, and finally the remaining onions.

Make a white sauce by melting margarine in saucepan; stir in flour with a wire whisk and gradually add milk. Pour over broccoli and onions which have been layered in casserole dish. At this point, this dish may be refrigerated until ready to cook.

Place casserole in preheated oven and immediately reduce heat to 300° F. Bake for 30 minutes or until sauce bubbles. Remove from oven; pour tomatoes over top of casserole and return to oven for 10 more minutes. Remove from oven and serve.

Serves 8.

Linda's Christmas Carrot Pudding

A marvelous way to end a delicious, festive meal.

1   cup granulated sugar
½   cup unsalted margarine
1   egg
1   cup carrots, ground
1   cup apples, ground
1   cup unsalted bread crumbs
½   cup skim milk
1   cup unbleached flour
1   teaspoon baking powder substitute (¾
         teaspoon in altitudes above 4,000 ft.)
1   teaspoon baking soda substitute
1   teaspoon ground cinnamon
1   teaspoon ground nutmeg
½   teaspoon ground cloves
1   cup candied mixed fruit*
1   cup raisins
1   cup nuts, chopped

Cream sugar and margarine in a large steel mixing bowl; add egg. Add remaining ingredients and mix well. Leaving mix in bowl, cover bowl tightly with aluminum foil. Place on wire rack in a 6-quart kettle. Add boiling water to kettle around and under the bowl until it reaches the top of the rack. Steam for 3 hours. Serve warm or at room temperature with Hard Sauce.

Serves 8-12.

*Your local bakery is a possible outlet for candied mixed fruit without preservatives.

Hard Sauce

½   cup granulated sugar
¼   cup unsalted margarine
2   cups hot water
4   tablespoons cornstarch
⅓   cup water or orange juice
1   teaspoon vanilla

In a one-quart saucepan, carmelize sugar and margarine for 7-10 minutes over medium high heat until mixture is brown. Add hot water gradually. Continue to stir to dissolve. Add cornstarch and water or juice and cook stirring constantly. Sauce will lose cloudy look as it cooks. Cook about 5 minutes. Add vanilla. Stir to mix. Spoon a few tablespoonfuls over each serving of Linda's Christmas Carrot Pudding.

Traditional Easter Menu

Easter Lamb
Easter Bread
Minted Zucchini
Wheat or Barley Pilaf
Sesame Romaine Salad
Apple Crumb Pie

Serves 8.

Easter Bread

A treat that makes the extra time and effort worthwhile.

⅓   cup raisins
2   tablespoons (2 packages) yeast
⅔   cup granulated sugar
1   cup very warm (110°-115° F.) half and half
        (milk and cream)
6   egg yolks
4   cups unbleached flour
1   tablespoon vanilla extract
1   teaspoon almond extract
1   tablespoon grated lemon rind
¼   pound (1 stick) unsalted butter, melted
1   cup confectioners' sugar
1   tablespoon lemon juice
1   tablespoon water

Put raisins in a one-quart saucepan. Cover with water. Simmer, covered, until raisins plump. Drain. Place the yeast in a small bowl. Add 2 tablespoons of the sugar and the heated half and half; stir and let stand in a warm place until doubled in size.

In a large mixing bowl, beat egg yolks with remaining sugar. Add yeast mixture, flour, vanilla extract, almond extract and lemon rind. Knead dough for 5 minutes. Add butter gradually. Knead another 5 minutes or until smooth. Add raisins and knead.

Divide dough in half and place in two greased bundt pans. Place in oven preheated to 100° F. Cover with towel and leave oven door ajar. Let stand for one hour or until doubled in size. Remove from oven. Preheat oven to 350° F. When oven is 350° F., return pans to oven. Bake for 45 minutes or until lightly browned. Remove from oven. Turn bread out of pans onto wire rack. Cool.

Mix confectioners' sugar, lemon juice and water together in a small bowl for icing. Spread over cakes, allowing icing to drip down sides.

The bread freezes well. If freezing bread, do not ice. Put icing on after it has thawed.

Easter Lamb

1   large leg of lamb (about 8-10 pounds)
6   bay leaves
2   tablespoons dried mint leaves *or* 6 drops
            mint extract
¾   cup unbleached flour
½   teaspoon garlic powder
2   teaspoons paprika
¼   teaspoon ground black pepper
½   cup plus 1 tablespoon cold water

Trim the lamb of any excess fat. Make 3 deep gashes, about ¼" deep in 3 evenly spaced places on top of the lamb. Turn the leg over and repeat procedure. Stuff each gash with one bay leaf and one tablespoon of mint leaves that has been divided into 6 parts. Place the lamb on the rack of a broiler pan, fat side up.

In a small bowl, mix the remaining one tablespoon mint leaves, flour, garlic powder, paprika and black pepper. Gradually add cold water until a very thick paste is formed. Seal the holes on the underside of the lamb with some of the flour paste, and then spread with the back of a spoon the remaining paste onto the entire top of the leg of lamb.

Place in oven and cook at 325° F. at the ratio of ½ hour per pound. (An 8-pound roast would take approximately 4 hours to produce a "medium" roast.)

Serves 8-10 people.

Apple Crumb Pie

Terrific any time of year, for any occasion.

6-8   tart apples
1   10-inch unsalted pastry shell, unbaked
¾   cup granulated sugar
1   teaspoon ground cinnamon
½   cup granulated sugar
¾   cup unbleached flour
⅛   teaspoon ground nutmeg
¼   cup unsalted margarine

Pare apples. Cut into bite-size pieces and place in the pastry-lined pie plate. In a small bowl, mix ¾ cup granulated sugar and the cinnamon together; sprinkle over apples.

In a small bowl, mix the ½ cup sugar, flour and nutmeg together. Cut in margarine until the mixture is crumbly. Sprinkle over apples. Bake in a 400° F. oven for 50 minutes, or until filling bubbles up. Top will get browned.

Makes one 10-inch pie.

Minted Zucchini

2   pounds small zucchini
1   medium onion
¼   cup unsalted margarine
1   teaspoon sweet basil
½   teaspoon dehydrated mint, crushed
⅛   teaspoon black pepper

Wash zucchini and cut into ⅓-inch rounds. Slice onion into rings. In a large skillet, sauté zucchini and onion in margarine. Sprinkle with basil, mint and pepper. Cook until just tender. Serve at once.

Makes 8 servings.

Wheat or Barley Pilaf

An excellent side dish for the large Easter meal!

¼   cup (½ stick) unsalted margarine
3   tablespoons vegetable oil
1   clove garlic, minced
1   green pepper, chopped
½   onion, chopped
½   teaspoon black pepper
1   stalk celery, chopped
1   cup broccoli, chopped
1   cup almonds, ground or slivered
1   cup uncooked cracked wheat or pearl barley
1   unsalted beef bouillon cube
1   tablespoon vegetable seasoning powder
1   teaspoon lemon juice
2½   cups water
2   green onions, chopped
2   fresh tomatoes, chopped

In a large frying pan, melt margarine and oil. Add garlic, green pepper, onion, pepper, celery and broccoli; sauté. Add almonds, cracked wheat and remaining ingredients, except for green onions and tomatoes. Pour into 3-quart casserole dish. Bake in a 350° F. oven for 45 minutes. Remove from oven. Garnish with tomatoes and green onions.

6-8 servings.

Sesame Romaine Salad

2	medium heads Romaine lettuce, washed and torn into bite-size pieces
1	pint cherry tomatoes, washed, remove stems
¼	head red cabbage, washed and shredded
½	red onion, sliced thinly
¼	cup sesame seeds
¼	recipe Vinaigrette Dressing (pg. 99)

Mix ingredients, except for dressing, in salad bowl which has been rubbed with a clove of garlic. Add Vinaigrette dressing just before serving and toss lightly.

    8 servings.

Father's Day Dinner

Stuffed Cornish Hens
Spiced Peaches
Fresh Cooked Broccoli
Mixed Green Salad (see Salads)
Strawberry Shortcake

Serves 4-6

Stuffed Cornish Hens

4	Rock Cornish Game Hens
3	tablespoons unsalted margarine
1	stalk celery, diced
1	small onion, diced
1	medium apple, cored and diced
½	cup pecan pieces, chopped
1	teaspoon crumbled sage leaves *or* ½ teaspoon ground sage
½	teaspoon paprika
3	sprigs fresh parsley, chopped
1	egg
½	pound unsalted bread, cubed and toasted
1	cup chicken or vegetable broth*
1	orange
Garlic powder	
Paprika	

Thaw and wash the Game Hens. Dry the insides and place in a 9x13-inch baking dish.

In a large skillet, sauté the celery, onion and apple in the margarine until the onion is transparent. Add the pecan pieces, sage, paprika, parsley and egg. Toss lightly with the bread cubes and broth.

Stuff each hen with some of the bread mixture. Squeeze the juice of the orange over the hens and sprinkle with a slight amount of garlic powder and paprika.

Bake in a 325° F. oven. Lightly cover with aluminum foil for the first one hour of cooking. Uncover for the remaining ½-1 hour. Cook until the legs wiggle rather loosely and the skin is crisp, brown, and beginning to shrink in appearance.

If there is any stuffing left after filling the hens, place in a greased casserole dish and bake, covered, the last one-half hour of the cooking time for the hens. Serve as a side dish with the meal.

Serves 4-6.

*Make broth using one unsalted chicken bouillon cube and one-half teaspoon vegetable broth seasoning mix in one cup of boiling water.

Spiced Peaches

These peaches are an easy do-ahead project!

24 hours to 3 days before serving:
2   large cans of peach halves, in light syrup
3   whole cloves
1   stick of cinnamon
1   tablespoon brown sugar
½   cup water
1   teaspoon brandy flavoring or extract

Remove the peaches from the syrup, reserving liquid. Add all the remaining ingredients, except brandy, to the syrup in a 3-quart saucepan and heat to boiling. Place peaches in a medium-sized bowl or deep casserole dish; mix in brandy or extract. Pour the liquid over the peaches.

Cover and refrigerate until ready to serve. Drain and place on a relish dish to serve.

Serves 4-6.

Fresh Cooked Broccoli

2   medium bunches broccoli, trimmed and
        cut into spears
2   tablespoons lemon juice
½   cup Blender Mayonnaise (pg. 90)

In a 6-quart kettle, cook the broccoli in water until it is just barely tender. Drain and sprinkle with the lemon juice. Spread the mayonnaise over the spears and cover the broccoli in the pan with a lid. Let stand 5 minutes. Remove to a serving dish and serve immediately.

4-6 servings.

Strawberry Shortcake

1½   quarts fresh strawberries
3   tablespoons granulated sugar
2   cups unbleached flour
6   teaspoons baking powder substitute (5 tea-
        spoons in elevations above 4,000 ft.)
1   tablespoon granulated sugar
½   cup shortening *or* unsalted margarine
1   egg, beaten
½   cup skim milk
Non-dairy whipped topping or whipped cream

In a medium-sized bowl mix the fresh strawberries that have been washed, hulled and sliced with the 3 tablespoons of sugar. Let stand until ready to serve.

In another medium-sized bowl mix the flour, baking powder substitute and granulated sugar. Cut in shortening until mixture is like coarse crumbs. Combine egg and milk, add to the dry ingredients, and stir until just moistened. Divide dough into two parts. Dust the bottom of two 8x1½-inch ungreased round pans with flour. Put half the dough into each pan, spreading lightly to fit the pan.

Bake at 425° F. for approximately 15 minutes or until toothpick inserted in center comes out clean. Immediately turn out layers on a plate, placing half the strawberries between the layers and the remaining berries and juice on top. Top with whipped cream or non-dairy whipped topping. Serve immediately!

6 servings.

Fourth Of July Summer Barbeque

Strawberry Cooler
Barbequed Chicken (see Marinade
    for Meats and Chicken)
Confetti Sweet-Sour Relish
    (see Pickling, Canning)
Baked Beans
Potato Salad
Chocolate Chip Mint Ice Cream
Fresh Raspberry Ice Cream
Country Vanilla Ice Cream

Serves 4.

Strawberry Coolers

This makes one Cooler—increase ingredients as necessary.

5	strawberries
1	tablespoon lime juice
3	teaspoons granulated sugar
½	cup crushed ice

Blend in blender for each individual serving. This may be doubled easily.

Baked Beans

The longer the cooking time, the more mellow and blended the flavors become. 24 hour cooking—adding more liquid—makes the beans taste even more like "old fashioned goodness."

1½	cups dried small white or great northern beans, soaked and cooked according to directions in the introduction to Ethnic Dishes section. (Reserve cooking liquid.)
2	tablespoons minced dehydrated onion
1	large onion, chopped
¼	cup light molasses
1	tablespoon dry mustard
3	tablespoons unsalted prepared mustard
1	cup reserved bean water
1	cup apple cider
3	tablespoons cider vinegar
10	drops tabasco sauce
½	cup brown sugar, packed
1	6-ounce can unsalted tomato paste
½	teaspoon seasoned salt substitute
1	whole onion

Place all the above ingredients, except whole onion, in a greased large bean pot or slow cooker. Cover and bake for 5-8 hours at 250° F. Then, slice the onion thinly and arrange attractively on the top of the beans. At this point, if the beans are runny they should be cooked uncovered for one hour. If the beans are dry, add more apple cider or reserved bean water until of desired consistency and cook for one more hour.

Serves four.

Potato Salad

Sure to be a favorite with your guests!

6	potatoes
1	large onion, chopped or 1 medium bunch green onions, chopped
4	hard cooked eggs, chopped
2	stalks celery, chopped
⅔	cup unsalted French Dressing (pg. 97)
2	tablespoons unsalted prepared mustard
½	cup unsalted mayonnaise or Blender Mayonnaise (pg. 90)
2	tablespoons lemon juice
¼	teaspoon paprika
¼	teaspoon seasoned salt substitute
¼	cup chopped fresh parsley
2	red radishes, sliced

Wash and quarter potatoes. Place in 3-quart saucepan and cover with water. Bring to a full boil, cover pan and lower heat to a low boil. When the potatoes have been cooked, immediately skin them while they are still hot. Chop potatoes into bite-size pieces and put into a large mixing bowl. Add the remaining ingredients except the parsley and radishes. Mix thoroughly. Arrange the parsley and radishes over the top of the salad. Cover and refrigerate for a few hours to let flavors blend. 4-6 servings.

Fresh Raspberry Ice Cream

For special occasions deserving delectable treats — homemade ice cream!

5	eggs, beaten
2¾	cup granulated sugar
3	cups whipping cream
2	cups whole milk
2	cups skim milk
2	teaspoons vanilla
3	cups fresh raspberries

In a large mixing bowl, gradually add sugar to beaten eggs using high speed on electric mixer. Continue to beat until mixture is very stiff. This may take 5-7 minutes. Add the whipping cream. Pour into a gallon or 6-quart ice cream freezer. Add the remaining ingredients except raspberries. Churn according to freezer directions for about 15 minutes or until ice cream has frozen to a mushy consistency. Add the raspberries and continue to churn. Freeze as directed.

Country Vanilla Ice Cream

This is a basic recipe.

5   eggs, beaten
2¼   cups sugar
3   cups whipping cream
3   cups whole milk
3   cups skim milk
5   teaspoons vanilla

In a large mixing bowl, gradually add sugar to beaten eggs. Use a high speed on the electric mixer. Continue to beat until mixture is very stiff.* Add whipping cream. Pour this mixture into a gallon or 6-quart ice cream freezer. Add remaining ingredients and stir well. Freeze according to freezer directions.

*For Chocolate Chip-Mint Ice Cream, add 1½ cups grated milk or semi-sweet chocolate. Omit the vanilla and add instead 1½ teaspoons mint extract.

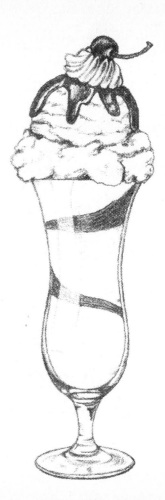

Canning, Pickling and Preserving

For the person on a low-sodium diet, the common commercially prepared condiments are strictly "off limits"! Ketchup, pickles, relishes and mustard are higher in sodium than allowed on the low-sodium diet. Many low-sodium condiments can be purchased in health food stores, and some markets carry selections of low-sodium condiments in the diet section. Yes, home canning can be accomplished without salt, and these foods can be safe to store and eat. In many recipes, one may replace salt with sugar, vinegar, or uniodized salt-substitute, and the acid content will be what is needed to help preserve food.

There are three basic canning methods: open kettle; hot water bath; pressure canning. Open kettle method is only safe to use for jams and jellies. The hot water bath can be used with a relatively small financial investment. Pressure cooking canning is faster, but the initial financial investment is more than the other two methods. Pressure canning may be more dangerous and may require some expertise. None of the following recipes in this section require pressure canning.

Steps in canning:

1. Assemble all your equipment: jars, new lids, screw rims, a deep canning kettle, a large mouth funnel, tongs, hot pads, wire racks, paper towels.

2. Choose only choice, fresh food to can. Blemished food, even with the blemishes cut out may still have organisms that promote spoilage.

3. Wash all fruits and vegetables with cold clear water, using a scrubbing vegetable brush when necessary to get all crevices clean.

4. Wash all jars, lids and rims in steaming, soapy water, rinsing well. Dishwashers work well to sterilize jars and screw rims (not lids). If you do not have a dishwasher, boil the jars inside and out to be sure of sterilization. Lids should always be put in a saucepan and simmered gently for a few minutes before sealing.

5. Do not use a copper kettle for pickling or canning.

6. Fill jars with the food to no higher than ½-inch from the top. This is called ½-inch head space. Run a knife around the inside of the jar to eliminate air bubbles. Wipe the rim of the jar with a clean, moist paper towel. This insures that the seal will be tight. Place the wet, steaming lid on the jar and screw down tightly.

7. Place the partially sealed jars in boiling water deep enough to cover one inch over tops of lids. Start counting processing time the moment the water comes again to an active boil.

8. When the processing time is up, remove the jars from the boiling water using tongs and hot pad gloves.

9. Read the label directions on the canning lid box to determine if you have a perfect seal. If not, store in refrigerator aud use quickly.

10. To cool, set jars on wire cake racks with enough space between them so they can cool quickly. Cool at room temperature and avoid drafts. Cooling rapidly produces a less mushy produce.

11. For pickles:

a. Crispiness comes from soaking for prolonged periods in *cold* salt water. Use salt-substitute that has no iodine added instead. Alum is another suggested source to produce crispness.

b. Process cucumbers for pickles within 24 hours of picking. This keeps flavor high, spoilage lower, and also produces a more crisp pickle.

c. "Salty" pickle recipes may not require a hot water bath. We suggest a 5-minute hot water bath to insure a tight seal and inhibit spoilage.

d. Too much fresh garlic in recipes or in dill pickles may produce a gas which will cause the seal to rupture as much as two weeks to a month after originally sealing.

e. Chilling any pickle before serving improves its eating quality 100 percent.

12. When water bath required is longer than 20 minutes, increase the time 2 minutes for every 1,000 ft. elevation. When the total water bath time is 20 minutes or less, add 5 minutes to the total cooking time.

For Jams and Jellies: Some packaged pectin products have salt products in them. Read labels very carefully if your favorite recipes call for pectin.

For preserves that use no pectin thickening is obtained by longer cooking times. Thickening also comes from the sugar. See Potpourri of Flavor section: "Invert Sugar", pg. 32. We include a few preserves that are unusual and are guaranteed to give you rave notices!

Use cane sugar instead of sugar made from sugar beets, whenever possible, in all your preserving, but especially in jellies, jams and preserves. Cane sugar dissolves more readily and will not tend to "sugar up" or crystallize in the jars after sitting a while.

Label carefully in the summer and fall. In the winter you can review your handiwork with a continual feeling of accomplishment and pride.

Home canned products make wonderful gifts.

Pickled Beets

8-10 medium-sized fresh beets
1   large onion, sliced
2   cups water
1   cup cider vinegar
1½   cups brown cane sugar
¼   teaspoon uniodized salt substitute

Wash the beets and remove the tops. Place in a large 6-quart kettle and cover with water. Bring to a boil and cook until a fork inserted in the beets pierces them without much resistence. Do not overcook. Beets should still be firm. Drain water. Slip the skins off each beet.

In the same kettle (washed thoroughly) place the onion, water, vinegar, sugar and salt substitute. Heat until the sugar is dissolved. Slice the beets, or chunk, and place in the kettle with the remaining ingredients. Heat just to boiling. At this point beets can be placed in a bowl, covered and refrigerated for immediate use. Or, they may be canned.

To Preserve:

Continue boiling beets in liquid for 5 minutes. Ladle beets, onions and liquid into hot sterilized pint jars. Wipe jar rims and threads. Place lids on according to manufacturer's directions. Process 5 minutes in water bath (10 minutes for 4,000-5,000 ft. altitudes).

To Use Commercially Canned Beets:

Cans of unsalted beets may be purchased in the supermarket. Pickled beets may be made to refrigerate by using the beet liquid instead of water and following the above directions (except the preserving directions). Two to three 16-ounce cans would be equivalent to the above quantity of raw beets.

Martha's Never Fail Dill Pickles

1   quart white vinegar
3   quarts water
4   tablespoons uniodized salt substitute
         (look in pharmacy section, labeled
         "potassium chloride")
6   garlic cloves
6   sprays dill
Small cucumbers (process within 24 hours of
         picking)
6   quart jars, sterilized

In a 6-quart kettle, boil vinegar, water and salt substitute. Put *one* clove of peeled garlic and one spray of dill in each hot sterilized quart jar. Pack very freshly picked small cucumbers in jars.* Pour boiling liquid in jar until liquid covers pickles. Leave one-inch head space. Check to make sure jars are sealed. Process in hot water bath 3-5 minutes. Let set 2 or more months before opening to use.

**Important:* Loosely pack pickles in the jar. When jars are filled too full or more than one clove garlic per jar is used, the jars may unseal—even weeks later!

Canned Stewed Tomatoes

Useful in Mexican dishes, Quick Macaroni (pg. 136) and Cheese, Basic Hot Sauce (pg. 149), or as a vegetable dish.

10   large green peppers, chopped
7   large onions, chopped
¾   bushel tomatoes
21   quart canning jars

In each sterilized quart jar put:
1   tablespoon white vinegar
1   teaspoon granulated sugar
3   heaping tablespoons each green pepper
         and onion

In a large 6-quart kettle, boil water. Dip each tomato in boiling water until the skins pop. Remove and dip in a cold water bath. The skins will slip off the tomatoes. Remove the spurs. Quarter each tomato.

In each jar put vinegar, sugar, peppers and onions in quantities prescribed above. Pack each jar with tomatoes, leaving a one-inch head space. Clean rims; cover with sterilized hot lids and screw tops according to manufacturer's directions. Process in a hot water bath for 50 minutes. (One hour at 4,000-5,000 ft. elevation.)

Let cool and check for seal. Store in a cool dark place.

Peach Preserves

Using the pits in processing these peach preserves adds a rich, nut-like taste. This method will become a "must" for you and your family.

12 cups ground peaches, skins on (3 quarts — about 25-30 peaches, if small)
7 cups granulated cane sugar
1 cup brown cane sugar
¼ cup lemon juice
1 teaspoon ground cinnamon
20 peach pits

Wash the peaches well, removing as much fuzz as possible. Cut out all bruised portions. Chunk and put in a food grinder. Place ground peaches in a large bowl or kettle. Add the remaining ingredients and mix well. Pour into two 9x13x2-inch baking dishes. Place in the oven and bake at 325° F. for 1-3 hours, stirring every 15-20 minutes. When mixture is a bit more runny than desired remove from oven. The color of the preserve will be an amber color. (Preserve will thicken some in jar after cooling.) Immediately ladle into steaming sterilized jars, making sure each jar receives at least one peach pit. Clean rims and seal according to manufacturer's directions.

Makes 8-10 pints.

Sweet Cucumber Pickles

8 cups cucumbers, unpeeled, sliced
1 head cauliflower, cut into flowerettes (optional)
2 green peppers, seeded and chopped
1 large onion, sliced
1 tablespoon uniodized salt substitute
Water and ice cubes
3 cups white vinegar
3 cups granulated cane sugar
1 tablespoon celery seed
1 tablespoon mustard seed *or* whole pickling spices
½ teaspoon turmeric
6 hot, sterilized pint jars

Place prepared vegetables in a large bowl. Sprinkle with the salt substitute. Cover with cold water and a few ice cubes. Allow to stand 3 hours. Drain well. In a 6-quart kettle, bring remaining ingredients to boil; add vegetables, bring to a boil, and cook 10 minutes. Fill hot pint jars with pickles and liquid to one inch from the top. Cover with sterilized lids and screw rings, according to manufacturer's instructions. Place in boiling water bath for 5 minutes. (10 minutes for 4,000-5,000 ft. elevation.) Remove and let cool. Check seal.

Makes about 5-6 pints. This recipe doubles well to yield about 10-12 pints.

Aunt Jenny's Pear Preserves

A good accompaniment anytime, but especially with Aunt Jenny's Potato Refrigerator Rolls (pg. 58).

8   cups peeled, diced pears (not extremely ripe or soft)
7   cups granulated cane sugar
¼   teaspoon ground cloves

In a large heavy-bottomed kettle cook the pears and sugar, stirring frequently. (The pieces of the diced pears should be about ¼-inch to ½-inch square.) Continue cooking the mixture for several hours or until the mixture comes off the spoon in a solid "thread" instead of drips.* Add the cloves. Stir well. Prepare the jars and lids.

Ladle the preserves into sterilized ½-pint or pint jars. Seal according to manufacturer's directions.

Makes about 5 pints.

*If this is cooked too long the preserves will become "gummy" in the jars. It tends to thicken as it cools and sits. To check for proper consistency, place a teaspoonful of preserves on a small plate. If it mounds slightly as it cools it is ready.

This is *not* a thick preserve, but rather the texture of honey with chunks of pear in it.

Plum Conserve

6   cups ripe purple plums
2   lemons
2   oranges
4½   cups granulated sugar
3   cups raisins
1   cup walnuts, chopped

Wash plums. Remove pits and cut into small pieces. Put into large 6-quart kettle. Grate rind off of lemons and oranges; add to kettle. Squeeze juices from oranges and lemons, remove seeds, and put into kettle also. Add sugar and raisins. Bring to a boil; reduce heat and simmer, stirring occasionally, until conserve becomes thick (about one hour). Be careful not to scorch. Stir in walnuts.

Pour conserve into hot, sterilized jars, leaving a ½-inch head space. Wipe rims of jars carefully and top with hot sterilized new lids. Put clean bands on jars and seal. Invert jars for a few seconds and then place on clean towels in a draft-free area. Check for seal after jars have cooled.

Yields 11-12 half-pint jars.

Sweet Pickle Relish

For sandwiches, salads, or salad dressings.

15-20 large cucumbers (4 quarts ground)
5   onions (3 cups ground)
2   green peppers
3   sweet red peppers
1   green or red tomato
2   tablespoons uniodized salt substitute
1   quart cider vinegar
1   quart granulated cane sugar
3   tablespoons celery seed
½   teaspoon allspice
2   tablespoons mustard seed
1   teaspoon black pepper
½   teaspoon nutmeg
½   teaspoon ground cloves
1½   teaspoons turmeric
¼   teaspoon cardamom or ground cinnamon
10-11 sterilized pint jars

Grind the cucumbers, onions, peppers and tomatoes. Place in a large bowl or pan and sprinkle with salt substitute. Let stand at least one hour or up to 12 hours. Drain well. Combine all the remaining ingredients in a large (6-quart) preserving kettle. Add the drained vegetables. Simmer 15 minutes, stirring constantly, or until the mixture loses its bright green color. Ladle the relish into the steaming, sterilized jars to ½-inch of each top. Wipe off the tops and threads of the jars with a damp cloth. Put on prepared lids and seal as the manufacturer directs. (15-20 minutes at elevations above 4,000 ft.) Cool on towels. Wipe jars clean and store in a dark place after checking to be sure all lids have sealed.

Makes 10-11 pints.

Refrigerator Pickles

7   cups unpeeled cucumbers or zucchini, sliced
1   cup sliced onions
1   green pepper, chopped
2   cups granulated sugar
1   cup white vinegar
2   tablespoons celery seed
½   teaspoon seasoned salt substitute

In a 2-quart saucepan, heat the vinegar and sugar until liquid is clear. In a very large bowl mix remaining ingredients together and let stand one hour. Put in hot sterilized jars and keep in refrigerator indefinitely.

Piccalilli Relish

Excellent condiment for beef dishes.

8   cups chopped cabbage
8   cups chopped green tomatoes
3   cups chopped green peppers
1   cup chopped sweet red peppers
3   cups chopped onion
6   cups cider vinegar
4   cups granulated cane sugar
6   teaspoons dry mustard
2   teaspoons ground ginger
1   teaspoon ground cinnamon
1   teaspoon ground mace
2   tablespoons mustard seed
½   teaspoon dried, crushed hot red chili
       pepper (tied in cheesecloth bag)
14 pint-sized canning jars, sterilized, hot

Combine chopped vegetables in a large 6-quart kettle. Add remaining food ingredients.

Stir over medium heat until sugar is dissolved. Increase heat and cook rapidly for 25 minutes, stirring frequently. Remove cheesecloth bag.

Ladle hot relish into hot jars, leaving ½-inch head space. Place lids on according to manufacturer's directions.

Put each jar as it is filled onto rack in canner or deep kettle. When canner is filled, add hot water to cover jars 1-2 inches.

Cover canner and bring water to boil. Reduce heat to hold water at a steady boil. Start processing time when water reaches a full boil.

Process in boiling water bath 10 minutes (15 minutes for 4,000 to 5,000 ft. elevation).

Makes about 14 pints.

Confetti Sweet-Sour Relish

6   cups finely chopped carrots
1½   cups finely chopped green pepper
        (about 2 large peppers)
1¼   cups finely chopped red pepper
        (about 1½ large peppers)
1½   cups finely chopped cabbage
3   cups finely chopped red onion
        (about 2 large onions)
Boiling water
4   cups cider vinegar
3   cups honey
1   teaspoon seasoned salt substitute
3¼   teaspoons mustard seed
3¼   teaspoons celery seed
6   pint jars, sterilized, hot

In 6-quart kettle, place carrots, green and red peppers, cabbage and onion. Cover with boiling water; let stand 5 minutes.

Drain mixture well. Return to kettle; stir in vinegar, honey, seasoned salt substitute, mustard seed and celery seed. Stirring frequently, bring to boil over medium heat. Reduce heat.

Stirring occasionally, continue boiling gently about 20 minutes or until mixture thickens. Ladle hot mixture into clean hot ½-pint jars, leaving a ½-inch head space.

Place jars on rack in kettle, add hot water to cover jars by one inch. Bring to a boil and process 10 minutes (15 minutes at 4,000-5,000 ft. elevation). Remove jars from water and cool. Store in a cool place.

Makes six pint jars.

Virginia's Chili Sauce

This is a sweet tomato sauce and not in the least bit "hot" flavored. It is delicious on hamburgers, meat sandwiches and scrambled eggs.

3   quarts ground tomatoes (about 30)
1   quart ground apples (12)
1   pint ground onions (2-3)
3   cups ground green peppers (6-7)

1½ quarts granulated cane sugar
1   quart brown apple cider vinegar
2   teaspoons ground cinnamon
2   teaspoons ground cloves
1   teaspoon ground red pepper
10 pint jars, sterilized

Peel tomatoes. (See Stewed Tomatoes pg. 224.) Grind all vegetables in food grinder or processor. Place all ground vegetables in an 8-quart heavy-bottomed kettle. Add sugar, vinegar and spices.

Gently simmer, uncovered, for at least four hours or longer for thicker consistency. It should be thick (thick enough to stay in a little mound on a plate). Put into steaming pint jars. Clean rims and threads of jars. Seal with hot sterilized lids according to manufacturer's directions. Process in hot water bath for 5 minutes (10 minutes for 4,000-5,000 ft. elevation).

Makes about 10 pints. This recipe doubles well. Do not cook in enamel pans as it tends to stick.

Additional notes: When a small amount of this chili sauce is added to unsalted mayonnaise it tastes very much like the "Secret Sauce" at hamburger places.

The cost per pint is 38.6 cents *or* 2 cents per ounce. This cost for homemade chili sauce is one-fifth the cost of purchasing chili sauce.

Sources of Information

American Heart Association of Washington, *"Flavor Without Salt: Low-Sodium Recipes,"* 333 First Avenue West, Seattle, WA 98119

Bagg, Elma W., *Cooking Without a Grain of Salt,* New York: Bantam Books, 1972. $1.95.

Brown, W. J., *Cook To Your Heart's Content: On A Low-Fat, Low-Salt Diet,* Van Nos Reinhold. $6.95.

Brunswick, J. Peter, Dorothy Love, and Assa Weinberg, M.D., *How To Live 365 Days a Year the Salt-Free Way,* New York: Bantam Books, Inc., 1977. $1.95.

Conason and Metz, *Salt Free Diet Cook Book,* Grosset & Dunlap. $1.95.

Jones, Jean, *Secrets of Salt Free Cooking,* 101 Productions. $5.95.

Kraus, Barbara, *The Dictionary of Sodium, Fats and Cholesterol,* New York: Grosset and Dunlap. 1976. $3.95.

Lloyd, Nancy, *Salt Free Recipes to Save Your Life,* Great Britain: Thorsons Publishers Limited, 1977. $1.95.

Margie, Joyce and James Hunt, *Living With High Blood Pressure,* New Jersey: H.L.S. Press, Inc., 1978. About $15.00.

Morrison, Lester, M.D., *The Low-Fat Way to Health and Longer Life,* New York: A.R.C. Books, Inc., 1971. $1.65.

Payne and Callahan, *The Fat and Sodium Controlled Cookbook,* Little Brown and Co. $8.95.

Psychology Today, *"The New Food Consciousness",* October 1978.

Roth, June, *Salt-Free Cooking with Herbs and Spices,* Chicago: Contemporary Books, Inc., 1975. $3.95.

Thornburn, A. H., *Living Salt Free and Easy!* New American Library. $1.50.

Wolke, Mark, Deborah Kidushim and Rose Dosti, *Light Style: The New American Cuisine,* New York: Harper and Row, October 1979.

Free Low-sodium Recipe Booklets

Delicious Dimensions in Low Sodium Cookery. Write: Campbell Soup Company, Box 355, Dept. DD, Collingswood, New Jersey 08108

Delicious Low-sodium Diets. Write: Standard Brands, Inc., Education Service, P.O. Box 2695, New York, New York 10017

Low-sodium Recipes with High Appetite Appeal. Write: Angostura International, Ltd., Dept. H., 1201 Corbin Street, Elizabeth, N.J. 07201

Low-sodium Spice Tips. Send a self-addressed envelope to: American Spice Trade Association, P.O. Box 1267, Englewood Cliffs, New Jersey 07632

Should You Shake Your Salt Habit? Write: Giant Food, Inc., P.O. Box 1804, Washington, D.C. 20013

When the Doctor Says "Limit Sodium" Think First Lemon and a wallet-sized sodium reminder. Send a self-addressed envelope to: Sunkist Growers, Inc., Division 21, Box 7888, Van Nuys, California 91409

Sensible Ways to Cut Down on Sodium: Send a self-addressed envelope to: Adolph's Salt Substitutes, P.O. Box 2003-T, Jefferson City, MO 65101

Sodium Content of Your Food, Home and Garden Bulletin 233. Write: SEA Publications Requests and Distribution USDA, Room 6007 South Building, Washington, D.C. 20250.

INDEX